How to Write a Grant Proposal

How to Write a Grant Proposal

CHERYL CARTER NEW
JAMES AARON QUICK

WILEY

John Wiley & Sons, Inc.

About the CD-ROM

Introduction

When you purchased this book, you also received a CD-ROM containing sample files for your use to help you prepare your own grant proposals.

The CD-ROM contains Word and Excel files for each of the four complete proposals described throughout this book—an After School Program, a Senior Citizen Wellness Center, a Fire Station, and an Inner City Drug & Alcohol Abuse Program—all easily downloadable and customizable.

Each proposal contains 18 specific elements that make up a complete proposal. All of the 18 elements for each project are organized into four separate folders. Although the examples provided here are for very specific projects, the Word and Excel documents can be used as templates—or a starting point—that you can customize for any other project.

In addition, a fifth folder contains checklists of important points to remember for each of the 18 proposal elements. These can be printed out for easy reference.

Software Requirements

The files on the enclosed CD-ROM are saved in Microsoft Excel 97 and Microsoft Word for Windows 97. In order to use the files, you will need to have spreadsheet software capable of reading Microsoft Excel 97 files and word processing software capable of reading Microsoft Word 97 files.

System Requirements

- IBM PC or compatible computer
- CD-ROM drive
- Windows 95 or later
- Microsoft Word for Windows 97 or later or other word processing software capable of reading Microsoft Word for Windows 97 files*

Publisher's note: Wiley publishes in a variety of print and electronic formats and by print-on-demand. If this book refers to media such as a CD or DVD that is not included in the version you purchased, you may download this material at http://booksupport.wiley.com. For more information about Wiley products, visit www.wiley.com.

*Users who do not have Microsoft Word for Windows 97 on their computers can download the free viewer from the Microsoft web site. The URL to the viewer is: *http://office.microsoft.com/downloads/9798/wdvw9716.aspx*. This download is for users who don't have Word; it allows them to open and view Word 97 documents.

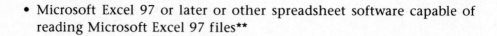

• Microsoft Excel 97 or later or other spreadsheet software capable of reading Microsoft Excel 97 files**

Using the Files

Loading Files

To use the files, launch your spreadsheet or word processing software. Select **File, Open** from the pull-down menu. Select the appropriate drive and directory. A list of files should appear. If you do not see a list of files in the directory, you need to select Word Document (*.doc) or Microsoft Excel Files (*.xls) under Files of Type. Double-click on the file you want to open. Use the file according to your needs.

Printing Files

If you want to print the files, select **File, Print** from the pull-down menu.

Saving Files

When you have finished editing a file, you should save it in a new directory on your C:/ drive by selecting **File, Save As** from the pull-down menu.

User Assistance

If you need assistance with installation or if you have a damaged disk, please contact Wiley Technical Support at:

Phone: 201-748-6753
Fax: 201-748-6450 (Attention: Wiley Technical Support)
URL: *www.wiley.com/techsupport*

To place additional orders or to request information about other Wiley products, please phone: 800 225-5945.

** Users who do not have Microsoft Excel on their computers can download the free viewer from the Microsoft web site. The URL to the viewer is: *http://office.microsoft.com/Downloads/ 2000/xlviewer.aspx.*

Use of the program with an earlier version of Microsoft Excel or other spreadsheet software might result in some formatting and display anomalies that we cannot support.

The Microsoft Excel 97/2000 Viewer is recommended for use with a stand-alone computer that does not have Microsoft Excel installed. This product allows the user to open and view Excel 97 and Excel 2000 spreadsheet files. The viewer is not suitable for use on a server.

About the Authors

James Aaron Quick is the Chief Executive Officer for Polaris, a South Carolina Corporation. He has served in this capacity since 1989. As the Senior Instructional Specialist for Polaris, he has spoken before thousands of potential grant seekers from the fields of education, healthcare, and nonprofit management. He has written successful grant proposals for over 10 years, for projects ranging from $10,000 to $7.9 million to grant makers including federal sources, foundations, and corporations. He is coauthor of many Polaris publications as well as the best-selling trade book on grant seeking entitled *Grant Seeker's Toolkit: A Comprehensive Guide to Finding Funding* (New York: John Wiley & Sons, 1998) and *Grant Winner's Toolkit: Management and Evaluation of a Granted Project* (New York: John Wiley & Sons, 1999). Jim also writes nonfiction articles and books, as well as novels and short stories.

Cheryl Carter New is the President of Polaris Corporation. She is the founder of the company, which was incorporated in 1984. Her background includes instruction at kindergarten, primary, and middle school levels; administration at kindergarten and primary school levels; and curriculum, course development, and instruction at the college level. She wrote her first successful grant proposal in 1969 and has continued to be active in the field to the present. She has written numerous articles in the field as well as on negotiation, management issues, and strategic planning. She has spoken on the subjects of grants acquisition and negotiations at many national, regional, and state conferences. She is the developer of several college level courses and workshops in the field of grant seeking, offered and presented in 45 states. She is coauthor of many Polaris publications as well as the best-selling trade book on grant seeking entitled *Grant Seeker's Toolkit: A Comprehensive Guide to Finding Funding,* published by John Wiley & Sons, and the upcoming *Grant Winner's Toolkit: Management and Evaluation of a Granted Project,* also to be published by Wiley. Cheryl also writes and illustrates children's books. More information about Polaris and free information for grant seekers can be found at *www.polarisgrantscentral.net.*

Contents

Contents

Contents

Contents

Contents

Contents

Introduction

To date, we have written three books about how to be successful in acquiring grants. This is our fourth book. One would think we would have exhausted the subject by now. On the contrary, the subject of grant acquisition is such a complex subject that we have more books yet to write.

There are so many different types of grants with so many different facets that one can spend a lifetime studying all the possibilities. Most people think of two things when they think of grants—either scholarships or entitlements such as Social Security. But there are so many other types. There are government grant programs for individual needs through various departments and agencies. There are small business grants and small business innovation research grants. There are research grants—probably the best-known grants. There are also project grants, which make up the bulk of grants to organizations.

Each grant maker has its individual "personality." Federal grants vary by department and agency. One might fund traditional research, while another funds wildly innovative programs. State grants can be highly political and personal. Foundations run the gamut from very hands-on to almost aloof. Corporation grants usually reflect their management and can be the toughest to get because of the many ways they can be approached.

Funders all have two things in common. Their business is investing money, and they all want to solve one or more problems. That is why they are in business—to solve problems. Some grant makers have been established by a person who experienced a life-changing event. As a result, the grant making focuses on a particular issue. Some respond to public awareness that a problem needs solving. Whatever the reason, they are all focused on one problem or another.

As grant seekers, it is our job to study the problems within our organization's mission. When we discover an unmet need for our client population, we analyze a possible solution. Our solution requires action— as such it is a project. A project is an undertaking made up of activities leading to a positive conclusion. Once we have projects developed, then we search for funders wanting to solve the same problems. The connection with the funder is the desire to solve the same problem.

The way we tell the funder about our project is through a proposal. In fundraising, we might send letters to a thousand people or organizations requesting donations. That is not the way the world of grants works. With grants, you write an individual proposal to an individual funder. You follow the funder's directions for writing that proposal to the letter.

Many people make the mistake of writing a single proposal, getting a list of names and addresses, and sending that proposal around. Then they wonder why they never get funding. They only think they are writing a grant proposal. Funders disregard such proposals as "non-responsive." Those people have not understood about the investment the funder is trying to make in a project that will solve the problem in which they are interested.

Grant seeking is 80% project development, research, and positioning. The rest is writing. One should never write the first line of a proposal until the project is fully developed. Otherwise you really have nothing about which to write. Once your project is developed, then the proposal writes itself.

Grant seeking is hard work but infinitely rewarding. When you have a good project that helps people, and you can see the fruits of your labor, the work does not seem like a burden. We have helped many organizations acquire grant funding. We have taught tens of thousands of people in our workshops. We never tire of seeing the happy faces of children who have a second chance as a result of a grant. We never tire of knowing that women will get timely cancer screening as a result of a grant. We never tire of knowing that people are getting counseling as a result of a grant. We never tire of answering grant questions online. This work is rewarding indeed.

Publisher's note: Wiley publishes in a variety of print and electronic formats and by print-on-demand. If this book refers to media such as a CD or DVD that is not included in the version you purchased, you may download this material at http://booksupport.wiley.com. For more information about Wiley products, visit www.wiley.com.

Chapter 1

Cover Letter

**The advantage of love at first sight is that
it delays a second sight.**

Natalie Clifford Barney[1]

At a Glance

What Else Is It Called?

- Transmittal letter or letter of transmission

When Is It Used?

A cover letter should be sent whenever it is not prohibited. With some requests for proposal, there is a strict page limitation with explicit directions to follow for every page. In this case, a cover letter is not usually appropriate. However, you can leverage a cover letter to make an excellent first impression so it should be included whenever possible. Normally with proposal to a foundation or a state program, a cover letter can be included. Often with a federal grant program, a cover letter is not included.

Why Is It Used?

A cover letter is an introduction. It is a lot like making introductions in person. It is a way of getting started on the right foot by introducing yourself instead of launching into the request right away.

Key Concepts

- Brief.
- Positive and confident.

---

[1] Natalie Clifford Barney (1876–1972), U.S.-born French author, *Samples from Almost Illegible Notebooks,* no. 299 (London: Adam, 1962).

- Concise and inviting.
- Thank you.

Formatting Issues

Make the letter one page only, keeping it as brief as possible. The letter should be printed on original letterhead. The type should be a 12-point text font, and the margins should be generous, which means at least one inch. We suggest you not fully justify your text (straight margins on both left and right). Use left justification and leave the right margin ragged (rag right). There should be a reference line between the inside address and salutation that clearly identifies the grant program for which the proposal is being submitted.

The salutation should be to a specific person. You may not use "To whom it may concern" or "Dear Colleague" salutations. They show that you have not done the basic research to determine the grant program contact person. The letter should come from (be signed by) the highest ranking person possible in your organization (the correspondent). The letter should be signed by a person, not a machine or a computer and preferably with blue ink. A letter signed with blue ink is indisputably an original. Don't forget to include the "prepared by" line at the bottom of the letter. Show professionalism in all ways—including the smallest.

Detailed Discussion

A cover letter is an opportunity for you to make an inviting introduction to the grant maker about your organization and also about your project. This is a place for creativity but not elaborate language. You want to warmly invite the reader to read about your excellent project.

The cover letter is one place to push the most obvious "hot buttons." What is a hot button? It is an issue that is critical to the funder. As we have explained in detail in our other books, you must meet the funder's agenda to receive an award. By reading every bit of information you can find on the funder, you will see recurring topics and themes. Perhaps the funder is particularly interested in diversity, or projects that promote preventive health care, or projects that promote family unity. These are hot buttons—issues that are at the heart of the reason the funder has gone to the trouble of setting up funds to grant.

Funders do not just decide to offer grants willy nilly. There is a problem or several problems they want to solve. If they had enough funding to solve the problem themselves, they would certainly try to do just that. For example, assume one grant maker wants to stop drug and alcohol abuse in the United States. How much money would it take to do that? More than even our federal and state governments have. So with the funds the grant maker has, they "seed" projects that, in their opinion, have a good chance of making an impact. They fund projects that can be modeled by other groups to help in their communities. Do they fund projects to set up animal shelters? Or water conservation? No, they fund projects that obviously and rationally directly impact drug and alcohol use in this country. This is just one reason why it is a huge mistake to write one proposal and send it to dozens of funders—you are wasting your time if your project does not match the hot buttons of the funder.

How do you find out about a given funder's hot buttons? You read their literature—all of it. You read about projects they have funded in the past. You read any articles you can find about the funder. Most funders have an Internet presence now and that makes it a lot easier, but some are glad to mail you information about their programs. Funders do not keep their key agendas secret and they are not playing a game with you—they want to invest in the very best projects they can.

Let's look at a couple of examples from actual information published by grant makers.

The Ford Foundation[2] is a resource for innovative people and institutions worldwide. Our goals are to:

- *Strengthen democratic values,*
- *Reduce poverty and injustice,*
- *Promote international cooperation and*
- *Advance human achievement*

This has been our purpose for more than half a century.

A fundamental challenge facing every society is to create political, economic and social systems that promote peace, human welfare and the sustainability of the environment on which life depends. We believe that the best way to meet this challenge is to encourage initiatives by those living and working closest to where problems are located; to promote collaboration among the nonprofit, government and business sectors, and to ensure participation by men and women from diverse communities and at all levels of society. In our experience, such activities help build common understanding, enhance excellence, enable people to improve their lives and reinforce their commitment to society.

The Ford Foundation is one source of support for these activities. We work mainly by making grants or loans that build knowledge and strengthen organizations and networks. Since our financial resources are modest in comparison

[2] The Ford Foundation, 320 E. 43rd St., New York, NY 10017, *www.fordfound.org.*

to societal needs, we focus on a limited number of problem areas and program strategies within our broad goals.

Let's look at what the Ford Foundation says about itself. What are its hot buttons? The obvious ones are the four bulleted items, but what are the less obvious issues critical to the grant maker, the Ford Foundation?

First of all they write, "we believe the best way to meet this challenge is to encourage initiatives by those living and working closest to where problems are located." What does this mean? It means that the Ford Foundation wants to fund efforts at the grassroots level. It is not going to look kindly on a proposal by a think tank in California wishing to solve a literacy issue in the rural Midwest. It will, however, consider a proposal that meets one or more of the obvious criteria (the ones in bullets) and that is submitted by a group of organizations actually located in the rural Midwest.

So how do you use this information in a cover letter? Well you might write an initial paragraph like the one below.

> *Our project will go a long way to effectively offering literacy education classes right in the communities in which our most rural citizens live. Our organization is located centrally among five counties with the highest poverty ratings and lowest educational achievement in the state. Our illiterate citizens have failed in school and thus do not want to go to a school house for help. They are much more comfortable in their churches, grange halls, and local grocery stores. So we are taking our programs to them.*

Here is another example from the David and Lucille Packard Foundation.[3]

> *The mission of the Conservation Program is to ensure a healthy future for all life on earth. The Conservation Program embraces an ecological approach that draws together the people, institutions, resources, and ideas that can best address our environmental crisis. Our primary goal is to conserve biodiversity resources in our core geography of California, Cascadia, Hawaii, the Western Pacific, and Mexico. To accomplish that, we support field-based projects in those areas. In addition, other program areas address some of the drivers of biodiversity loss and environmental decline; these program areas include Marine Fisheries, Energy, Western Land Use, and, in conjunction with the Population Program, Population-Environment.*

The primary goals are pretty well clarified in this statement. However, take notice of the phrase, "draws together the people, institutions, resources,

---

[3] The David and Lucille Packard Foundation, 300 2nd St., Ste. 200, Los Altos, CA 94022, *www.packfound.org.*

and ideas that can best address." This indicates that this grant maker subscribes to the practice of partnering to solve a problem. This is a growing issue among grant makers around the world. The theory is that partnerships make best use of all resources and reduce redundancy in the use of resources. The following is a paragraph for a cover letter that addresses both the primary issues and the hot button.

In our coastal area, pollution from area industry has raised temperatures of the bay so that the native fish and shellfish are dying or are contaminated by bacteria. This interrupts the ecosystem and interrupts the carefully and environmentally sound management of our fishing industry. Through a coalition of concerned citizens, managers of the local fish processing plants, representatives of the fishermen, and key top managers of the local industries, we believe we have developed a solution to the problem—one with lasting effect.

What have you done with this introductory paragraph in your cover letter? You have let them know that you understand their agenda, and moreover, you meet the essence of their standard. In doing this, you are predisposing them to like your proposal because you clearly understand their key considerations and, moreover, you agree with them.

What is another thing your cover letter accomplishes? It places your organization and project in the state, country or world. You know your community intimately. But remember, the readers who read your proposal may not know anything about your type of community. Many government grant makers bring in people from all parts of the country and not one may be from your part of the world. Even within a state, one part of the state may not know a thing about the problems and pressures of living in another part of the state. So one thing you do in a cover letter is try to give a thumbnail picture of your part of the world and the target population your project intends to serve.

> **Remember:** A grant maker intends to solve a problem. Your project must be targeted to solve the problem that interests the grant maker. The proposal is the way you describe your project so that the grant maker knows enough about it to be sure it is a good investment. Your project must serve a target population—it must benefit someone—so it is important that you describe your target population so the grant maker can picture the beneficiaries.

Here is an example of how you might briefly describe your location and target population in a cover letter.

Our area is rural and our population is diverse due mostly to a large number of migrant workers. There are few cohesive communities with recognizable structure. Our people mostly work the land or work in the few small industries scattered across the three counties we intend to serve. Most adults reached no more than eighth grade and most clearly live in poverty.

Here is another example from a different type of environment.

We are a second tier city of half a million people. Most of our citizens work in steel or heavy manufacturing facilities. During a significant portion of the year, the climate is such that citizens rarely get out except to go to work. Loose communities surround each manufacturing plant. Other than school, there is little for our young people to do and there are many hours of isolation without adult supervision. For these and other reasons, we have a growing alcohol abuse problem both with adults and, significantly, with our young people.

It is also important to state your purpose for submitting a proposal. You do not need to go into detail but you need to say something more than "we need money." They know that. Few, if any, funders will fund the entire budget of a project. This is not a money issue as much as a philosophy issue. If the grant maker funds the entire budget, what will happen after the grant funding inevitably runs out? The project will die. Other than entitlements, grant funding is not intended to go on forever. It has a limited time span and no grant funder wants to fund a project that dies when the funding runs out. They want to fund lasting efforts that are good investments.

So the grant maker wants to see your investment, and that of all the other partners and stakeholders in the effort. This is the overall project budget. There is a smaller budget that represents what you are asking of the grant maker. Here is an example of what you might say as a purpose for submitting the proposal.

Though we have funding internally and from our partners for the planning phase and for the actual structures within which the project will run, we do not have enough funding to cover all of the equipment necessary to accomplish the project mission.

Here is another example of a concise statement of purpose.

Our project is designed so that once it is implemented, project income and donated staff from our partners will insure continuation. However, for the project to be initiated, we need funding for staff training, for resource materials for our community resource center, and for the technology to manage the continuing project.

Next to last, it is important to thank the grant maker for the opportunity to submit a proposal. Everyone likes to be thanked and the representatives of the grant maker are no exceptions. It is an opportunity that you would not have if the people that set up the fund had not worked hard, first of all, to establish the fund and, second, to review, select and evaluate worthy projects.

Finally, give information on the project contact person. The project contact person is the one person in your organization who knows more about the project than anyone else. At this time, the contact person is probably the proposal writer rather than the project director. It is also probably not the cover letter correspondent. The contact person must be able to answer questions about the project, especially budget questions. Give the name, telephone number, fax number, and e-mail address for the contact person. If there are any special directions for making contact, such as time restrictions, include this information also.

Putting It All Together

Now that we have discussed all the pieces of the cover letter, what is an appropriate order in which to organize them? Your one-page cover letter should probably consist of four paragraphs in the following order. Each paragraph should contain this information:

1. Introduction to your organization, community, and target population.
2. Statement about the project that includes the two key hot buttons.
3. Purpose for submitting the proposal.
4. The "thank you" for the opportunity to submit the proposal and the contact person information.

Authorship

The question arises, "Who should write this letter?" The answer is that the proposal writer should craft the letter. Submit a carefully crafted letter to the correspondent as a "draft" for changes. Make any changes, print on letterhead, and return to the correspondent for signature. Almost no one will turn down the offer of someone else writing a draft from which to work.

Checklist—Cover Letter[4]

✔ On letterhead.

✔ One page.

✔ 12-point, text font.

✔ Generous margins.

✔ Left justified.

✔ Reference line.

✔ Salutation to a specific person.

✔ First paragraph introducing the organization, community, and target population.

✔ Paragraph about the project including two key hot buttons.

✔ Paragraph explaining the purpose for submitting proposal.

✔ Final paragraph expressing thanks and providing contact information.

✔ Correspondent is the highest ranking person possible in the organization.

✔ Signed by a human with blue ink.

✔ "Prepared by" line.

✔ Enclosure line.

Last Words

The cover letter is the first impression the funder has of your organization. It is important to take the opportunity to make points by indicating your fit with the funder's agenda. This can be done subtly by showing that you are an organization that can handle the project, that you fit with the funder's hot buttons, and that you understand what the funder is looking for. Writing cover letters is something of an art because you need to say a lot in a little space.

Examples of Cover Letters for Four Projects

The following four examples (1.1 to 1.4) offer sample cover letters used by four diverse organizations to request a grant. The elements described within this chapter have each been implemented in the letters.

---

[4] Remember that a grant maker's directions (instructions/guidelines) take precedence over any and all other considerations. You must absolutely, positively follow the grant maker's directions exactly, precisely, and painstakingly.

EXAMPLE 1.1

After School Program—Cover Letter

Sunnyvale School District
One Academy Lane • Sunnyvale, Mississippi 39200

August 31, 2004

Sarah Smith, Ph.D., Director
After School Grant Program
Office of Elementary and Secondary Education
U.S. Department of Education
Washington, D.C. 20500

REF: September 1, 2004—After School
Grant Program Competition

Dear Dr. Smith:

Sunnyvale School District serves 12,000 students from a rural, largely farming area in north central Mississippi. Our five middle schools serve 4,000 students, 1,200 of which we propose to serve with our After School Program. We propose to serve those middle school students most at risk of failure due to academic or behavior problems.

Our proposed After School Program includes student activities in three areas: academic, recreational, and social. We have established a community-wide consortium of 16 stakeholder organizations both public and private.

Focus groups held throughout the district identified as needing immediate attention, the problem of children with no adult supervision between the time school is out and parents return home from work. The district's long-term plan is to implement after school programs in all grades. To begin the process, we are requesting financial assistance to begin the process in our middle schools.

(continues)

EXAMPLE 1.1   *(Continued)*

After School Program—Cover Letter, page 2

We appreciate this opportunity to compete to be among the growing number of schools nationwide providing a quality after school alternative for the youth of their communities. For the answers to any questions you may have, please contact Jane Jones: voice 999-555-1111, fax 999-555-2222, or e-mail *jjones@ssd.k12.ms.us.*

Sincerely,

John J. Doe, Ph.D.
Superintendent

JJD/kbf

Enclosures: Proposal, 1 original with original signatures
                    Proposal, 6 copies

EXAMPLE 1.2

Senior Citizen Wellness Center—Cover Letter

 The Senior Citizen Wellness Center
100 Main Street
AnyTown, AnyState 99999

August 31, 2004

Cynthia Smyth, Director
Geriatric Grant Programs
Gigantor Health Care Foundation
One Funding Way
Grants Pass, Oregon 97526

REF: September Cycle—Geriatric Grant Programs

Dear Ms. Smyth:

The Senior Citizen Center has been created to serve our large
and growing elderly population through a partnership between
the city and several service organizations, both public and private.
Our midsized city is in the early stages of economic revival, but is
experiencing the problems inherent with an older than average
population.

We propose to use a comprehensive approach to the problems
of the elderly, including activities aimed at health, wellness, life
skills, and social enrichment. We also propose to create a single
entry point to all the various services available to the elderly
through a series of partnerships with local service providers.

The lead agency for this effort, the city, intends to place a bond
referendum before the voters in 2006 for long-term funding of
the Senior Citizen Center. We are requesting financial assistance to
enable us to establish a pilot program that demonstrates the benefits
of success thereby improving the chances of success with the
referendum.

(continues)

EXAMPLE 1.2 *(Continued)*

Senior Citizen Wellness Center— Cover Letter, page 2

We are indebted to Gigantor Health Care Foundation for the guidance and help we have been provided in the development of our project and the enclosed proposal. Win or lose, we have benefited already from our relationship. Aspects of our planning will move ahead regardless of outside funding, though our efforts would be enhanced greatly by your assistance. For answers to questions about our proposed project, please contact Jennie Carter: voice 999-555-3333, fax 999-555-4444, e-mail *jcarter@email.com.*

Sincerely,

Jack J. Doe
Director

JJD/kbf

Enclosures: Proposal, 1 original with original signatures
Proposal, 3 copies

EXAMPLE 1.3

Fire and Rescue Project—Cover Letter

Quad-County Fire and Rescue Association
123 Middle Junction Road
Central City, AnyState 12345

August 31, 2004

Don Jones, Director
Fire and Rescue Improvement Grant
Federal Emergency Management Agency
500 C Street, SW
Washington, D.C. 20472

REF: September 1, 2004—FRIG Competition

Dear Mr. Jones:

Quad-County Fire and Rescue Association is a cooperative effort of the 47 volunteer fire and rescue departments in Washington, Adams, Jefferson, and Madison counties. The purpose of the association is to pool scarce resources to improve training, recruitment, and community programs and outreach.

The purpose of the proposed project is to improve our abilities and capacity in fire prevention, fire fighting, and emergency medical services. The activities we will undertake in pursuit of this purpose include neighborhood fire prevention programs, a junior fire marshal program in the schools, centralized training, centralized recruitment, and improved purchasing power through standardization and coordination.

We need assistance in expanding the collaborative effort on behalf of the fire and rescue departments in the Quad-County area. It is widely accepted that the association concept has promise, but for the true strength of the association to become real, we need to show concrete results. FEMA assistance will enable us to overcome this hurdle.

(continues)

EXAMPLE **1.3**   *(Continued)*

Fire and Rescue Project—Cover Letter, page 2

Thank you for the opportunity to apply for the funds to improve fire and rescue services in our service area. Please contact me for answers to any question that may arise: voice 999-555-4321, fax 999-555-9876, or e-mail *moleary@quad-cnty-fire&rescue.org.*

Sincerely,

Mabel M. O'Leary,
Executive Director

MMO/kbf

Enclosures: Proposal, 1 original with original signatures
                   Proposal, 12 copies

EXAMPLE 1.4

Alcohol and Drug Abuse Program—Cover Letter

INNER CITY ALCOHOL AND
DRUG PREVENTION COMMISSION
44 RIVER ROAD • RIVER CITY, ANYSTATE 12345

August 31, 2004

Bernard Benrard, Director
Substance Abuse Prevention Initiative
Mega-Industries
100 Mega Circle
Mega, New York 12080

REF: September Cycle—Substance Abuse Prevention
     Grant Initiative

Dear Mr. Benrard:

Our Alcohol and Drug Prevention Commission serves the old inner city portion of River City. Our population consists of older, long time residents and young families and singles. We do not have many middle-aged citizens, though this segment of the population is slowly increasing as our economic base revitalizes.

The proposed project uses a community-wide consortium of partners including schools, community centers, business and industry, and substance abuse service providers, both public and private. Project activities include education outreach into schools and communities, a hot line and 24-hour crisis team, and a performance art group to dramatically disseminate the message against substance abuse.

(continues)

EXAMPLE 1.4   *(Continued)*

Alcohol and Drug Abuse Program— Cover Letter, page 2

The Commission receives funding from state, city, and federal sources for its regular programs and activities. The proposed project combines expansion of existing work (outreach), a new communication effort (hot line), and a cutting edge effort to get the message out (performance art).

On behalf of the commission and its partners, thank you for the help you have provided to us during the application development process. Even if we are not awarded a grant, we have benefited greatly from Mega-Industries involvement. We are grateful for the opportunity to become a Mega-Industries Anti-Substance Abuse Community. For answers to questions about our application, please contact Sue Smithson: voice 999-555-8888, fax 999-555-7777, e-mail *ssmithson@email.com.*

Sincerely,

John J. Jingleheimer
Executive Director

JJJ/kbf

Enclosures: Proposal, 1 original with original signatures
             Proposal, 4 copies

Chapter 2

Table of Contents

**Buying books would be a good thing if one
could also buy the time to read them in:
but as a rule the purchase of books is mistaken
for the appropriation of their contents.**

Arthur Schopenhauer[1]

At a Glance

What Else Is It Called?

- Contents or guide to contents
- Abbreviated TOC

When Is It Used?

Always include a table of contents. In a federal proposal, it is required. Always include one in a document with clearly defined parts and multiple pages (more than seven). Always include a table of contents in a document with supplementary information or appendix.

Why Is It Used?

First, it clearly shows you have included all the information the funder requested. Second, it shows a map of a complex document. If the reader is particularly interested in one section over another, the reader can turn to it quickly. It is important always to remember to make it easy on the reader.

---

[1] Arthur Schopenhauer (1788–1860), German philosopher. *Parerga and Paralipomena,* vol. 2, ch. 23, sct. 296a (1851).

Key Concepts

- Include every item requested by the funder in the order in which it was requested.
- Include every major heading in your document (headings should describe a body of content).
- Include all key parts of the proposal and all supplementary information.

Formatting Issues

The table of contents should be readable; do not use tiny type to keep it from spilling over to two pages. It should be in 12-point type, just as in the main body of the document. Main headings should be clearly marked with page numbers. Subheadings should be indented under main headings and should also have page numbers. A dotted line between headings and page numbers helps the reader match headings with pages. If the table of contents is long, include a heading *Table of Contents, continued* on the second page.

Psychology and Organization

The table of contents (TOC) looks like an easy section, but there is real psychology in setting up a TOC. Why? There are several reasons. First of all, funders have very little time to read your document—your deathless prose. Yes, it is true; reviewers may not read all of your proposal. Moreover, different people may read different parts. If a funder has clearly stated what has to be in a proposal, and an item is left out of the TOC, the funder is likely to assume it is not in your proposal. Funders, on seeing a part left out, may choose not to even review your proposal at all, declaring it unresponsive. No amount of argument or discussion on your part will prompt a funder to review it during the next round of competition once it has been rejected.

Most funders, as you know, have guidelines, at least, if not a full request for proposal, stating the information they want in a proposal. In our book *Grantseeker's Toolkit: A Comprehensive Guide to Finding Funding,*[2] we told our readers to carefully outline the content required in the proposal. This is your base outline for the table of contents. You will add special features of your project, appendices and supplementary information to your TOC.

Not only include everything in the table of contents that the funder requests, but also include it in the order in which they requested it. They

---

[2] Cheryl Carter New and James Aaron Quick, *Grantseeker's Toolkit: A Comprehensive Guide to Finding Funding* (Hoboken, NJ: John Wiley & Sons, 1998).

expect to see their own form of organization, even if you think they have the cart before the horse. Organize it the way they expect to see it, or they may miss the fact that you have all the anticipated parts. If you include additional topics, organize them logically with the topics they expect to see. Be careful that their major headings appear boldly and clearly. Again, make it easy on the reader.

> **Always:** Include everything the funder requested in the Guidelines or Request for Proposal in the Table of Contents.

Examples

Here are a couple of good examples. First, from the Charles Stewart Mott Foundation.[3]

Specific Program Guidelines: Pathways Out of Poverty

The Pathways Out of Poverty program suggests that in many cases it may be preferable to submit a letter of inquiry in lieu of a full proposal. Such letters should describe the purposes, objectives, general methodology and total costs of the project. This allows the team to determine the relevance of the project and whether a full proposal is desired.

The following checklist should be used when submitting a full proposal to the Pathways Out of Poverty program:

✔ *A cover letter signed by the individual ultimately responsible for signing grant contracts on behalf of the grant applicant. The letter should describe briefly the proposed project as well as the amount of money requested and the grant period.*

✔ *An explanation of the need or problem project addresses.*

✔ *A description of how the project fits within the objectives of the specific program area(s) under which funds are requested.*

✔ *The population served by the project.*

✔ *The methodology and plan of work describing activities to be undertaken and possible limiting factors that can affect project progress.*

✔ *The timetable for activities.*

✔ *Anticipated results of the project.*

✔ *The plan for dissemination of project results.*

✔ *Anticipated follow-up, including an explanation of future funding if the project is to continue.*

---

[3] Charles Stewart Mott Foundation, Mott Foundation Building, 503 S. Saginaw St., Suite 1200, Flint, MI 48502-1851.

✔ *An evaluation plan to determine how the project will meet its proposed objectives, or indication of grantee's willingness to participate in a Foundation-sponsored evaluation.*

✔ *An annotated, line-item budget that includes a written explanation of each amount. (For example, "Salaries and Wages" should include the number of full-time equivalent positions and the duties of each FTE.) In addition, the project budget should identify the other sources of funding by amount and donor, and indicate whether that funding is anticipated or committed.*

✔ *A summary of the institutional budget, based on the applicant's fiscal year, if the applicant is not a major educational institution or unit of government.*

✔ *Appendices such as institutional background, qualifications of main project personnel, and proof of tax-exempt 501(c)(3) status by the IRS.*

The table of contents for a Charles Stewart Mott Foundation proposal would look something like Exhibit 2.1.

Next we can look at a federal program table of contents from the Smaller Learning Communities Program.[4] The requirements of the program are as follows:

1. ***Application for Federal Assistance.*** *Use ED Form 424. The first page is the standard application face page on which you provide basic identifying information about the applicant and the application. Please note that the requirement for the employer identification number has been revised. Please indicate your D-U-N-S number. If you are unfamiliar with that number or how to obtain one, instructions are included in the package. Please include the e-mail address of the contact person, if available.*

2. ***Coversheet for the Smaller Learning Communities (SLC) program application package.*** *The second page of your application consists of the SLC cover page indicating the name and address of each school included in the application.*

3. ***Budget Form.*** *Use the enclosed ED Form 524 (Budget Information, Non-Construction Programs) to provide a complete budget summary for each year of the project.*

4. ***Program Abstract.*** *Begin with a one-page abstract summarizing the proposed Smaller Learning Communities project, including enrollment data on each eligible high school and a short description of the population to be served by the project and a description of the project's objectives and activities.*

---

[4] Academic Improvement and Demonstration Programs, Office of Elementary and Secondary Education (OESE), Office of Vocational and Adult Education, CFDA #84.215L.

EXHIBIT 2.1

Sample Table of Contents— Charles Stewart Mott Foundation

Table of Contents

5. *Table of Contents. Include a table of contents listing the parts of the narrative in the order of the selection criteria and the page numbers where the parts of the narrative are found. Be sure to number the pages.*

6. *Program Narrative. Applicants are strongly encouraged to limit the application narrative to no more than 25 double-spaced, standard-type pages. Describe how the applicant meets the competitive priority, if applicable. Describe fully the proposed project in light of the selection criteria in the order in which the criteria are listed in the application package. Do not simply paraphrase the criteria.*

7. *Budget Narrative. Please provide a* brief *narrative that explains: (1) the basis for estimating the costs of professional personnel salaries, benefits, project staff travel, materials and supplies, consultants and subcontracts, indirect costs, and any projected expenditures; (2) how the major cost items relate to the proposed activities; (3) the cost of evaluation; and (4) a detailed description, as applicable, explaining in-kind support or funding provided by partners in the project.*

8. ***Compliance with General Education Provisions Act (GEPA), Section 427.*** *Include a section that describes how the program narrative (Part III) describes its compliance with GEPA's Section 427—equitable access to and participation in federally assisted programs for students, teachers, and other program beneficiaries with special needs.*

9. ***Assurances and Certifications.*** *Each of the forms and assurances provided in this application package (4 total) must be completed and included in the application.*

10. ***Appendices.*** *Applicants must include baseline data on student outcomes for one year, as Appendix A. Applicants may also include supporting documentation as appendices to the narrative. This material should be concise and pertinent to the competition. Note that the Secretary considers only information contained in the application in ranking applications for funding consideration. Letters of support sent separately from the formal application package are not considered in the review by the peer review panels.*

The table of contents from the Smaller Learning Communities Program would then look like Exhibit 2.2.

> The table of contents may not look very important, but it may be critical to whether or not you actually get funded. Prepare it with significant forethought.

Checklist—Table of Contents[5]

✔ Grant maker's order.

✔ Grant maker's names.

✔ A separate line entry for each application part named by grant maker.

✔ All forms.

✔ Project narrative broken into multiple, indented sub-headings.

✔ Separate line entry for each budget year's form and narrative.

✔ Separate line entry for each item in appendix.

---

[5] Remember that a grant maker's directions (instructions/guidelines) take precedence over any and all other considerations. You must absolutely, positively follow the grant maker's directions exactly, precisely, and painstakingly.

EXHIBIT 2.2

Sample Table of Contents—Smaller Communities Learning Program

Table of Contents

Last Words

Many grant makers publish, usually in the application guidelines, the proposal evaluation criteria, including the point value assigned to each part of the proposal. This grading rubric is the single best source for establishing the organization of your proposal. From it you get the order of the parts and what to name them. Two unbreakable rules apply.

1. Always put the parts of a proposal in the order shown in the application guidelines.
2. Always use the grant maker's names for the parts of a proposal.

It makes no difference what order makes the most sense. It makes no difference what a proposal section is normally called. There is one and only one authority in these matters, and that authority is the grant maker.

Examples of Tables of Contents for Four Projects

The following four examples (2.1 to 2.4) are sample tables of contents used by the same four diverse organizations profiled in Chapter 1. The specific elements described within this chapter are depicted in each table of contents.

EXAMPLE 2.1

After School Program—Table of Contents

Sunnyvale School District

Table of Contents

ED Form 424: Application for Federal Education Assistance . . . . .

Standard Form 424B: Assurances, Nonconstruction Programs . . .

ED80-0013: Certifications Regarding Lobbying; Debarment, Suspension, and Other Responsibility Matters; and Drug-Free Workplace Requirements . . . .

ED80-0014: Certification Regarding Debarment, Suspension, Ineligibility, and Voluntary Exclusion— Lower-Tier Covered Transactions . . . .

Standard Form LLL: Disclosure of Lobbying Activities . . . .

Executive Summary . . . .

Project Summary . . . .

Problem Statement . . . .

Goals and Objectives . . . .

Project Description . . . .

Management Plan . . . .

ED Form 524: Budget Information, Nonconstruction Programs . . .

Budget Justification . . . .

Continuation Plan . . . .

Evaluation Plan . . . .

Documentation Plan . . . .

Dissemination Plan . . . .

Key Personnel Biosketches . . . .

Timeline . . . .

Bibliography . . . .

Appendix A: Letters of Support . . . .

EXAMPLE 2.2

Senior Citizen Wellness Center— Table of Contents

The Senior Citizen Wellness Center

Table of Contents

Executive Summary . . . .

Project Summary . . . .

Problem Statement . . . .

Goals and Objectives . . . .

Project Description . . . .

Management Plan . . . .

Budget . . . .

Budget Justification . . . .

Continuation Plan . . . .

Evaluation Plan . . . .

Documentation Plan . . . .

Dissemination Plan . . . .

Key Personnel Biosketches . . . .

Timeline . . . .

Bibliography . . . .

Appendix A: Letters of Support . . . .

EXAMPLE 2.3

Fire and Rescue Project—Table of Contents

Quad-County Fire and Rescue Association

Table of Contents

EXAMPLE 2.4

Alcohol and Drug Abuse Program— Table of Contents

INNER CITY ALCOHOL AND DRUG PREVENTION COMMISSION

Table of Contents

Chapter 3

Executive Summary

**When you give power to an executive
you do not know who will be filling that position
when the time of crisis comes.**

Ernest Hemingway[1]

At a Glance

What Else Is It Called?

- Executive brief or overview

When Is It Used?

Always include an executive summary when approaching a foundation or corporation unless it is specifically prohibited in fact or by severe page limitation. Most often a federal program will severely limit the type and content of pages so unless it asks for an executive summary, you would normally not include one.

Why Is It Used?

It shows the reader at a glance what you are requesting. Many times, especially with regard to a corporate proposal, your proposal will be routed to the appropriate person based on the executive summary. You are always dealing with people who have very little time to waste. They do not have time to read your whole proposal to find out what it is about and what you are requesting of them. An executive summary allows the reader to gain a clear idea of your project without reading through pages of text.

---

[1] Ernest Hemingway, "Notes on the Next War: A Serious Topical Letter," *Esquire* (September 1935), as quoted in *By-Line Ernest Hemingway,* ed. William White.

Key Concepts

- Provides a description of the project and expected results. Concentrates on the essence of your project, not all the side issues and ramifications.
- Gives the pertinent contact information.
- Clearly states what you expect of the funder.
- Clearly states what your organization and others are investing in the project (remember no funder will fund the project's entire budget).

Formatting Issues

The executive summary is never more than one page in length. It is formatted in 12-point type with clear headings as shown in this chapter. Do not try to cram more words in by extending margins or by making type smaller. This is to be a very concise (with no extraneous words) component of the proposal.

Project Title

Your project title should be descriptive and memorable. It should not be so cute that it sounds silly and unprofessional, neither should it be so full of jargon that the average person could not tell what the project was about. This is not the time for double-talk.

Contact Person

This should be the person who is always available to talk to the funder—the person who knows the most about the project. Administrative assistants should be alerted to get this person any time the funder calls. You do not want to keep the funder waiting for days for a return call.

Proposal Submitted By

The official agency or entity that is responsible for managing the funds, if awarded, should be entered along with the full street address.

Mission Statement

What is the ultimate mission of your project if everything works out perfectly? Are you trying to eliminate drugs from your community? Will you increase the quality and length of life for your senior citizens? What is the ultimate result? A mission is not to build a swimming pool. That is not a valid mission. With regard to the swimming pool, a valid mission might be "eliminate youth aggression through productive activity." Or "maintain a healthier senior population." The swimming pool is simply a tool to be used to attain a mission. Your mission is what you ultimately hope to accomplish.

Summary of Problem Statement and Project Synopsis

Since this whole executive summary is no more than one page in length, you need to describe your project in one or two paragraphs. This requires, not just a vague idea of what you intend to do, but a well-developed project that is completely thought through and has action steps to accomplish over a specific time frame. Of course you should never write a proposal until you have planned every aspect of your project. But this fact bears repeating. Simply put, you state the main ingredients of your project.

In one sentence—state the problem you are addressing. The following are examples:

- *Our young people ages 12 to 19 have an increase in criminal activity that is tenfold what it was five years ago.*
- *The incidence of heart disease in our county is 80% higher than the state average.*
- *Our rural children have little exposure to classical studies and the arts because of the lack of community resources which hampers them when competing for entry to major colleges and universities.*

After stating the problem, proceed to tell concisely what you intend to do about the problem. Have you designed a counseling and mentoring project? Is your project a community education, exercise and nutrition program? What are the key elements of your project and main focus?

The following shows examples of problem statements with an example project synopsis for each.

- ***Our young people ages 12 to 19 have an increase in criminal activity that is tenfold what it was five years ago.***

  Through a cooperative effort of the local sheriff's department, police department, school system, department of health and human services, and local churches, students at risk will be identified. Trained counselors and master social workers will be assigned to each group of ten children. Some counselors and social workers will be paid out of agency budgets, and some will be paid from the project budget. Each student will be assessed, using formal and proven tests and assessments. A team of professionals working directly with the child will create an individual development plan. This plan will include special classes, counseling, community volunteering, an assigned mentor, tutoring, family counseling, and supervision for all hours of the day.

- ***The incidence of heart disease in our county is 80% higher than the state average.***

  A county-wide free screening program will be available through all churches, schools, community centers, and clinics in the county so that screening is accessible to every person in the county. This will be accomplished over two months of weekdays and weekends. Those individuals that are found to be at risk will be invited to attend classes offered in the same locations as the screenings. These classes include: nutritional grocery buying, heart healthy cooking, home exercise techniques, and heart healthy lifestyle changes. Support groups will be set up for smokers who wish to stop, couch potatoes, and those with depression or other emotional or physical issues that affect heart health. All community centers will be fitted with exercise equipment, a walking track, and licensed, qualified health professionals to monitor and guide each participant. Each week the churches will serve a heart-healthy meal to all participants free of charge and provide recipes.

- ***Our rural children have little exposure to classical studies and the arts because of the lack of community resources. This hampers them when competing for entry to major colleges and universities.***

  With the assistance of the state arts council, both state universities, and with virtual access through the Internet and via satellite, we plan to provide our students classes, lectures, arts experiences, and virtual laboratories for exploration and learning. Visiting artists will expose our students to various arts media and will be funded both by the state arts council and the university system. Classes in various aspects of the arts, including arts appreciation, piano, stringed instruments and wind instruments, will be provided by master's students through the university system during our summer program. Lectures will be sought from major museums and galleries throughout the region. We plan a dedicated arts lab with guided and supervised tours of all the major art centers in the United States and worldwide. Students will use a satellite system to take courses from our state universities and others across the country. Older students will prepare lessons to present to younger students.

Expected Results

Write a summary of the results expected from your project. Look at the information on missions, goals, and objectives in Chapter 6 and on evaluation plans in Chapter 10 for a thorough discussion of outcomes and results. Provide an overall statement of the expected outcome of your project mission. Write one sentence that states the outcome of each goal. The following is an example.

Our ultimate mission is to eliminate drugs from our middle and high schools. We intend to do this through a combination of counseling, education and law enforcement. Our counseling program should advise and educate 1,250 students a year with 75% quitting drugs for at least a year. Follow-up is weekly and aggressive. We will launch an education campaign in every classroom with all children having been actively taught about dangers of drug use. In addition, a parent campaign to educate parents about signs and symptoms, as well as intervention, will reach 90% of the parents. Law enforcement representatives will discuss penalties and give case examples of people who use and deal drugs and the legal system. A law enforcement officer will be stationed at each school and will help counsel students.

Funding Request

State the overall budget for the project, then state the amount of your request. A funder will not fund every dollar for a project because the funder wants to see an investment by the submitting organization. The funder also wants to see either an in-kind or real dollar investment by the partners. For a further discussion of in-kind, see the discussion of budget in Chapter 15. The following is an example.

Our total project budget is $325,760. Our request from ABC Foundation is for $152,750 of that figure.

Your Investment

Discuss your investment in the project in dollar terms. Also outline the amounts partners are contributing. Be brief. The following is an example.

Our organization is investing $75,000 in the project and an additional $35,000 in in-kind contribution. The department of social services is contributing $22,500 and $3,200 in in-kind. The local police department is contributing $37,310 in in-kind.

Checklist—Executive Summary[2]

✔ One page.
✔ Heading for each topic.

---

[2] Remember that a grant maker's directions (instructions/guidelines) take precedence over any and all other considerations. You must absolutely, positively follow the grant maker's directions exactly, precisely, and painstakingly.

✔ Project title.

✔ Contact person information.

✔ Applicant information.

✔ Mission statement.

✔ Problem statement.

✔ Project summary.

✔ Expected results.

✔ Applicant's investment.

✔ Funding request.

Last Words

The most common question about the executive summary is: "What's the difference between the project summary and the executive summary?" The answer is simple. The project summary deals exclusively with project activities. The executive summary is a snapshot of all major aspects of the project. The executive summary includes information about the applicant, the problem, and finances—topics not covered in a project summary. In fact, a project summary is part of an executive summary, but only part, perhaps one quarter of the contents.

For most proposal writers, a summary is the most difficult part of a proposal to write. It often takes an uninvolved person to stand back and make the hard choices about the small amount of information that can go into a summary. The choice is not to make a summary longer. The choice is to leave out extraneous material, and that is the problem. The person who developed the project and wrote the proposal is often so emotionally involved with the work that it is impossible to make the hard choices about what to leave out. Everything seems important. Only an outsider can bring the dispassionate view that is necessary.

Examples of Executive Summaries of Four Projects

The following four examples (3.1 to 3.4) are sample executive summaries for each of the four diverse organizations that have been profiled in the book thus far. The specific elements described within this chapter are illustrated in each example.

EXAMPLE 3.1

After School Program—Executive Summary

Sunnyvale School District

Project Title

After School Program

Contact Person

Jane Jones (voice 999-555-1111, fax 999-555-2222, or e-mail *jjones@ssd.k12.ms.us*)

Applicant Information

Sunnyvale School District
One Academy Lane
Sunnyvale, Mississippi 39200

Mission Statement

The mission of the After School Program for middle school students is to improve academic performance, reduce the incidence of behavioral problems, increase recreational and social opportunities, and promote positive parental involvement.

Problem Statement

Sunnyvale school district faces problems similar to many rural school districts across the nation. In summary, the problems are low academic achievement, high drop out rate (low graduation rate), low self-esteem, increasing incidents of violence, increasing use of alcohol, tobacco, and other drugs, few chances for organized recreation, and insufficient positive parental involvement in education.

Project Summary

The After School Program for middle school students has five main components:

1. Improve academic performance with supervised homework completion, tutoring, and supplemental academic instruction.

2. Provide applied learning activities such as cooking and carpentry.

(continues)

EXAMPLE **3.1** *(Continued)*

After School Program— Executive Summary, page 2

3. Provide recreational activities such as soccer and chess.

4. Provide social and health activities such as anger management and drug and alcohol prevention.

5. Provide parental involvement activities.

Participants will be served a nutritious, after school snack, and transportation home will be provided. Supplemental academic instruction will be provided by teachers certified in various subjects. Applied learning, recreational, and social and health activities will be provided by specialists such as 4-H leaders, home economics and vocational education instructors, city parks and recreation staff, and alcohol, tobacco, and other drug commission counselors.

Expected Results

Middle school students' grades and test scores improve. Participants become proficient in an applied life skill. Incidence of substance abuse and violence decrease. Parents become more involved in their children's education. Participants have the opportunity for a daily supervised recreational activity of their choice.

Our Investment

The district and its partners contribute $1,046,414 to the budget of the project during year one. This amount increases each year until, in project year 5, the share of the budget borne by the district and its partners is 86% of the budget.

Funding Request

For project year 1, the grant request is $1,022,723, less than 50% of total project cost. The amount requested goes down each year until, in project year 5, the grant request is $224,609, less than 14% of total project cost.

EXAMPLE 3.2

Senior Citizen Wellness Center— Executive Summary

The Senior Citizen Wellness Center

Project Title

Senior Citizen Center

Contact Person

Jennie Carter (voice 999-555-3333, fax 999-555-4444, e-mail *jcarter@email.com*)

Applicant Information

The Senior Citizen Center
100 Main Street
AnyTown, AnyState 99999

Mission Statement

The mission of the Senior Citizen Center project is to enhance health, wellness, and social activity, and to provide a single point of entry into the world of services for the elderly.

Problem Statement

The elderly population of our city is a much larger percentage of the total population than in the country as a whole. The problems of the elderly are well documented. Health and wellness head the list. Physical decline inhibits the elderly from moving about easily, making the normal functions of life, such as shopping, difficult or impossible. Mental decline makes the elderly susceptible to mistakes with medication and dealing with the complications of life, such as taxes and paying bills. Lack of mobility also decreases the opportunity for social interaction, which furthers mental decline.

Project Summary

Health and wellness activities are provided through partnerships with the city hospital, the public health department, and the ATOD (Alcohol, Tobacco, and Other Drugs) Commission. Health activities include screenings for heart disease, diabetes, and several other conditions. Screenings are followed by referral to

(continues)

EXAMPLE 3.2   *(Continued)*

Senior Citizen Wellness Center— Executive Summary, page 2

appropriate care. Wellness activities include exercise programs, weight room, and other supervised activities. Cooking classes teach how to prepare food for specialized diets.

Social activities include meals, games with a game room, dances, and a foster grandparent program in partnership with local schools. Combination social and health activities are support groups for those seniors with emotional or mental issues such as loss or substance abuse.

The single point of entry provides seniors with a simplified way to access all the various services for the elderly, both public and private, through a single location and with a single counselor or helper.

Expected Results

The health and wellness of our city's elderly improves. Seniors benefit mentally and emotionally from improved social activities. Seniors have an effective single point of entry to the providers of services to the elderly.

Our Investment

The Senior Citizen Center will provide all needed support except that detailed in the grant request. A major effort will go into a positive outcome for the bond referendum for permanent funding for the project staff positions.

Funding Request

We are requesting funds to provide five staff positions for three years as well as equipment and renovation for program start-up.

EXAMPLE 3.3

Fire and Rescue Project—Executive Summary

Quad-County Fire and Rescue Association

Project Title
Fire and Rescue Project

Contact Person
Mabel M. O'Leary (voice 999-555-4321, fax 999-555-9876, e-mail *moleary@quad-cnty-fire&rescue.org*)

Applicant Information
Quad-County Fire and Rescue Association
123 Middle Junction Road
Central City, AnyState 12345

Mission Statement
The mission of the Fire and Rescue Project is to increase community outreach and improve training, recruitment, and purchasing.

Problem Statement
Volunteer firefighters are our communities' first line of defense against fires, medical emergencies, chemical, biological, and terrorist threats, hazardous materials incidents, and trench collapses. They also provide high and low angle and other types of specialized rescues. Over the past twenty years, the number of emergency calls has increased dramatically along with the training requirements necessary to keep pace with expanding responsibilities. Volunteer fire and rescue departments are having increasing difficulty raising sufficient funds to keep pace with the cost of training and equipment necessary to meet the expanded range of emergencies to which communities expect them to respond. In addition, recruitment and retention are becoming serious problems. Since the early 1980s, the number of volunteer firefighters has decreased by almost 10%, while the number of calls to which they respond and the type of emergencies has increased dramatically. After-incident

(continues)

EXAMPLE **3.3** *(Continued)*

Fire and Rescue Project— Executive Summary, page 2

investigations show that over half of the fires could have been prevented with a relatively small investment of time, and generally, almost no expense.

Project Summary

The purpose of the Quad-County Fire and Rescue Project is to reduce the incidence of fires and injuries due to fires by increasing community outreach and improving training, recruitment, and purchasing.

Community outreach is to be improved through 47 neighborhood fire prevention programs and grade-appropriate junior fire marshal programs in 22 schools.

Training, recruitment, and purchasing is to be improved by centralizing the activities of 47 volunteer departments through a consortium of fire and rescue departments. The consortium creates, in effect, a fire and rescue department equivalent in size to a second-tier city such as Denver or Indianapolis.

Expected Results

Community members gain knowledge about fire prevention, and the number and the severity of fires decreases. Fire and rescue personnel are better trained. Recruitment and retention goals are met. The cost to member departments of purchases and purchasing decreases.

Our Investment

The consortium will fund the staff positions and provide the facility.

Funding Request

The grant request is to fund start-up funding for one year.

Example 3.4

Alcohol and Drug Abuse Program— Executive Summary

INNER CITY ALCOHOL AND DRUG PREVENTION COMMISSION

Project Title

ATOD (Alcohol, Tobacco, and Other Drugs) Prevention Project

Contact Person

Sue Smithson (voice 999-555-8888, fax 999-555-7777, e-mail *ssmithson@email.com*)

Applicant Information

Inner City Alcohol and Drug Prevention Commission
44 River Road
River City, AnyState 12345

Mission Statement

The mission of the ATOD Prevention Project is to reduce ATOD abuse among school students, provide intervention services, and effectively take the ATOD prevention message to the community.

Problem Statement

ATOD use among school-aged youth is increasing. Our community has no publicly available ATOD intervention and response resource. Members of the community have grown apathetic and bored with the anti-abuse message and are, therefore, *tuning out.*

Project Summary

The purpose of the community ATOD Prevention Project is to reduce ATOD abuse among school students, provide enhanced intervention services, and effectively take the ATOD prevention message to the community.

Substance abuse by children will be addressed through an educational outreach into the community's schools. The ATOD commission and the school district have partnered for a vigorous and ongoing in-school effort.

(continues)

EXAMPLE 3.4 *(Continued)*

Alcohol and Drug Abuse Program— Executive Summary, page 2

Intervention services will be enhanced with a 24-hour hotline and 24-7 crisis teams. Trained hotline operators and crisis team members will apply experience-proven intervention techniques to solve problems.

Performance art will be used to dramatically and effectively publicize the substance abuse prevention message to the community. A troupe of performance artists will perform publicly throughout the community to dramatize the anti-substance abuse message.

Expected Results

We expect that our project will increase students' and community members' knowledge about substance abuse. We expect that ATOD use will decrease. We expect drug overdoses and alcohol-related crimes and accidents to decrease.

Our Investment

The ATOD Commission is funding three of the six staff positions.

Funding Request

The grant request is for three staff positions and start-up expenses during project year 1.

Chapter 4

Project Summary

**A synopsis is a cold thing. You do it
with the front of your mind. If you're going
to stay with it, you never get quite the
same magic as when you're going all out.**

J.B. Priestley

At a Glance

What Else Is It Called?

- Project synopsis
- Project abstract
- Project overview

When Is It Used?

Most grant makers require a synopsis. It may be required in a space on the cover page or it may be requested on a separate, dedicated page.

Why Is It Used?

It has many purposes—if you are awarded a grant, it is used in publicity pieces, annual reports and on Web sites. This component is important because it is a way the funder can tell at a glance if you meet the criteria for funding. If something in the synopsis is outside the funder's agenda, then the reader may not read further. It is critical that you review the synopsis (as well as the entire proposal) from the funder's viewpoint. Is it clear that you qualify for an award based on a match between your project and the information published by the funder?

Key Concepts

- Brief but clear.
- Contains all major project components, if only in a list.
- Contains a mention of everything the funder requires in the project.
- Include the one, best, most creative aspect ("hook") of your project.
- Write it last.

Formatting Issues

You must absolutely adhere to required space limitations. If the directions say 500 words, then do not make it 501 and do not hyphenate words to cheat. Use normal margins and 12-point type as with the rest of the proposal.

Use Goals to Describe the Project

It is important that you write the project synopsis last because, as you develop the proposal, you will undoubtedly revise and change components. The synopsis must match your project. If you write it first or in the middle, you may have a synopsis that talks about one project and a proposal that discusses something significantly different. It is never good to confuse the reader.

Mention all significant project components. Suppose your project is to create a drug counseling service for your community. It is logical that you would have to house the counseling service, staff it, develop an intake system and a payment system, implement counseling, evaluate its effectiveness and track the participants. How would you describe all of this in a project synopsis? The following is an example.

> *Our project is to set up a successful community drug counseling program. The program will be housed in the same building as the Community Health Center. Staff will be three full-time licensed counselors, a social worker, a family physician, a physician's assistant and support staff. Intake will be based on referral from all public and private organizations that encounter and treat drug-related problems. Counseling services are for both drug abusers and their family members in individual and group sessions. Payment will be a sliding scale based on family income. Private and public insurances will be used to defray individual costs. Patients will be followed for a period of five years after release from counseling to determine recidivism rates and needs for further counseling.*

The previous synopsis is only 125 words, but it gives a clear picture of project components. Project synopses are not glamorous or poetic—just descriptive. But what if you only have a 50-word limit? The following is the synopsis for the same project, but with a 50-word limit.

> *The community drug counseling program will be housed with the Community Health Center, staffed by 3 counselors, a social worker, a physician, a physician's assistant and support staff. Participants are referred by community organizations. Services are for participants and family members. Insurance and sliding fees provide sustainment. Patients are tracked for five years.*

Notice that both synopses cover the same ground. The only difference is that the flow is terse and the details are sketchy in the second example. If the funder requests an extreme word limit, they know that only a few details are possible. Just think of what you can do with a 500-word limit.

If you have done a good job on your goals and they are clearly the major steps in your project, then they provide an outline for your project synopsis. Please refer to Chapter 6 in this book on writing goals and this point will become clear. In the meantime, here is an example using the same program in the other two examples.

> ***Goal 1:*** *House and staff program with nine professional staff including five professional staff and four support staff.*
>
> ***Goal 2:*** *Design intake system and set up agreements with private and public community organizations for referral.*
>
> ***Goal 3:*** *Design individual and group counseling activities for both participants and family members.*
>
> ***Goal 4:*** *Process appropriate paperwork to set up private and public insurance payments and develop a sliding fee schedule.*
>
> ***Goal 5:*** *Implement counseling program.*
>
> ***Goal 6:*** *Evaluate project effectiveness by following patients for five years after they complete counseling objectives.*
>
> ***Goal 7:*** *Effectively manage administrative and fiscal components of project.*

Look back at the synopsis examples and then look carefully at the goals. Notice that the goals are in a rough chronological order. Goals should be major steps to completing your project. As such, they guide the development of the synopsis. This is a large program with many goals. Smaller, shorter-term projects may have fewer goals. The funder may call what we list as goals, objectives—the wording does not matter, as we will discuss in the section on mission, goals, and objectives.

Examples

Here are some examples of how a potential funder asks for a project synopsis.

From the Robert Wood Johnson Foundation[1]

The unsolicited proposal letter should be sent on your institution's letterhead, should not exceed five typed pages, and should contain the following:

- *A 3–4 paragraph overview, including an explicit statement of what would constitute success for the project*

From the Mary Owen Borden Foundation[2]

Part A: Project Summary *(if possible, Part A should be limited to one page but should not exceed two pages):*

- *Briefly summarize the project, identifying its need and its long- and short-term goals.*
- *Identify the services to be provided and the community that will benefit from them (estimate the number of individuals served). Describe where your services are provided in Monmouth and/or Mercer counties.*
- *Describe the methodology used to evaluate the project.*

From the MacArthur Foundation[3]

The one-page summary should provide:

- *Information regarding who will carry out the work*
- *Name of your organization (and acronym if commonly used)*
- *Name of parent organization, if any*
- *Name of chief executive officer or person holding similar position*
- *Organization's address (and courier address if different)*
- *Organization's phone number, fax number, and e-mail address, if any*
- *Name and title of the principal contact person, if different from the above*
- *Address (and courier address if different), phone number, fax number, and e-mail address, if any, of principal contact*
- *Web address, if any.*

---

[1] The Robert Wood Johnson Foundation, P.O. Box 2316, College Road East and Route 1, Princeton, NJ 08543-2316.

[2] Mary Owen Borden Foundation, 160 Hodge Road, Princeton, NJ 08540-3014.

[3] The John D. and Catherine T. MacArthur Foundation, Office of Grants Management, 140 S. Dearborn Street, Chicago, IL 60603-5285.

As you can see, some potential funders require a lot of information in a small space. As we said, do not cheat, either by widening margins or downsizing the font size. Keep within the funder's limitations and include every bit of information they require, in the order they request it.

Checklist—Project Summary[4]

✔ Mention[5] of each significant project component.

✔ Mention of key grant maker requirements.

✔ Mention of a "big-ticket" budget item.

✔ Mention the "hook."

✔ Not one word over word count.

✔ Normal margins.

✔ 12-point, text font.

Last Words

This is usually the first thing the reviewer (the person who reads and grades your grant proposal) reads. This is your first and only chance to make a good first impression. The sad fact is that the project summary is often a rushed afterthought, slapped together in a mad dash to get the published proposal out the door in time for overnight delivery to the grant maker—a big, big mistake.

Think of a summary as the opportunity to set the stage for the rest of the proposal. Realize that the way most proposals are structured, it is difficult, if not impossible, to understand what is truly going on with a project without reading a large part of the proposal. A well-structured project summary gives the reader the big picture before diving into the sometimes difficult to follow detail of the proposal itself.

A big-ticket budget item is one that expends 40% or more of the requested grant amount on a single purchase. A purchase this size makes this one of the central aspects of the entire grant proposal. Don't try to hide the expense. Don't give cost in the project summary, but do mention the item in the context in which it will be used.

---

[4] Remember that a grant maker's directions (instructions/guidelines) take precedence over any and all other considerations. You must absolutely, positively follow the grant maker's directions exactly, precisely, and painstakingly.

[5] Note carefully that it is "mention"—not describe. You do not have space to describe.

Every project has (or should have) a creative feature, a "cool" something, an innovation—the hook. Tell the reader right up front about the hook. Get the reader ready for it. Prepare the reader's mind for the twist that makes your project stand out from the crowd. That puts the coming project description in a different and better perspective for the reader.

Examples of Project Summaries for Four Projects

The following four examples (4.1 to 4.4) are sample project summaries for each of the four diverse organizations profiled in this book. The specific elements described within this chapter are illustrated in each exhibit.

Example 4.1

After School Program—Project Summary
(125-word limit)

Sunnyvale School District

The After School Program for middle school students has five main components.

1. Improve academic performance with supervised homework completion, tutoring, and supplemental academic instruction.
2. Provide applied learning activities such as cooking and carpentry.
3. Provide recreational activities such as soccer and chess.
4. Provide social/health activities such as anger management and drug and alcohol prevention.
5. Provide parental involvement activities.

Participants will be served a nutritious, after school snack, and transportation home will be provided. Supplemental academic instruction will be provided by teachers certified in various subjects. Applied learning, recreational, and social and health activities will be provided by specialists such as 4-H leaders, home economics and vocational education instructors, city parks and recreation staff, and alcohol, tobacco, and other drug commission counselors.

EXAMPLE 4.2

Senior Citizens Wellness Center— Project Summary (250-word limit)

The Senior Citizen Wellness Center

The purpose of the Senior Citizen Center Project is to improve seniors' health and wellness, increase seniors' opportunities for social activity, and provide a single point of entry into the community's large number of services for the elderly.

Health and wellness activities are provided through partnerships with the city hospital, public health, and the ATOD commission. Health activities include screenings for heart disease, diabetes, arthritis, blood pressure, bone density, skin cancers, muscle weakness, and other conditions. Screenings are followed by referral to appropriate care. Wellness activities include exercise programs, weight room, dance, swimming, walking path and jogging track, all professionally supervised. Cooking classes teach how to prepare food for specialized diets such as diabetic, high blood pressure, or heart disease.

Social activities include meals, games with a game room, dances, and a foster grandparent program in partnership with local schools. Combination social and health activities are support groups for those seniors with emotional or mental issues such as loss or substance abuse.

The single point of entry provides seniors with a simplified way to access all the various services for the elderly, both public and private, through a single location and with a single counselor/helper. The elderly access the single point of entry system three ways.

1. Walk-in, counselor-aided assistance at the Senior Center.
2. Walk-in, self-service assistance via computer at the Senior Center.
3. Home visit by counselor.

Improving the health and well-being of our community's elderly translates into financial savings for the city and substantial enhancement of the community's overall economic development effort.

EXAMPLE 4.3

Fire and Rescue Project—Project Summary (100-word limit)

Quad-County Fire and Rescue Association

The purpose of the Quad-County Fire and Rescue Project is to reduce the incidence of fires and injuries due to fires by increasing community outreach and improving training, recruitment, and purchasing.

Community outreach is to be improved through 47 neighborhood fire prevention programs and grade-appropriate junior fire marshal programs in 22 schools.

Training, recruitment, and purchasing is to be improved by centralizing the activities of 47 volunteer departments through a consortium of fire and rescue departments. The consortium creates, in effect, a fire and rescue department equivalent in size to a second-tier city such as Denver or Indianapolis.

EXAMPLE 4.4

Alcohol and Drug Abuse Program—
Project Summary (125-word limit)

*INNER CITY ALCOHOL AND
DRUG PREVENTION COMMISSION*

The purpose of the Community ATOD Prevention Project is to reduce ATOD abuse among school students, provide enhanced intervention services, and effectively take the ATOD prevention message to the community.

Substance abuse by children will be addressed through an educational outreach into the community's schools. The ATOD Commission and the school district have partnered for a vigorous and ongoing in-school effort.

Intervention services will be enhanced with a 24-hour hotline and 24-7 crisis teams. Trained hotline operators and crisis team members will apply experience-proven intervention techniques to solve problems.

Performance art will be used to dramatically and effectively publicize the substance abuse prevention message to the community. A troupe of performance artists will perform publicly throughout the community to dramatize the message against substance abuse.

Chapter 5

Problem Statement

**A problem is something you have hopes
of changing. Anything else is a fact of life.**

C. R. Smith[1]

At a Glance

What Else Is It Called?

- Needs statement
- Statement of need
- Needs assessment
- The problem

When Is It Used?

Always—your project must be a solution to a problem. The absence of something is not a problem. "We do not have a swimming pool so we need a swimming pool" is not a problem statement.

Why Is It Used?

Your connection to the funder is that you both want to solve the same problem. If you do not match the funder's desire to solve a specific problem, you do not have a chance for funding. The problem is the foundation on which your project is built. If your project does not clearly provide a potential solution to the problem in which both you and the funder are interested, then funding is not likely.

---

[1] *Publishers Weekly*, September 8, 1969.

Key Concepts

- A problem is the reason for a project.
- Well thought-out and backed by statistics.
- Logical and specific.
- Provide comparative data.
- Short pithy sentences—do not ramble.

Formatting Issues

Use normal margins, clear headings and subheadings and 12-point type to divide and highlight statistical data. Use tables, charts, or graphs to display large amounts of numerical data. Many numbers contained in text can be difficult to understand, resulting in the reader missing key relationships.

Describe the Problem

Any project must start with a problem statement. It is the basis for your project. Your connection with the funder is that you both want to solve the same problem. The lack of something is not in and of itself a problem. Let's expand these thoughts. They are very important to the success of your proposal.

The Problem Is the Basis for Your Project

Why go to the trouble of doing a project at all? The answer is to solve a problem. Even the most esoteric project has a problem at its core. Why establish a museum? It solves the problem of preserving history for future generations. Why implement a senior information center? Because seniors need complex information and there are so many resources that can be confusing. Why paint your house? It prevents deterioration and rot. Why make a ham and cheese sandwich? It solves the problem of a growling stomach. Projects are based on solving a problem.

You might not think of the problem right away, but if you think through your life—your projects are all based on solving a problem in one way or another. As grants consultants we get questions every day; we invite them through our Web site and answer them for free. Fully nine-tenths of the questions begin, "we need . . ."

When we get a "we need" question, we work with the person to determine what problem they are trying to solve. Do you need a swimming pool for your community? Why? Is it because you want to promote a healthy, exercise-oriented life for your young people? Is it because you want to provide a safe place for youth to gather so they will not get in trouble? Do you want to initiate a water-aerobic exercise program for your numerous senior citizens? What is the reason you want a community swimming pool?

Only if you identify a legitimate problem, can you match a funder and acquire a grant. See the next section for expansion of this concept.

The Problem Is Your Connection with the Funder

Why do people and organizations give away money? Foundations and corporate giving programs have to submit a set of bylaws that clearly and specifically state why they are in business to give away money. This is part of the official papers they send in to receive their nonprofit status. In the case of an individual who establishes a foundation, normally there is a life event or a personal philosophy that drives the problem the individual wants solved and upon which the foundation is based. Sometimes this is a person who has become ill with a disease so the foundation focuses on curing mental illness, researching cancer cures, or taking care of crippled children. Sometimes this is a particular philosophy such as improving the quality of life for people in Africa, improving the quality of education, or influencing world leaders to end nuclear armament.

In the case of government programs, an issue that gets the public's attention is normally a driving force because government programs are highly political. When you read in more than one popular media site that there is a huge teen pregnancy problem, you can bet there will be a funding program to solve that problem. If you read that alcohol consumption is killing college students, then you can bet there will be a funding program to combat that problem. Government programs are designed to solve problems that are certainly real but also that have captured the attention of the public or of a group with a significant or a distinctive presence within a society. Let us reiterate—this is not to say the problems are not real—they certainly are—but they have to gain a certain public profile usually before funding follows.

Funders have an agenda—to award funds based on their own interests and on the purposes for which they were established. They will only fund solutions to problems they have identified as being important. Many people confuse fundraising, where one letter requesting money for a good cause is mailed to many organizations or individuals, with grant seeking. Grant makers are not swayed by good causes other than those in which they already have an interest. Some allow unsolicited proposals. Others have set grant projects where they formally solicit proposals for a particular effort. Still others do both. It is therefore critical that a potential grant seeker thoroughly research a potential funder to determine exactly what the funder is interested in before deciding to send a proposal.

Your problem—the problem for which your project is a potential solution—must match a critical interest for the funder in order for your proposal to be considered. Research on funders is discussed in our best-seller, *Grantseeker's Toolkit: A Comprehensive Guide to Finding Funding*.[2]

Lack of Something Is Not a Problem

The lack of something is not equivalent to the problem. You cannot tell a funder that you lack playground equipment, money for the technology to do research, a symphony orchestra, or a swimming pool; therefore, please give money to correct this lack. This is circular reasoning.

You have to lay the groundwork to match the funder's interests. Let's see how this could be done with a few examples.

Playground equipment—*The real problem is that children in your community play in the streets because there is no other place to play. The income level of families in the area where the playground is to be located is extremely low. Land was donated between housing developments to serve as the playground. Local volunteers cleaned up the property. Children of poverty need a safe, supervised place to play. Now you have a problem that will match an interest of a potential funder.*

Technology to do research—*Technology is not the issue. Your research is the issue. Technology is just a tool. You are studying Lou Gehrig's Disease (ALS) to determine if oxidative stress is a potential cause of the death of motor neurons. You now have a problem that will match funders who are interested in cutting edge medical research or in motor neuron diseases or specifically in Lou Gehrig's Disease. Technology appears as a tool in the budget.*

A symphony orchestra—*You want to introduce young people in your community to classical music and masters such as Bach, Beethoven, Handel and others. In your rural community there is no resource for hearing such music firsthand. You want to tour schools and community centers and teach children about the classics. You need funds to get the program started. Afterward public concerts in surrounding townships and funds from schools will sustain the operation. Funders interested in music education, the arts, or providing a quality education are potential sources for funding.*

A swimming pool—*Your community has a high crime rate among teenagers. There is nothing for them to do in the community—no gathering place and*

---

[2] Cheryl Carter New and James Aaron Quick, *Grantseeker's Toolkit: A Comprehensive Guide to Finding Funding* (Hoboken, NJ: John Wiley & Sons, 1998).

no fruitful activity. Since you are in a tropical environment, you believe that a community swimming pool with adequate supervision and special programs to attract teenagers will help eliminate the crime problem by providing a place to go after school rather than wandering the streets in gangs. You have opened a lot of territory to match funders who are interested in youth, in crime reduction, and in health and exercise programs.

Include These Elements in the Problem Statement

Logical Narrative Description of the Problem

Hone in on your problem. Define it and clarify it before you start to write. Do not include extraneous problems. Suppose you have a high teen pregnancy rate in your community. Suppose it is growing and you want to initiate an education and counseling project to work with young women and young men in the community to help them understand the impact of their decisions. Stick to that subject.

Do not include that perhaps this is why the crime rate is higher in your community or perhaps this is the reason there are so many accidental deaths in children in the community. Do not include that there are an increasing number of people unemployed in your community. These are all related problems but cloud the issue as far as your project is concerned. You are not directly attacking the crime problem with your project. You are not counseling the young parents on preventing accidents with their children. You are not directly providing job counseling. Do not confuse your proposal readers. What you are doing is providing an education and counseling program to young people in the community to make them aware of the impact of their decisions. Lay the groundwork carefully for the project you intend to do, not for a variety of projects that could be done on related problems.

Here is an example of part of a problem statement that would lay a good foundation for the teenage pregnancy counseling and education project example above.

The United States has the highest teenage pregnancy rate of all developed countries. About 1 million teenagers become pregnant each year; 95% of those pregnancies are unintended, and almost one third end in abortions. Public costs from teenage childbearing totaled $120 billion from 1985–1990; $48 billion could have been saved if each birth had been postponed until the mother was at least 20 years old.

Though birth rates for teenagers declined for all races and ethnic groups in the United States in past years, the rates are growing in our community (see following table). They are growing in all social groups and in all ethnic groups.

Teen Pregnancy Rates (Pregnancies Per 1,000 Girls)	Our State	Our State Rank	United States	Our Community
15 to 19 year olds	−11%	29	−13%	+23%
Girls age 14 or younger	−23%	10	−11%	+13%
15 to 17 year olds	−10%	33	−13%	+25%
18 to 19 year olds	−11%	28	−11%	+30%

• Rank of 1 = lowest rate

In a survey of all youths age 14 to 19, there was an appalling lack of understanding of how decisions made today affect one's life in the future. Moreover, there was a general feeling that someone else would deal with the consequences of their decisions. Following is a chart of the questions and percentages of young people answering each option as well as a chart of the most common comments by those questioned.

As you can see, the problem statement directly points to the solution we are offering to the problem.

Statistical Backups and Comparisons

In any problem statement, one data point will not do. What if I said, alcohol abuse increased by 100% in our community this year? Does this shocking bit of data mean anything? Perhaps not. What if you had one case of alcohol abuse in your community of 200,000 last year and one more this year for a total of two? Does this constitute a severe problem? Of course not.

Data is only pertinent and has an impact if it is comparative so that the reader can relate the statistic to something. It is only important if the reader can clearly see its relevance in light of known data about the problem.

You need to place your data within the range of data known about the problem in general. It is good to compare your community's problem to the problem in the state and the nation. The Internet is an extremely valuable tool to get state and national statistics. Use a good search engine like Google *(www.google.com)*, enter keywords or a brief phrase of the information you want, and you will surely find it if any agency or organization collects that data.

Grant makers, unless they are local, are not that interested in providing a solution to a problem in your community. What they are interested in is providing a potential solution to a problem that can be replicated in communities like yours in other parts of the country. If your problem is unique to your community only a local group is likely to fund you. Part of your task is to depict your community as similar to many other communities across the nation. Remember, most proposal readers will not be familiar with your community. Even if your community is New York City, how many false ideas are there of life in New York? Many. Even if you think your community is well-known it is important for you to place your community's problem firmly in the minds of the potential funder.

> **Wrong**—*Our community has a shocking level of B.A.D. bacteria in the groundwater. This obviously affects our community by causing a potential for serious illness. Our local health department reports an increase of both infection and pneumonia that we believe can be traced to our groundwater bacteria. We are most concerned about our more than 300 children below the age of five and our senior population.*

> **Right**—*Our community has a level of B.A.D. bacteria at more than one part per liter. Our community is heavily industrialized with krypton fabrication plants from which seepage causes B.A.D. bacteria to flow into groundwater used for drinking and bathing. There are numerous communities like ours in every state with the exception of two in the nation. The lessons we learn in our project can easily be transferred to other communities like ours. According to the most recent EPA study (Groundwater Danger, October 2000), one in five communities with krypton fabrication plants have the potential to have B.A.D. bacteria in groundwater. At the level of bacteria in our system, infection and pneumonia are serious health concerns. In fact, in the past year the health department reports an increase in bacterial infection of 45% and in pneumonia of 32%.*

In the second case, the reader knows that this is a serious problem, and also that it affects many communities other than the one seeking funding. Statistical data is provided that is professional and credible. The funder can clearly see that if the project works in this community, it will benefit many others.

Results of Local Needs Assessments

If you have a survey or local report that backs up your case, by all means, include it in your problem statement. This shows local investment in solving the problem you are addressing, especially if the study was done by another organization in the community.

All grant makers are concerned with your own and your community's investment in the project. Why? Because, with more groups involved in your project, there is more chance for success and for continuation after grant money runs out, as it surely will.

What constitutes a local needs assessment?

- A study by a local group.
- A survey by your organization.

- Results of a related project in the community that provided a part of the information necessary to the success of your project.
- Results of a previous project by your organization.
- A regular report by a credible agency or group in your community.

Historical Data—How Did This Occur?

If there is a pertinent progression that has caused the problem, then a description of this will provide background to contribute to the proposal reader's knowledge. Almost any information that clarifies the problem, and thus the project, is valuable for the person reading the proposal.

For example, what if your problem is that younger and younger children are involved in committing crimes in your community? Now let's look at an example of the history that may have contributed to this situation.

> As you can see from statistical data, younger and younger children in our community are stealing, vandalizing and becoming addicted to drugs. The only thing that has changed in our community during the last few years is the advent of an industrial park providing jobs for very nearly every member of the community. Before the small industries moved in, most households had at least one member at home when children came home from school. Now there is no one home. Before children were supervised after school. Now they tend to gather with older children and young adults in the street. As we have seen, this is a recipe for disaster. Younger children are becoming gang mascots and participating in gang activity. They are exposed to the drug habits of the older young adults. Our after school program and third shift program will provide supervision and counseling for these youngest of criminals so they are steered away from trouble before it starts.

Let's take another example. What if your local river has become polluted in recent years whereas it was not in the past? What is the history behind this event?

> In the last three years our local river has become polluted. Once there was a state park along the river with a nice campground, nature trails, and a nature education program for local school children. In a state funding cutback, the programs and campground were abandoned. With no policing and no organized activities, people have become careless and are dumping camp sewage and trash all along our river. Our project to reestablish and expand the programs of the past will reestablish the river environment and protect it.

Readers can identify in some way with your situation if you take the time to explain it logically and professionally.

Statement of Impact of Problem

This would seem to go without saying, but few proposal writers bother to explain what will be the natural result, if the problem is not solved. Thus, they have a difficult time explaining the positive outcome of their project.

Do not be dramatic. But, what is the logical result if your project is not solved? What is the social, medical, psychological or physical impact?

Let's look at the two previous examples and formulate a logical conclusion.

> ***First, the example of young children involved in criminal activity***—*The problem is growing. Our local police force is understaffed and cannot provide oversight of these children. If the problem is not solved, children will be apt to advance to more complex and dangerous activity as time goes by and they get older. It is imperative that we intervene while the children are young and can be redirected.*

> ***Second, the example of the polluted river***—*Our river carries water to neighboring communities. The more time that goes by, the more polluted our river becomes, and the more dangerous, not only to our community but to those downstream. Moreover, the more polluted the river, the more impact for the flora and fauna along its borders.*

Problem impact is a good way to end the problem statement.

Checklist—Problem Statement[3]

- ✔ Describe broad problem—the major symptom of the real problem(s).
- ✔ Describe causes of broad problem—the real problem(s).
- ✔ A problem cited for each project component.
- ✔ Statistics and citations for each assertion.
- ✔ Statistics placing your situation in perspective with state and nation.
- ✔ Extensive numerical data in tables.
- ✔ Local needs assessment, survey results, focus group results.
- ✔ Historical perspective.
- ✔ Impact of problem.

---

[3] Remember that a grant maker's directions (instructions/guidelines) take precedence over any and all other considerations. You must absolutely, positively follow the grant maker's directions exactly, precisely, and painstakingly.

Last Words

Let's get something really, really straight. From the viewpoint of the grant maker, you do not have problems. Your organization or agency does not have problems. Only people in target populations have problems. You may call your target population participants, or patients, or clients, or students, or patrons, or visitors or any other such term. A target population is that group of people whom you intend to impact positively through the activities of your organization. They have the problems—always and only.

Can your organization benefit through renovation, equipment purchase, professional development for staff, or other such improvement? Of course it can, but any benefit to your organization occurs for one and only one reason—to help your target population.

This is why your problem may *not* be the lack of things, such as computers, or staff, or space, or training. Your target population may languish because you do not offer computer-assisted services. Your target population may need more personnel to work with it. Your target population may need more space in which to be served. Your target population may need better trained people assisting them. Your target population can need almost anything, but you need nothing of and by yourself. You exist to serve, to serve your target population.

Getting this straight keeps your problem statement on track. Stay focused like a laser beam on your target population.

One more thing, projects are solutions to problems. Therefore, the goals, objectives, and activities of your project flow naturally from your problem. Astute reviewers have a good idea of the activities that should be in a project after reading the problem statement. If you make the point that a change in your target population necessitates additional staff training, then that staff training had better show up in the project. Otherwise, why did you bring it up in the problem statement? The problem statement provides the basis for the project. That means it defines the problems that will be solved by accomplishment of the project's activities. Projects begin with and flow from the problem statement.

When you start describing your project, every aspect should trace its origin back to the problem. Otherwise, why are you doing it? Activity for activity's sake is a complete and total waste of both your time and the grant maker's money. If you want that grant, use the problem statement to show clearly that the activities in the project are worth the time and the money.

Examples of Problem Statements for Four Projects

The following four examples (5.1 to 5.4) are sample problem statements for each of the four diverse organizations profiled in this book. The specific elements highlighted in the chapter are reflected in each example.

EXAMPLE 5.1

After School Program— Problem Statement

Sunnyvale School District

Sunnyvale School District faces problems similar to many rural school districts across the nation. In summary, the problems are low academic achievement, high dropout rate (low graduation rate), low self-esteem, increasing incidents of violence, increasing use of alcohol, tobacco, and other drugs, few chances for organized recreation, and insufficient positive parental involvement in education.

On the state-mandated Academic Achievement Assessment (AAA) in both language arts and mathematics, district middle school students score in the lowest quartile of state school districts. In language arts, the district's middle school students placed 61st out of 64 districts. In mathematics, the district's middle school students placed 55th.

On the California Achievement Test (CAT), district middle school students performed below both state and national averages. Scores are shown in the following table.

	Language Arts	Mathematics
National Average	112.8	108.5
State Average	98.6	104.2
District Average	93.3	102.1

The dropout rate for our state is among the highest in the nation. Our school district's dropout rate is 21st out of 64 districts, making our dropout rate one of the highest in the country.

Low self-esteem manifests itself, for our purposes, in the belief that things will always be the way they have been, that the student's life will be the same as their parents' life. Students from homes in which the adults did not graduate from high school tend to be resigned to the same fate. Students who come from homes in which the adults either do not work at all, or work at manual or menial labor, tend to the same future (Walker and Jones, "Influence of Home Factors on School and Work," *Education USA*, June, 1999).

For incidents of violence, the district's rate is low when compared to large urban areas. When compared to similar rural areas, however, the district's rate of violent incidents is above average (*U.S. Census, 2000*). More troubling is that the rate has been on the increase for five straight years (*County Juvenile Court Summary Report: 2001*).

EXAMPLE 5.1   *(Continued)*

After School Program—
Problem Statement, page 2

After almost ten years of declining use of alcohol, tobacco, and other drugs (ATOD), the district began to see increases in 1998. The rate of use has now climbed back to rates not seen here since the early nineties *(County Juvenile Court Summary Report: 2001)*. The reasons are not understood, but the disruptive results to both academics and behavior are clear.

As is typical for rural areas, the opportunities for organized recreation are limited. The sheriff's office reports that the time frame during which the vast majority of incidents of juvenile (middle school age) violence and ATOD infractions occur is between 3:00 and 5:30 P.M., the time between school letting out and caretaker adults arriving home from work. The major cause is the lack of supervised after school activities to take the place of no adult supervision at home. An additional problem is the supervision of young children by their only slightly older siblings.

The literature clearly shows the relation between positively involved parents and success of their children in school, both academically and behaviorally. There is also a correlation between the income and education of parents and their involvement. The more educated the parents, the more they are involved in their children's education. The reasons are complex. For our purposes, we can summarize that those parents who themselves failed to do well in school as children, tend to avoid contact with school as adults. Walking down school hallways, sitting in school rooms, and talking to teachers brings back a set of learned negative reactions from the time when school was a place of disappointment and failure ("The Influence of Parent's School Experience on Involvement with their Children's Education," *Journal of Education Psychology,* January, 2002). Milk, Spoon, and Peaches).

Results from our community focus groups show that the vast majority of parents (for all practical purposes, all parents), regardless of income or education want their children to do well in school. The problem is one of not knowing how to help. The desire is there. The parent focus groups identified four main barriers. (1) Meetings are at school, a place with bad connotations for many. (2) Teachers "talk down to us and don't listen." (3) Meetings are scheduled at the school's convenience. The work schedules of many people are such that they need flexibility. (4) A substantial minority of caretakers lack transportation to get to and from meetings.

EXAMPLE 5.2

Senior Citizen Wellness Center—Problem Statement

The Senior Citizen Wellness Center

The elderly population of our city is a much larger percentage of the total population than in the country as a whole.

The median age of the U.S. population is 35.3 years. The median age of our city's population is 49.2 years *(U.S. Census, 2000)*.

Of the overall population of the United States, 12.4% are 65 years and over. Our city's population is 23.8% 65 years and over *(U.S. Census, 2000)*.

The average household size of owner-occupied housing in the United States is 2.7 persons. In our city, this average household size is 1.4 persons *(U.S. Census, 2000)*.

The problems of the elderly are well-documented. Health and wellness head the list. Physical decline inhibits the elderly from moving about easily, making the normal functions of life, such as shopping, difficult or impossible. Mental decline makes the elderly susceptible to mistakes with medication and dealing with the complications of life, such as taxes and paying bills. Lack of mobility also decreases the opportunity for social interaction, which furthers mental decline *(Aging and its Effects on Everyday Living, AARP, 2000)*.

The federal government, the state, the city, and private organizations offer a wide variety of services to the elderly, ranging from help with utilities to mental health counseling. In our city, we have identified 24 such programs. This variety causes very real problems for the elderly since each program has its own eligibility requirements, application procedures, paperwork, and follow-up.

A survey undertaken by the Senior Citizen Center found that the average senior has knowledge of only seven programs, with Social Security, Medicare, Medicaid, and Meals on Wheels consistently being four of the seven. A further result of the survey was that 75% of the seniors found the experience of applying for the benefits of the average program to be "terrible." There was no real variation among sources whether federal, state, city, or private. The application experience was uniformly rated as bad to terrible *(Senior Citizen Center Survey: What Seniors Think, 2002*—see appendix for a copy of the survey questionnaire and compilation of results.)

Comments given by survey respondents found application processes to be "made for much younger folks" and "confusing and demeaning." The general consensus was that they had worked hard all their lives and deserved better at this stage of their lives than to be demeaned by "begging" for the means to live.

EXAMPLE 5.3

Fire and Rescue Project—Problem Statement

Quad-County Fire and Rescue Association

Three quarters (75%) of the firefighters in the United States are volunteers. These volunteer firefighters protect 43% of the nation's population. Of the approximately 31,500 fire departments in the country, 89% are all, or mostly, volunteer.

In many communities across the country, volunteer firefighters are the first line of defense against fires, medical emergencies, chemical, biological, and terrorist threats, hazardous materials incidents, and trench collapses. They also provide high and low angle rescues, and other types of specialized rescue. Over the past twenty years, the number of emergency calls has increased dramatically, along with the training requirements necessary to keep pace with expanding responsibilities.

Volunteer fire and rescue departments are having increasing difficulty raising sufficient funds to keep pace with the cost of training and equipment necessary to meet the expanded range of emergencies to which communities expect them to respond (*Report on the National Volunteer Fire Summit*, National Volunteer Fire Council, 1999).

In addition, recruitment and retention are becoming serious problems. Since the early 1980's, the number of volunteer firefighters has decreased by almost 10% while the number of calls to which they respond and the type of emergencies has increased dramatically (*Fire Report on Recruitment and Retention in the Volunteer Fire Service*, National Volunteer Fire Council, 1999).

Nationally, after-incident investigations show that over half of fires could have been prevented with a relatively small investment of time and generally almost no expense. (*National After-Incident Reporting Findings*, National Fire Academy, 2001). Review of five years of incident reports from the 47 fire and rescue departments in the quad-county area yield the same conclusion.

EXAMPLE 5.4

Alcohol and Drug Abuse Program— Problem Statement

INNER CITY ALCOHOL AND DRUG PREVENTION COMMISSION

During the late eighties and most of the nineties, alcohol, tobacco, and other drug (ATOD) use declined among all age groups. The past few years, however, have seen an increase in the use of alcohol, of tobacco, and of certain drugs, mostly among school-age children. The problem extends down into the middle school grades, which begin at either 5th or 6th grade. The problem varies from state to state and even from school district to school district (*Demographic Subgroup Trends for Various Licit and Illicit Drugs: 1975–2001,* Institute for Social Research, University of Michigan, 2002).

Experts disagree on the causes of this latest upward trend, but some consensus does exist. A decade of declining ATOD abuse figures caused substance abuse organizations to grow lax about getting the word out, about spreading the message. Programs against substance abuse in the schools have grown old and stale. They have not kept up, and an alarming number of today's children are ignoring the message (John J. Master, "Why Now: What's Causing our Kids to Light Up, Chug Down, and Get High?" *Health Care Digest,* April, 2002).

Additionally, a decade of shrinking numbers caused the intervention and response capacity of many anti-abuse organizations to weaken. As demand declined, these organizations naturally reallocated resources to other issues. In our community, no publicly available ATOD intervention and response resource exists.

Chapter **6**

Mission, Goals, and Objectives

**Success is a consequence and
must not be a goal.**

Gustave Flaubert[1]

At a Glance

What Else Are They Called?

- Project outcomes
- Activities, tasks, or action items

When Are They Used?

Always. In one form or another, every funder wants to see the major steps to accomplish your project. No matter what they call them (mission, goal, objective, activity, action item or task), they are the key components of your project and show the flow of activity and targets for success. More and more, funders are requiring accountability by asking that your goals and objectives be measurable with clear outcomes.

Why Are They Used?

Unless you have planned the major and minor steps in your project, you really do not have a project—only a vague idea. Grant funders do not fund vague ideas—only well-developed projects. You should completely plan out your project, including goals and objectives, before you search for funders. Only if you match the funder's agenda, will you receive

---

[1] Gustave Flaubert (1821–1880), French novelist, translated by William G. Allen, *Pensées de Gustave Flaubert* (Conard, 1915), p. 82.

funding. If you do not know the details of your project, you cannot know if you meet the funder's agenda. It is a good idea to make project development—problem solving—a consistent part of your organization's planning process.

Key Concepts

1. Detailed and measurable.
2. Goals are steps to accomplish your mission.
3. Objectives are steps to accomplish each goal.
4. Goal statements should include the following components: (a) what you are going to do, (b) using what approach, (c) when you are going to do it, (d) for how many for by how much, and (e) with what results (outcomes).
5. Objective statements should include the following components: (a) what you are going to do, (b) using what approach, (c) who is responsible, (d) for how many, for by how much, and (e) with what results (outcomes).

Formatting Issues

Goal statements should be very detailed to show the funder exactly what you intend to do to accomplish your mission. The mission is a "reach for" statement. Goals and objectives should be concrete. Use 12-point type and normal margins.

A Goal by Any Other Name[2]

Developing (writing) the goals and objectives for projects and proposals is a difficult task for many grant seekers. Why? One reason is the lack of standard definitions, ones on which everyone agrees. At one extreme, goals are lofty statements such as "cure world hunger" or "peace on earth." At the other extreme (where you will find us), goals are concrete, realistic, and measurable. Naturally, people tend to hold that their own definition is the correct one. A person's definition usually derives from the field in which the person works, and different fields use the words differently.

To illustrate the point, a list of interchangeable words (synonyms according to *Webster's Collegiate Dictionary*) includes goal, objective, target,

---

[2] Cheryl Carter New and James Aaron Quick, *Workbook II: Goals and Objectives, Analyzing RFPs, and Parts of Proposal*, Polaris Grantseeking Fundamentals Workshop, 2001.

purpose, and intent. *Roget's Thesaurus* adds to the list aim, design, ambition, and destination. Some groups use strategy in place of objective. Some groups organize ideas by objective, then strategy, then activity. Some call the lowest level under objectives a job, and others call that level a task. To complete the circle, find task in a thesaurus, and you will find goal as a substitute.

The bottom line is this: in project development and in proposal writing, it does not matter which words are used, as long as the intended meaning is clearly conveyed to the reader. Goals and objectives simply are a way of explaining what you want to do, for whom, and with what result. Writing goals and objectives is a way to organize your project. Writing goals is very similar to making an outline.

Rarely do grantors define exactly what they mean by goal and objective (or the other words they may use instead). Whatever grantors' own definitions, they assume you use the same ones, or at least that you understand theirs. *The way to insure that you are communicating with the reader is to clearly explain your definition of a mission, a goal, and an objective so the reader knows what to expect.* The ultimate purpose is to give the reader as much information as possible with which to judge the structure and value of your project. The best way to avoid problems is to eliminate any possibility of confusing the reader.

In this section, we describe a logical structure and give clear definitions. Feel free, however, to use a methodology familiar to you, perhaps one used in your field, or by your agency, or organization.

The model we use is one that combines fundamental principles from business, industry, and government. Whether your proposal goes to a corporation, a foundation, or a federal agency, you will provide the reader with a logical structure, and enough information for your project to be judged fairly.

Graphical Representation of the Mission, Goal, and Objective Progression

As you can see from Exhibit 6.1, goals are steps to achieving your mission and objectives are steps to achieving each goal.

Mission

Your project mission is your ultimate aim. It is what you want to happen in the best of all cases. The mission statement is the converse of the

EXHIBIT 6.1

Mission, Goal, and Objective Progression

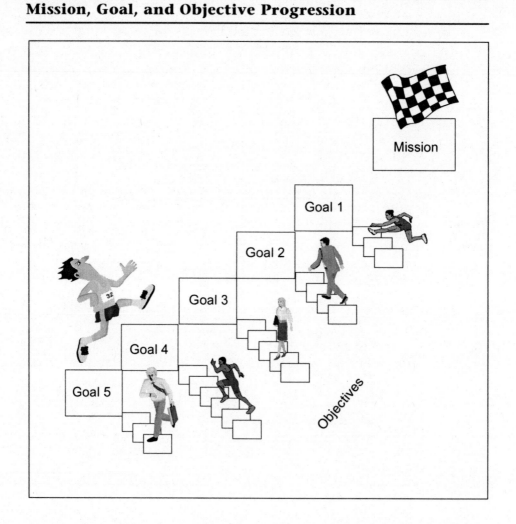

problem statement. If your problem is that drug abuse is growing in your high school, then your mission is that there will be no drug abuse in your high school. If your problem is that there are hungry people in Zambia, then your mission is that there is no more hunger in Zambia. If your problem is that there is a rise of careless boating deaths on the Florida coast, your mission is to eliminate careless boating deaths.

It is important that every project has a mission. It is the ultimate purpose for your project. It is what everyone is working to accomplish.

You may not fully succeed at accomplishing your mission, but it is your target.

Goal

Goals are the steps to accomplish the mission. They should be in logical order, according to what you would do first, second and third. If two things are being done at approximately the same time, then just choose one to be placed first. Project goals are doable. They are not just something vague at which to aim. Project goals are always concrete and measurable. They form the basis for your project management. If you think through the goals and objectives properly, you should be able to hand a set to your project coordinator who will then know how to manage the project.

Goals should have five parts:

- What you are going to do (the steps toward your mission)?
- Using what approach (methodology)?
- When it will be done (timeline)?
- For how many, or by how much (measurement)?
- With what result or outcome (evaluation)?

We like to chart our goals even if we are going to turn the chart into a statement. Sometimes there is room in the proposal for the chart itself. If so, funders appreciate seeing our entire plan. The following is an example.

Goal 2

What?	What approach?	When?	How many or how much?	Result/outcome
Review software to include in a children's nature library.	Expert committee including education professors, master teachers, librarian curriculum specialists.	During project month two.	To serve a community of 30,000.	Software selections include the 100 titles selected according to skill level, presentation, user friendliness, and content.

If we were to write this in a statement, it might look something like this.

Goal 2: *During project month two, an expert committee will review software to include in a children's library to serve a community of 30,000 with the outcome that 100 titles will be selected.*

The other information in your boxes will help you with the project description, evaluation plan, and other sections of your proposal.

The following is another example.

Goal 4

What?	What approach?	When?	How many or how much?	Result/outcome
Create a natural habitat for Kodiak bears.	Study the native habitat and include all natural elements and hidden viewing locations.	Project month 3.	For a family of four bears.	The habitat is as close to the home territory of the bears as possible including temperature, flora, geology, and water.

If we were going to write this in a statement, it might look something like this.

> **Goal 4**: *Research and create a natural habitat with hidden viewing locations during the project month for a family of four bears with the result that the habitat is as close to the home territory of the bears as possible.*

Objective

The objectives are steps for each goal. If you complete each objective, you should have completed the goal. They should also be in logical ascending order. Objectives should be concrete and measurable.

Objectives have five parts as follows:

- What you are going to do (the steps toward your goal)?
- Using what approach (methodology)?
- Who will do it (project management and supervision)?
- For how many or by how much (measurement)?
- With what result or outcome (evaluation)?

The following are examples for the two goals we stated earlier in this chapter.

> **Goal 2**: *During project month two, an expert committee will review software to include in a children's library to serve a community of 30,000 with the outcome that 100 titles will be selected.*

Objective 1

What?	What approach?	Who?	How many or how much?	Result/outcome
Form the expert committee and schedule meetings.	Gain commitment from 2 education professors, 2 master teachers, 2 curriculum coordinators, and 2 librarians.	Project coordinator.	Set up ten, three-hour sessions.	The expert committee is established and commitments are gained from all members for the scheduled meetings.

If we were to write an objective statement from this chart it would be as follows.

Objective 1: *The project coordinator will gain commitment from eight members for the expert committee and set up ten three-hour review sessions so that all committee members can be present.*

As with goals, the remaining information in the chart will be used elsewhere in the proposal, and also in your project management process. The following is an objective for the second goal we wrote.

Goal 4*: Research and create a natural habitat with hidden viewing locations during the project month for a family of four bears with the result that the habitat is as close to the home territory of the bears as possible.*

Objective 1

What?	What approach?	Who?	How many or how much?	Result/outcome
Research the habitat of the Kodiak bears.	Access National Geographic experts on bears, consult with wildlife agency head in the Kodiak Archipelago and the bear expert at the University of Alaska.	Project coordinator and animal management department head.	Habitat for a family of four bears.	The flora, geology, water resources, and temperature are known for the native habitat.

The objective statement can be written as follows.

Objective 1: *The project coordinator and animal management department head will research the natural habitat of the Kodiak bears with experts in the* *field with the result of knowing all pertinent information about flora, geology, water and temperature.*

Checklist—Goals and Objectives[3]

✔ What will happen?

✔ How will it be accomplished (approach, methodology, strategy)?

✔ When will it happen (in project time)?

✔ Who is responsible and who will do the work?

✔ For how many, or how much (measurability)?

✔ With what result, outcome, or benefit (why is the activity being done)?

Last Words

With over fifty years of combined experience dating back to 1969, we have seen changes come and go. No subject has seen greater swings of opinion than project organization, what we are calling goals and objectives. Supposedly new ideas crop up every few years. Largely, these new ideas are the use of new words to describe old concepts. There is basically nothing new here. One can change nomenclature and talk about outcomes rather than results, or strategy rather than methodology, or any other choice of new labeling, but the reality of project organization and operation do not change.

Follow the progression in the following boxes. In our organizational scheme we put number 3 (when will it happen) in the goal and 4 (who will do it) in the objective. For the purposes of this discussion, they are shown together.

1	2	3	4	5	6
What will happen?	How will it happen? (approach, method, strategy)	When will it happen?	Who will do it?	For how many or how much?	With what result, outcome, or benefit?

---

[3] Remember that a grant maker's directions (instructions/guidelines) take precedence over any and all other considerations. You must absolutely, positively follow the grant maker's directions exactly, precisely, and painstakingly.

1. This is the entry point into any step at any level in an organizational plan—a basic, simple statement of something that will happen.

2. What is needed next is the answer to the logical question: "How will we do that?" The "how" can be dressed in fancy clothes and escorted to the spring cotillion, but underneath all the fancy language in the world it remains a "how."

3. No one argues about time frames. It does make sense to avoid the calendar, however. Use project months, quarters, and years. This way it makes no difference when the money shows up. The beginning of a project is always project time zero, and project time begins counting.

4. There are two aspects of the "who." Who is responsible that the activity takes place, from a management or supervisory viewpoint? Second, who will do the work? The same person may have both responsibilities. It is well to remember that if you cannot name who will do a thing, it will get done by one of two people—nobody or you. It may be helpful to avoid names and use titles. It is often easier to know the type of person who will do things rather than an actual named person.

5. Every activity must have some measurability attached to it. Don't overlook the simple measurability of a yes or no, the binary choice at the heart of the digital age. The activity could be to install a computer. The measurability is that the computer is installed and functioning properly.

6. The result, outcome, or benefit can prove difficult for some people. But it is, arguably, the most important part of the entire organizational step. At first glance, it may seem like a restatement of item 1. It is not. The outcome provides the reason for doing the work. The benefit provides the motivation for everything else. One of the main reasons that so much activity today accomplishes so little is that no clear end is defined before beginning. Always define clearly, and measurably, the desired outcome before beginning. This sounds like simple common sense, and it is.

If you develop an organizational plan including all the information shown in our plan, you will be able to answer any question a grant maker will ask you about your project. Just be careful to not get confused by terminology. Make the assumption that whatever they may ask, it cannot be something completely new. It is simply not possible. Look carefully at the model. You will find the answers.

Examples of Mission, Goals, and Objectives for Four Projects

The next page shows examples of mission statements, followed by examples (6.1–6.4) of goals and objectives for each of the four diverse organizations profiled in this book. The specific elements highlighted in the chapter are reflected in each example.

Mission Statements for All Four Organizations

After School Program—Sunnyvale School District

The mission of the After School Program for Middle School students is to improve academic performance, reduce the incidence of behavioral problems, increase recreational and social opportunities, and promote positive parental involvement.

Senior Citizen Center—The Senior Citizen Center

The mission of the Senior Citizen Center Project is to enhance health, wellness, and social activity, and to provide a single point of entry into the world of services for the elderly.

Fire and Rescue Project—Quad-County Fire and Rescue Association

The mission of the Fire and Rescue Project is to increase community outreach and improve training, recruitment, and purchasing.

ATOD Prevention—Inner-City Alcohol and Drug Prevention Commission

The mission of the ATOD (Alcohol, Tobacco, and Other Drugs) Prevention Project is to reduce ATOD abuse among school students, provide intervention services, and effectively take the ATOD prevention message to the community.

EXAMPLE 6.1

Goals and Objectives
for the After School Program

Sunnyvale School District

Goal 1

What will happen?	How will it happen? (Method/Strategy)	When will it happen?	For how many or how much?	With what result or benefit?
Develop necessary infrastructure.	Prepare facilities, hire staff, and recruit volunteers and contractors.	During first three project months.	Facilities for 1,200—1 project director, 5 site directors, 5 assistant site directors, 25 teachers, 5 snack coordinators, 150 tutors, 25 contractors.	Sufficient facilities and qualified staff.

Goal 2

What will happen?	How will it happen? (Method/Strategy)	When will it happen?	For how many or how much?	With what result or benefit?
Train program personnel.	Classroom, online, and self-study.	Begin project month two and ongoing thereafter.	Train all staff, volunteers, and contractors (see Goal 1).	Staff sufficiently trained to effectively handle all aspects of their activities.

Goal 3

What will happen?	How will it happen? (Method/Strategy)	When will it happen?	For how many or how much?	With what result or benefit?
Provide supplemental academic activities.	Classroom teachers identify academic needs—staff develop academic development plan.	Begin project month four and ongoing thereafter.	Supervised homework for 1,200, tutoring for 600, supplemental academic activities for 600.	Participants complete homework, grades of academic participants rise one letter grade.

EXAMPLE 6.1   *(Continued)*

Goals and Objectives
for the After School Program

Goal 4

What will happen?	How will it happen? (Method/Strategy)	When will it happen?	For how many or how much?	With what result or benefit?
Provide applied learning activities.	In partnership with 4-H, home economics, and vocational education.	Begin project month four and ongoing thereafter.	For 400 participants.	Participants become proficient in an applied life skill.

Goal 5

What will happen?	How will it happen? (Method/Strategy)	When will it happen?	For how many or how much?	With what result or benefit?
Provide recreational activities.	In partnership with parks and recreation and private providers.	Begin project month four and ongoing thereafter.	For all 1,200 participants.	Participants have daily opportunity to participate in choice of activity.

Goal 6

What will happen?	How will it happen? (Method/Strategy)	When will it happen?	For how many or how much?	With what result or benefit?
Provide social and health services and activities.	Partner with public health, ATOD, violence prevention project, and hospital.	Begin project month four and ongoing thereafter.	For 600 participants.	Incidents of substance abuse and violence decrease 50%— health care issues resolved.

Goal 7

What will happen?	How will it happen? (Method/Strategy)	When will it happen?	For how many or how much?	With what result or benefit?
Provide parental involvement activities.	Workshops, open houses, meetings, Web site, direct mail.	Begin project month four and ongoing thereafter.	For all 1,200 participants.	Positive parental involvement increases 100%.

(continues)

EXAMPLE 6.1   *(Continued)*

Goals and Objectives
for the After School Program

Goal 8

What will happen?	How will it happen? (Method/Strategy)	When will it happen?	For how many or how much?	With what result or benefit?
Evaluate After School Program.	Quantitative and qualitative measures and formative and summative measures.	Throughout term of program.	Assess all goals and objectives.	Determine effectiveness of activities, provide basis for changes to improve project, and report to stakeholders.

Goal 9

What will happen?	How will it happen? (Method/Strategy)	When will it happen?	For how many or how much?	With what result or benefit?
Manage After School Program.	Manage people and funds, disseminate information, continue project, consult advisory board.	Throughout term of program.	Attain all relevant numbers.	Successfully accomplish all goals and objectives.

Goal 1—and Objectives to Achieve Goal

What will happen?	How will it happen? (Method/Strategy)	When will it happen?	For how many or how much?	With what result or benefit?
Develop necessary infrastructure.	Prepare facilities, hire staff, and recruit volunteers and contractors.	During first three project months.	Facilities for 1,200—1 project director, 5 site directors, 5 assistant site directors, 25 teachers, 5 snack coordinators, 150 tutors, 25 contractors.	Sufficient facilities and qualified staff.

EXAMPLE 6.1 *(Continued)*

Goals and Objectives
for the After School Program

Objective 1

What will happen?	How will it happen? (Method/Strategy)	Who will do it?	For how many or how much?	With what result or benefit?
Hire project director.	State and district hiring practices.	Assistant superintendent.	1 project director.	Obtain qualified project director.

Objective 2

What will happen?	How will it happen? (Method/Strategy)	Who will do it?	For how many or how much?	With what result or benefit?
Hire site directors and snack coordinators.	State and district hiring practices.	Project director.	5 site directors and 5 snack coordinators.	Obtain qualified site directors and snack coordinators.

Objective 3

What will happen?	How will it happen? (Method/Strategy)	Who will do it?	For how many or how much?	With what result or benefit?
Hire teachers.	State and district hiring practices.	Project director and site directors.	5 teachers per site.	Obtain certified teachers for supplemental academic instruction.

Objective 4

What will happen?	How will it happen? (Method/Strategy)	Who will do it?	For how many or how much?	With what result or benefit?
Recruit tutors.	Recruit high school students per district volunteer recruitment practices.	Site directors.	30 tutors per site.	Obtain qualified tutors.

(continues)

EXAMPLE 6.1   *(Continued)*

Goals and Objectives for the After School Program

Objective 5

What will happen?	How will it happen? (Method/Strategy)	Who will do it?	For how many or how much?	With what result or benefit?
Complete agreements with private contractors.	State and district contractual agreement practices.	Project director and site directors.	25 contractors.	Obtain qualified practitioners for various contract areas.

Objective 6

What will happen?	How will it happen? (Method/Strategy)	Who will do it?	For how many or how much?	With what result or benefit?
Prepare facilities.	In accordance with federal and state mandates for After School Programs.	Site directors and school principals.	240 participants per site.	Each middle school prepared to host an After School Program.

Goal 2—and Objectives to Achieve Goal

What will happen?	How will it happen? (Method/Strategy)	When will it happen?	For how many or how much?	With what result or benefit?
Train program personnel.	Classroom, online, and self-study.	Begin project month two and ongoing thereafter.	Train all staff, volunteers, and contractors (see Goal 1).	Staff sufficiently trained to effectively handle all aspects of their activities.

Objective 1

What will happen?	How will it happen? (Method/Strategy)	Who will do it?	For how many or how much?	With what result or benefit?
Train personnel on accepted practices of dealing with after school participants. (Orientation)	Three hours of classroom instruction of existing district curriculum.	District professional development staff.	All original staff, volunteers, and contractor personnel and all incoming staff, volunteers, and contractor personnel during term of project.	No staff or personnel will work with participants without completion of this orientation training.

EXAMPLE 6.1 *(Continued)*

Goals and Objectives
for the After School Program

Objective 2

What will happen?	How will it happen? (Method/Strategy)	Who will do it?	For how many or how much?	With what result or benefit?
Train tutors.	*Online tutorial of existing district curriculum.*	*Supervised by site directors.*	*All original tutors and all incoming tutors during term of project.*	*No tutors may work with participants without completion of this training.*

Objective 3

What will happen?	How will it happen? (Method/Strategy)	Who will do it?	For how many or how much?	With what result or benefit?
Inform middle school personnel of their responsibilities toward After School Program.	*One-hour presentation with question and answer session.*	*Project director with site directors.*	*One primary session for each site and make-ups for personnel missing primary session.*	*All middle school personnel understand After School Program and their relation and responsibilities to it.*

Goal 3—and Objectives to Achieve Goal

What will happen?	How will it happen? (Method/Strategy)	When will it happen?	For how many or how much?	With what result or benefit?
Provide supplemental academic activities.	*Classroom teachers identify academic needs—staff develop academic development plan.*	*Begin project month four and ongoing thereafter.*	*Supervised homework for 1,200, tutoring for 600, supplemental academic activities for 600.*	*Participants complete homework, grades of academic participants rise one letter grade.*

(continues)

EXAMPLE 6.1   *(Continued)*

Goals and Objectives
for the After School Program

Objective 1

What will happen?	How will it happen? (Method/Strategy)	Who will do it?	For how many or how much?	With what result or benefit?
Recruit participants for after school supplemental academic activities.	Normal teacher-parent communications methods plus direct mail.	Site directors, assistant site directors, principals, and classroom teachers.	Up to 240 participants per site.	Enroll those students who are most in need of academic supplementation.

Objective 2

What will happen?	How will it happen? (Method/Strategy)	Who will do it?	For how many or how much?	With what result or benefit?
Tailor academic experience for each participant to meet individual needs.	Develop individual supplemental academic plan.	After school teachers with classroom teachers.	Up to 240 participants per site.	The academic activities serve to improve participants' academic performance.

Objective 3

What will happen?	How will it happen? (Method/Strategy)	Who will do it?	For how many or how much?	With what result or benefit?
Help with homework.	Provide supervised homework completion.	Tutors under supervision of site directors and assistant site directors.	Up to 240 participants per site.	All After School Program participants complete homework each day.

EXAMPLE 6.1 *(Continued)*

Goals and Objectives for the After School Program

Objective 4

What will happen?	How will it happen? (Method/Strategy)	Who will do it?	For how many or how much?	With what result or benefit?
Help with academic subjects.	Tutoring.	Tutors under supervision of site directors and assistant site directors.	Up to 240 participants per site.	Participants in need obtain the help needed to improve academically.

Objective 5

What will happen?	How will it happen? (Method/Strategy)	Who will do it?	For how many or how much?	With what result or benefit?
Provide language arts academic supplementation.	Classroom instruction.	After school teachers.	Up to 50 participants.	Participants improve language arts grades.

Objective 6

What will happen?	How will it happen? (Method/Strategy)	Who will do it?	For how many or how much?	With what result or benefit?
Provide mathematics academic supplementation.	Classroom instruction.	After school teachers.	Up to 50 participants.	Participants improve mathematics grades.

Goal 4—and Objectives to Achieve Goal

What will happen?	How will it happen? (Method/Strategy)	When will it happen?	For how many or how much?	With what result or benefit?
Provide applied learning activities.	In partnership with 4-H, home economics, and vocational education.	Begin project month four and ongoing thereafter.	For 400 participants.	Participants become proficient in an applied life skill.

(continues)

EXAMPLE 6.1   *(Continued)*

Goals and Objectives
for the After School Program

Objective 1

What will happen?	How will it happen? (Method/Strategy)	Who will do it?	For how many or how much?	With what result or benefit?
Determine the applied learning activities in which students will participate.	Determine interest during intake interview.	Site directors, assistants, and after school teachers.	80 participants per site.	Students participate in applied learning most appropriate for them.

Objective 2

What will happen?	How will it happen? (Method/Strategy)	Who will do it?	For how many or how much?	With what result or benefit?
Hold applied learning sessions.	Hands-on practical learning.	Contractors under supervision of site directors.	80 participants per site.	Participants learn a skill and gain confidence.

Objective 3

What will happen?	How will it happen? (Method/Strategy)	Who will do it?	For how many or how much?	With what result or benefit?
Recruit additional applied learning providers.	Determine needs from interviews of participants.	Site directors and after school teachers.	Add capacity for 20 participants per school semester.	Meet applied learning needs of participants.

Goal 5—and Objectives to Achieve Goal

What will happen?	How will it happen? (Method/Strategy)	When will it happen?	For how many or how much?	With what result or benefit?
Provide recreational activities.	In partnership with parks and recreation and private providers.	Begin project month four and ongoing thereafter.	For all 1,200 participants.	Participants have daily opportunity to participate in choice of activities.

EXAMPLE **6.1**   *(Continued)*

Goals and Objectives
for the After School Program

Objective 1

What will happen?	How will it happen? (Method/Strategy)	Who will do it?	For how many or how much?	With what result or benefit?
Determine the recreational activities in which students will participate.	Determine interest during intake interview.	Site directors, assistants, and after school teachers.	240 participants per site.	Students participate in recreational activities most appropriate for them.

Objective 2

What will happen?	How will it happen? (Method/Strategy)	Who will do it?	For how many or how much?	With what result or benefit?
Hold recreational sessions.	Supervised recreation.	Contractors and partners under supervision of site directors.	240 participants per site.	Participants participate in a recreational activity of their choice daily.

Objective 3

What will happen?	How will it happen? (Method/Strategy)	Who will do it?	For how many or how much?	With what result or benefit?
Recruit additional recreational providers.	Determine needs from interviews of participants.	Site directors and after school teachers.	Add variety of recreational activities.	Meet recreational desires of participants.

Goal 6—and Objectives to Achieve Goal

What will happen?	How will it happen? (Method/Strategy)	When will it happen?	For how many or how much?	With what result or benefit?
Provide social and health services and activities.	Partner with public health, ATOD, violence prevention project, and hospital.	Begin project month four and ongoing thereafter.	For 600 participants.	Incidents of substance abuse and violence decrease 50%— health care issues resolved.

(continues)

EXAMPLE **6.1** *(Continued)*

Goals and Objectives
for the After School Program

Objective 1

What will happen?	How will it happen? (Method/Strategy)	Who will do it?	For how many or how much?	With what result or benefit?
Determine the social and health services activities in which students will participate.	Determine need during intake process.	Site directors, assistants, and after school teachers, classroom teachers, and parents.	120 participants per site.	Students participate in needed social and health services activities.

Objective 2

What will happen?	How will it happen? (Method/Strategy)	Who will do it?	For how many or how much?	With what result or benefit?
Hold social and health services sessions.	Classroom instruction, workshop, and hands-on learning as appropriate.	Contractors and partners under supervision of site directors.	120 participants per site.	Participants participate in social and health services activities individually needed.

Objective 3

What will happen?	How will it happen? (Method/Strategy)	Who will do it?	For how many or how much?	With what result or benefit?
Recruit additional social and health services providers.	Determine needs from interviews of participants and parents.	Site directors and after school teachers.	Add needed number of social and health services activities.	Meet social and health services needs of participants.

EXAMPLE 6.1 *(Continued)*

Goals and Objectives
for the After School Program

Goal 7—and Objectives to Achieve Goal

What will happen?	How will it happen? (Method/Strategy)	When will it happen?	For how many or how much?	With what result or benefit?
Provide parental involvement activities.	Workshops, open houses, meetings, Web site, direct mail.	Begin project month four and ongoing thereafter.	For all 1,200 participants.	Positive parental involvement increases 100%.

Objective 1

What will happen?	How will it happen? (Method/Strategy)	Who will do it?	For how many or how much?	With what result or benefit?
Involve parents in After School Program.	Hold parent workshops.	Site directors and assistants.	One parent workshop per site per month.	Parents learn how to better help children improve academically and socially.

Objective 2

What will happen?	How will it happen? (Method/Strategy)	Who will do it?	For how many or how much?	With what result or benefit?
Involve parents in After School Program.	Hold open house.	Site directors, assistants, and after school teachers.	One open house per site per semester.	Parents learn how to better help children improve academically and socially.

Objective 3

What will happen?	How will it happen? (Method/Strategy)	Who will do it?	For how many or how much?	With what result or benefit?
Involve parents in After School Program.	Hold individual parent meetings.	After school teachers.	One meeting per participant per semester.	Help individual parents help their children.

(continues)

91

EXAMPLE 6.1   *(Continued)*

Goals and Objectives
for the After School Program

Objective 4

What will happen?	How will it happen? (Method/Strategy)	Who will do it?	For how many or how much?	With what result or benefit?
Communicate with parents on regular basis.	Develop and maintain after school page on district Web site.	Project director and assistant.	For anyone with access to Internet.	Inform parents and community about After School Program.

Objective 5

What will happen?	How will it happen? (Method/Strategy)	Who will do it?	For how many or how much?	With what result or benefit?
Communicate with parents on regular basis.	Direct mail with bi-monthly after school newsletter.	Project director.	1,200 participants.	Keep all participant parents informed about After School Program.

Objective 6

What will happen?	How will it happen? (Method/Strategy)	Who will do it?	For how many or how much?	With what result or benefit?
Involve parents in after school activities.	Solicit parents to attend after school activities.	Site directors and contractor personnel.	1,200 participants.	Parents participate in recreational, arts, and applied learning activities.

Goal 8—and Objectives to Achieve Goal

What will happen?	How will it happen? (Method/Strategy)	When will it happen?	For how many or how much?	With what result or benefit?
Evaluate After School Program.	Quantitative and qualitative measures and formative and summative measures.	Throughout term of program.	Assess all goals and objectives.	Determine effectiveness of activities, provide basis for changes to improve project, and report to stakeholders.

EXAMPLE **6.1** *(Continued)*

Goals and Objectives
for the After School Program

Objective 1

What will happen?	How will it happen? (Method/Strategy)	Who will do it?	For how many or how much?	With what result or benefit?
Develop evaluation questions.	Determine information needed by stakeholders to improve program and assess performance — quantitative and qualitative, formative, and summative.	Project director, site directors, and evaluator.	All goals and objectives.	Evaluation provides information needed to effectively assess program.

Objective 2

What will happen?	How will it happen? (Method/Strategy)	Who will do it?	For how many or how much?	With what result or benefit?
Determine data necessary to answer question.	Match type of data to evaluation question.	Project director, site directors, and evaluator.	All goals and objectives.	Appropriate data is collected.

Objective 3

What will happen?	How will it happen? (Method/Strategy)	Who will do it?	For how many or how much?	With what result or benefit?
Determine measurement methodology.	Match measurement methodology with type of data to be collected.	Project director, site directors, and evaluator.	All goals and objectives.	Appropriate data collection methodology is used.

(continues)

EXAMPLE 6.1 *(Continued)*

Goals and Objectives
for the After School Program

Objective 4

What will happen?	How will it happen? (Method/Strategy)	Who will do it?	For how many or how much?	With what result or benefit?
Obtain or develop measurement tools.	Purchase or create.	Evaluator.	All goals and objectives.	Appropriate measurement tools are available for data collection.

Objective 5

What will happen	How will it happen? (Method/Strategy)	Who will do it?	For how many or how much?	With what result or benefit?
Collect data.	Implement measurement techniques.	Evaluator working with project director, site directors, and other after school personnel.	All goals and objectives.	Sufficient data gathered to answer all evaluation questions.

Objective 6

What will happen?	How will it happen? (Method/Strategy)	Who will do it?	For how many or how much?	With what result or benefit?
Analyze data.	Match analysis methodology with type of data and information needed.	Evaluator.	All goals and objectives.	Data is appropriately analyzed to provide information about progress and outcomes of project.

Objective 7

What will happen?	How will it happen? (Method/Strategy)	Who will do it?	For how many or how much?	With what result or benefit?
Publish evaluation results.	Written evaluation report.	Evaluator.	For all stakeholders.	Pertinent information made available to stakeholders.

EXAMPLE **6.1**   *(Continued)*

Goals and Objectives for the After School Program

Goal 9—and Objectives to Achieve Goal

What will happen?	How will it happen? (Method/Strategy)	When will it happen?	For how many or how much?	With what result or benefit?
Manage After School Program.	Manage people and funds, disseminate information, continue project, consult advisory board.	Throughout term of program.	Attain all relevant numbers.	Successfully accomplish all goals and objectives.

Objective 1

What will happen?	How will it happen? (Method/Strategy)	Who will do it?	For how many or how much?	With what result or benefit?
Effectively manage project personnel, both staff and volunteer.	Use effective management techniques.	Project director and site directors.	All staff and volunteers.	Project participants express satisfaction with quality of work of staff and volunteers.

Objective 2

What will happen?	How will it happen? (Method/Strategy)	Who will do it?	For how many or how much?	With what result or benefit?
Effectively manage funds.	Apply state and district financial process.	Project director.	All funds and in-kind contributions.	No audit exceptions.

Objective 3

What will happen?	How will it happen? (Method/Strategy)	Who will do it?	For how many or how much?	With what result or benefit?
Constantly improve project.	Use formative evaluation results to review activities and make changes to project activities.	Project director and site directors.	All goals and objectives.	Efficiency and effectiveness of project activities improves during course of project.

(continues)

95

EXAMPLE 6.1   *(Continued)*

Goals and Objectives
for the After School Program

Objective 4

What will happen?	How will it happen? (Method/Strategy)	Who will do it?	For how many or how much?	With what result or benefit?
Disseminate information about project.	District staff presentations, newsletter, Web site, newspaper articles, cable access channel presentations, state and national conference presentations, reports to appropriate clearinghouses.	Project director.	District staff, community, and state and national peer audiences.	Demonstrate to district staff and community members the worth of the program.

Objective 5

What will happen?	How will it happen? (Method/Strategy)	Who will do it?	For how many or how much?	With what result or benefit?
Seek community involvement.	Advisory board.	2 parents, 2 community members, 2 business and industry representatives, 2 educators, district supervisor, project director.	Meets bimonthly.	Community oversight of and input to After School Program.

Objective 6

What will happen?	How will it happen? (Method/Strategy)	Who will do it?	For how many or how much?	With what result or benefit?
Continue project after term of grant funding.	Using evaluation results and dissemination activities, hold informational meetings with stakeholders.	Project director.	Approach all stakeholders.	Middle school After School Program continues and After School Program expanded into elementary grades.

EXAMPLE 6.2

Goals and Objectives for the Senior Citizen Wellness Center

The Senior Citizen Wellness Center

Goal 1

What will happen?	How will it happen? (Method/Strategy)	When will it happen?	For how many or how much?	With what result or benefit?
Perform all preparatory activities.	*Hire staff, recruit volunteers, train personnel, obtain materials.*	*Project months 1–2.*	*Facilities and personnel to accomplish other goals and objectives for 1,250 participants.*	*Facilities and personnel able to effectively accomplish other goals and objectives.*

Goal 2

What will happen?	How will it happen? (Method/Strategy)	When will it happen?	For how many or how much?	With what result or benefit?
Develop and implement health and wellness service enhancements.	*In partnership with hospital, public health, and ATOD commission.*	*Develop during project months 2–4, implement in project month 5.*	*1,250 participants.*	*Improve health and wellness of participants as measured on the Elderly Fitness Scale.*

Goal 3

What will happen?	How will it happen? (Method/Strategy)	When will it happen?	For how many or how much?	With what result or benefit?
Develop and implement social enrichment activity enhancements.	*In partnership with a variety of organizations, both public and private.*	*Develop during project months 2–4, implement in project month 5.*	*1,250 participants.*	*Improve participants' quality of life as measured by their opinions.*

(continues)

EXAMPLE **6.2** *(Continued)*

Goals and Objectives for the Senior Citizen Wellness Center

Goal 4

What will happen?	How will it happen? (Method/Strategy)	When will it happen?	For how many or how much?	With what result or benefit?
Develop and implement single point of entry to services for the elderly.	Establish collaborative relationships with service providers.	Develop during project months 2–4, implement in project month 5.	1,250 participants.	Participants have one stop shopping for services and a single personal counselor.

Goal 5

What will happen?	How will it happen? (Method/Strategy)	When will it happen?	For how many or how much?	With what result or benefit?
Monitor and manage project.	Evaluate, effectively manage people and funds, disseminate information, continue project, consult advisory board.	Throughout term of program.	Attain all relevant numbers.	Successfully accomplish all goals and objectives.

Goal 1—and Objectives to Achieve Goal

What will happen?	How will it happen? (Method/Strategy)	When will it happen?	For how many or how much?	With what result or benefit?
Perform all preparatory activities.	Hire staff, recruit volunteers, train personnel, obtain materials.	Project months 1–2.	Facilities and personnel to accomplish other goals and objectives for 1,250 participants.	Facilities and personnel able to effectively accomplish other goals and objectives.

Objective 1

What will happen?	How will it happen? (Method/Strategy)	Who will do it?	For how many or how much?	With what result or benefit?
Hire key personnel.	Use organization's approved hiring procedures.	Executive director.	Project director, single point of entry coordinator.	Obtain qualified key personnel.

EXAMPLE **6.2** *(Continued)*

Goals and Objectives for the
Senior Citizen Wellness Center

Objective 2

What will happen?	How will it happen? (Method/Strategy)	Who will do it?	For how many or how much?	With what result or benefit?
Hire project personnel.	Use organization's approved hiring procedures.	Project director and single point of entry coordinator.	Administrative assistant and 2 social workers.	Obtain project personnel.

Objective 3

What will happen?	How will it happen? (Method/Strategy)	Who will do it?	For how many or how much?	With what result or benefit?
Recruit volunteers.	Use organization's approved volunteer recruitment procedures.	Project director and single point of entry coordinator.	20 volunteers.	Obtain sufficient volunteers to perform project activities.

Objective 4

What will happen?	How will it happen? (Method/Strategy)	Who will do it?	For how many or how much?	With what result or benefit?
Train staff and volunteers.	Classroom instruction followed up with on-line continuing education.	Project director and consultant.	All staff and volunteers.	Staff and volunteers possess skills and knowledge to implement project activities.

Objective 5

What will happen?	How will it happen? (Method/Strategy)	Who will do it?	For how many or how much?	With what result or benefit?
Prepare facility for single point of entry activities.	Renovate a street-level front room of office.	Single point of entry coordinator and social workers and contractors.	Facility to handle three participant interviews at once with three more participants using computer access.	Inviting, workable facility for participants and staff.

(continues)

EXAMPLE 6.2 *(Continued)*

Goals and Objectives for the
Senior Citizen Wellness Center

Objective 6

What will happen?	How will it happen? (Method/Strategy)	Who will do it?	For how many or how much?	With what result or benefit?
Provide staff and volunteers with what they need to implement activities.	Obtain supplies, materials, and equipment.	Administrative assistant.	For all project activities.	Project personnel and volunteers have the supplies and materials they need for project activities.

Goal 2—and Objectives to Achieve Goal

What will happen?	How will it happen? (Method/Strategy)	When will it happen?	For how many or how much?	With what result or benefit?
Develop and implement health and wellness service enhancements.	In partnership with hospital, public health, and ATOD commission.	Develop during project months 2–4, implement in project month 5.	1,250 participants.	Improve health and wellness of participants as measured on the Elderly Fitness Scale.

Objective 1

What will happen?	How will it happen? (Method/Strategy)	Who will do it?	For how many or how much?	With what result or benefit?
Improve quality of life of center participants.	Screenings for heart disease, diabetes, arthritis, blood pressure, bone density, skin cancers, muscle weakness, and general health.	Organization staff in partnership with public health and hospital personnel.	800 participants.	Decrease serious effects of heart disease, diabetes, arthritis, high blood pressure, low bone density, skin cancers, and muscle weakness.

EXAMPLE 6.2 *(Continued)*

Goals and Objectives for the
Senior Citizen Wellness Center

Objective 2

What will happen?	How will it happen? (Method/Strategy)	Who will do it?	For how many or how much?	With what result or benefit?
Provide exercise activities.	Weight room, aerobic exercise room, dance sessions swimming pool exercise, walking paths, jogging.	Organization staff in partnership with city, YMCA, YWCA, and parks and recreation.	600 participants.	Physical fitness of participants is measurably improved.

Objective 3

What will happen?	How will it happen? (Method/Strategy)	Who will do it?	For how many or how much?	With what result or benefit?
Help those with substance abuse problems.	Counseling.	Organization staff in partnership with ATOD commission personnel.	150 participants.	Decrease use of alcohol, tobacco, and other drugs.

Objective 4

What will happen?	How will it happen? (Method/Strategy)	Who will do it?	For how many or how much?	With what result or benefit?
Help those with losses and disabilities.	Support groups.	Organization staff in partnership with social services staff.	300 participants.	Participants regain positive mental health.

(continues)

EXAMPLE 6.2 *(Continued)*

Goals and Objectives for the Senior Citizen Wellness Center

Objective 5

What will happen?	How will it happen? (Method/Strategy)	Who will do it?	For how many or how much?	With what result or benefit?
Food preparation activities.	Hands-on workshops and "eat-ins."	Organization staff in partnership with social service nutritionist.	300 participants.	Participants eat healthier.

Goal 3—and Objectives to Achieve Goal

What will happen?	How will it happen? (Method/Strategy)	When will it happen?	For how many or how much?	With what result or benefit?
Develop and implement social enrichment activity enhancements.	In partnership with a variety of organizations, both public and private.	Develop during project months 2–4, implement in project month 5.	1,250 participants.	Improve participants' quality of life as measured by their opinions.

Objective 1

What will happen?	How will it happen? (Method/Strategy)	Who will do it?	For how many or how much?	With what result or benefit?
Develop enhanced social activities.	Games, dances, dinners, chorus groups.	Organization staff in partnership with churches and retirement homes.	Serve 1,500 participants.	Enhanced social activities effectively organized.

EXAMPLE **6.2** *(Continued)*

Goals and Objectives for the
Senior Citizen Wellness Center

Objective 2

What will happen?	How will it happen? (Method/Strategy)	Who will do it?	For how many or how much?	With what result or benefit?
Develop foster grandparent program.	Develop recruitment, screening, training, and assessment procedures.	Organization staff in partnership with national foster parent organization and school district.	200 foster grandparents.	Foster grandparent program effectively organized.

Objective 3

What will happen?	How will it happen? (Method/Strategy)	Who will do it?	For how many or how much?	With what result or benefit?
Implement enhanced social activities.		Organization staff in partnership with churches and retirement homes.	Serve 1,500 participants.	Participants express increased satisfaction with available social activities.

Objective 4

What will happen?	How will it happen? (Method/Strategy)	Who will do it?	For how many or how much?	With what result or benefit?
Implement foster grandparent activities.	Recruit, screen, train, and oversee foster grandparents, recruit children, and assess effect of program.	Organization staff in partnership with national foster parent organization and school district.	200 foster grandparents.	Children and foster grandparents report positive experience.

(continues)

EXAMPLE 6.2 *(Continued)*

Goals and Objectives for the
Senior Citizen Wellness Center

Goal 4—and Objectives to Achieve Goal

What will happen?	How will it happen? (Method/Strategy)	When will it happen?	For how many or how much?	With what result or benefit?
Develop and implement single point of entry to services for the elderly.	Establish collaborative relationships with service providers.	Develop during project months 2–4, implement in project month 5.	1,250 participants.	Participants have one stop shopping for services and a single personal counselor.

Objective 1

What will happen?	How will it happen? (Method/Strategy)	Who will do it?	For how many or how much?	With what result or benefit?
Bring providers of services to the elderly together.	Establish collaborative agreements with service providers.	Mayor, executive director, project director and single point of entry coordinator.	The 23 service providers in the city.	Working collaborative arrangements exist with service providers.

Objective 2

What will happen?	How will it happen? (Method/Strategy)	Who will do it?	For how many or how much?	With what result or benefit?
Overcome obstacles to partners working together.	Resolve security and privacy issues.	Single point of entry coordinator and service providers.	23 service providers in the city.	Privacy and security issues are no longer barriers to partners working together.

EXAMPLE **6.2** *(Continued)*

Goals and Objectives for the
Senior Citizen Wellness Center

Objective 3

What will happen?	How will it happen? (Method/Strategy)	Who will do it?	For how many or how much?	With what result or benefit?
Set up communication among partners.	Develop information transfer protocols.	Single point of entry coordinator and service providers.	23 service providers in the city.	Provide for a smooth transfer of appropriate information.

Objective 4

What will happen?	How will it happen? (Method/Strategy)	Who will do it?	For how many or how much?	With what result or benefit?
Develop and implement outreach program to publicize service.	Radio and television public service ads, direct mailing, city information dissemination avenues (i.e. utility bills).	Single point of entry coordinator in partnership with service providers.	200 radio ads, 50 television ads, a direct mailing with 3 hits through city avenues.	75% of those in community over 65 (or their caretakers) know of single point of entry.

Objective 5

What will happen?	How will it happen? (Method/Strategy)	Who will do it?	For how many or how much?	With what result or benefit?
Develop operating procedures.	Develop procedures manuals.	Single point of entry coordinator in partnership with service providers.	Procedures manuals developed for each staff and volunteer position.	Procedures and methodology documented.

(continues)

EXAMPLE 6.2 *(Continued)*

Goals and Objectives for the
Senior Citizen Wellness Center

Objective 6

What will happen?	How will it happen? (Method/Strategy)	Who will do it?	For how many or how much?	With what result or benefit?
Implement single point of entry.	Walk-in facility with both counselors and self-service.	Single point of entry coordinator and social workers in partnership with service providers.	1,250 participants.	The elderly can obtain access to all services from one place with one counselor.

Goal 5—and Objectives to Achieve Goal

What will happen?	How will it happen? (Method/Strategy)	When will it happen?	For how many or how much?	With what result or benefit?
Monitor and manage project.	Apply effective and appropriate measures.	Throughout term of program.	Attain all relevant numbers.	Successfully accomplish all goals and objectives.

Objective 1

What will happen?	How will it happen? (Method/Strategy)	Who will do it?	For how many or how much?	With what result or benefit?
Evaluate project.	Formative and summative assessment with quantitative and qualitative measures.	Project director and outside evaluator.	All goals and objectives.	Assess formatively to improve ongoing operation; assess summatively to measure success.

EXAMPLE 6.2 *(Continued)*

Goals and Objectives for the Senior Citizen Wellness Center

Objective 2

What will happen?	How will it happen? (Method/Strategy)	Who will do it?	For how many or how much?	With what result or benefit?
Effectively manage project personnel, both staff and volunteer.	*Use effective management techniques.*	*Project director.*	*All staff and volunteers.*	*Project participants express satisfaction with quality of work of staff and volunteers.*

Objective 3

What will happen?	How will it happen? (Method/Strategy)	Who will do it?	For how many or how much?	With what result or benefit?
Effectively manage funds.	*Apply accepted accounting principles.*	*Project director.*	*All funds and in-kind contributions.*	*No audit exceptions.*

Objective 4

What will happen?	How will it happen? (Method/Strategy)	Who will do it?	For how many or how much?	With what result or benefit?
Constantly improve project.	*Use formative results to assess activities and make changes.*	*Project director.*	*All goals and objectives.*	*Project activities improve during course of project.*

Objective 5

What will happen?	How will it happen? (Method/Strategy)	Who will do it?	For how many or how much?	With what result or benefit?
Disseminate information about project.	*Newsletter, Web site, articles, cable access, present at conferences and clearinghouses.*	*Project director.*	*Community, state, and national peer audiences.*	*Buy-in from community, replication by peer audience.*

(continues)

EXAMPLE **6.2** *(Continued)*

Goals and Objectives for the Senior Citizen Wellness Center

Objective 6

What will happen?	How will it happen? (Method/Strategy)	Who will do it?	For how many or how much?	With what result or benefit?
Seek community involvement.	Advisory board.	Mayor; 4 community members, director of Council on Aging, hospital administrator, project director.	Meets bimonthly.	Community oversight of and input to program.

Objective 7

What will happen?	How will it happen? (Method/Strategy)	Who will do it?	For how many or how much?	With what result or benefit?
Continue project after term of grant funding.	Using evaluation results and dissemination activities, hold informational meetings with stakeholders.	Project director.	Approach all stakeholders for appropriate support.	Enhanced activities and single point of entry continue after term of grant.

EXAMPLE 6.3

Goals and Objectives for the Fire and Rescue Project

Quad-County Fire and Rescue Association

Goal 1

What will happen?	How will it happen? (Method/Strategy)	When will it happen?	For how many or how much?	With what result or benefit?
Perform project set-up activities.	*Hire staff, prepare facility, obtain materials.*	*Project months 1–2.*	*Develop facilities and personnel to accomplish other goals and objectives for 1,250 participants.*	*Facilities and personnel able to effectively accomplish other goals and objectives.*

Goal 2

What will happen?	How will it happen? (Method/Strategy)	When will it happen?	For how many or how much?	With what result or benefit?
Increase community outreach.	*Neighborhood fire prevention program and junior fire marshal program in schools.*	*Begin in project month three and ongoing thereafter.*	*47 community outreach programs, 22 junior fire marshal programs in schools.*	*Community knowledge about and opinion of fire and rescue increases.*

Goal 3

What will happen?	How will it happen? (Method/Strategy)	When will it happen?	For how many or how much?	With what result or benefit?
Improve training, recruitment, and purchasing.	*Centralization of training, recruitment, and purchasing of 47 fire and rescue departments.*	*Begin in project month three and ongoing thereafter.*	*1,050 fire and rescue personnel trained, 188 fire and rescue personnel recruited, 47 departments participate.*	*Fire and rescue personnel trained to measurably higher level; recruitment quotas met; and cost of purchases down.*

(continues)

EXAMPLE 6.3   *(Continued)*

Goals and Objectives for the Fire and Rescue Project

Goal 4

What will happen?	How will it happen? (Method/Strategy)	When will it happen?	For how many or how much?	With what result or benefit?
Monitor and manage project.	Apply effective and appropriate measures.	Throughout term of program.	Attain all relevant numbers.	Successfully accomplish all goals and objectives.

Goal 1—and Objectives to Achieve Goal

What will happen?	How will it happen? (Method/Strategy)	When will it happen?	For how many or how much?	With what result or benefit?
Perform consortium set-up activities.	Hire staff, prepare facility, obtain materials.	Project months 1–2.	Develop facilities and personnel to accomplish other goals and objectives for 1,250 participants.	Facilities and personnel able to effectively accomplish other goals and objectives.

Objective 1

What will happen?	How will it happen? (Method/Strategy)	Who will do it?	For how many or how much?	With what result or benefit?
Hire consortium director.	Contract with personnel service, interview finalists.	Committee of fire and rescue department chiefs.	Consortium director (director).	Qualified person hired to run consortium.

Objective 2

What will happen?	How will it happen? (Method/Strategy)	Who will do it?	For how many or how much?	With what result or benefit?
Hire consortium staff.	Advertise and interview.	Director.	Assistant director, administrative assistant, training coordinator, shipping and receiving person.	Qualified personnel hired to perform consortium activities.

EXAMPLE 6.3   *(Continued)*

Goals and Objectives for the Fire and Rescue Project

Objective 3

What will happen?	How will it happen? (Method/Strategy)	Who will do it?	For how many or how much?	With what result or benefit?
Prepare facility.	Renovate donated building and environs.	Director and contractors.	Office space for staff activities, space and setup for training.	Sufficient space and facility to perform all consortium activities.

Objective 4

What will happen?	How will it happen? (Method/Strategy)	Who will do it?	For how many or how much?	With what result or benefit?
Equip consortium.	Obtain materials, supplies, and equipment.	Administrative assistant.	See material, supply, and equipment list in budget.	Sufficiently equipped and supplied to perform all consortium activities.

Goal 2—and Objectives to Achieve Goal

What will happen?	How will it happen? (Method/Strategy)	When will it happen?	For how many or how much?	With what result or benefit?
Increase community outreach.	Neighborhood fire prevention program and junior fire marshal program in schools.	Begin in project month three and ongoing thereafter.	47 community outreach programs, 22 junior fire marshal programs in schools.	Community knowledge about and opinion of fire and rescue increases.

Objective 1

What will happen?	How will it happen? (Method/Strategy)	Who will do it?	For how many or how much?	With what result or benefit?
Develop neighborhood fire prevention program.	Focus group results from fire and rescue departments and community members with accepted standards.	Director and assistant director with local chiefs and personnel.	Develop a basic program with modifications as necessary for each community.	A tailored fire prevention program, fully developed and documented, ready for each of 47 communities.

(continues)

EXAMPLE 6.3   *(Continued)*

Goals and Objectives for the Fire and Rescue Project

Objective 2

What will happen?	How will it happen? (Method/Strategy)	Who will do it?	For how many or how much?	With what result or benefit?
Implement neighborhood fire prevention program.	Methodologies to be determined during development. (Objective 1)	Local fire and rescue department with support from consortium.	47 communities.	Reduction in number and severity of fires and fire injuries.

Objective 3

What will happen?	How will it happen? (Method/Strategy)	Who will do it?	For how many or how much?	With what result or benefit?
Develop junior fire marshal program for schools.	Focus group results from fire and rescue departments, educators, and students with accepted standards.	Director and assistant director with local chiefs and personnel, and school personnel.	Program procedures documented for three age groups: primary grades, middle schools, and high schools.	Age-appropriate junior fire marshal program fully developed and documented.

Objective 4

What will happen?	How will it happen? (Method/Strategy)	Who will do it?	For how many or how much?	With what result or benefit?
Implement junior fire marshal program for schools.	Methodologies to be determined during development. (Objective 3)	Local fire and rescue department with support from consortium.	22 schools.	School-age children demonstrate increased fire safety knowledge.

EXAMPLE 6.3   *(Continued)*

Goals and Objectives for the Fire and Rescue Project

Goal 3—and Objectives to Achieve Goal

What will happen?	How will it happen? (Method/Strategy)	When will it happen?	For how many or how much?	With what result or benefit?
Improve training, recruitment, and purchasing.	*Centralization of training, recruitment, and purchasing of 47 fire and rescue departments.*	*Begin in project month three and ongoing thereafter.*	*1,050 fire and rescue personnel trained, 188 fire and rescue personnel recruited, 47 departments participate.*	*Fire and rescue personnel trained to measurably higher level, recruitment quotas met, and cost of purchases down.*

Objective 1

What will happen?	How will it happen? (Method/Strategy)	Who will do it?	For how many or how much?	With what result or benefit?
Develop centralized training.	*Determine training and delivery method, obtain or develop curricula, determine trainers.*	*Training coordinator with local chiefs and trainers.*	*Needed training for 47 departments fully developed.*	*Provide higher quality training at less cost than available prior to consortium.*

Objective 2

What will happen?	How will it happen? (Method/Strategy)	Who will do it?	For how many or how much?	With what result or benefit?
Develop centralized recruitment.	*Interview fire and rescue personnel to determine what works (what recruited existing personnel).*	*Director and assistant director with local chiefs.*	*Procedures for recruitment fully developed and documented.*	*Recruit sufficient personnel to maintain local departments fully staffed.*

(continues)

EXAMPLE 6.3 *(Continued)*

Goals and Objectives for the Fire and Rescue Project

Objective 3

What will happen?	How will it happen? (Method/Strategy)	Who will do it?	For how many or how much?	With what result or benefit?
Develop centralized purchasing.	Internet-based purchasing process centralized at consortium.	Director and assistant director.	Procedures documented for ordering, receiving, shipping, and documentation.	Provide cost savings to member fire and rescue departments.

Objective 4

What will happen?	How will it happen? (Method/Strategy)	Who will do it?	For how many or how much?	With what result or benefit?
Implement centralized training.	Classroom, hands-on, and online continuing education.	Training coordinator and selected trainers.	Provide needed training for 1,050 fire and rescue personnel.	Provide higher quality training at less cost than available prior to consortium.

Objective 5

What will happen?	How will it happen? (Method/Strategy)	Who will do it?	For how many or how much?	With what result or benefit?
Implement centralized recruitment.	Methodology determined during development. (Objective 2)	Director and assistant director with local chiefs.	188 new recruits.	Recruit sufficient personnel to maintain local departments fully staffed.

Objective 6

What will happen?	How will it happen? (Method/Strategy)	Who will do it?	For how many or how much?	With what result or benefit?
Implement centralized purchasing.	Ordering, receiving, shipping, and documenting.	Director, assistant director, and shipping and receiving person.	47 departments.	Provide cost savings to member fire and rescue departments.

EXAMPLE 6.3   *(Continued)*

Goals and Objectives for the Fire and Rescue Project

Goal 4—and Objectives to Achieve Goal

What will happen?	How will it happen? (Method/Strategy)	When will it happen?	For how many or how much?	With what result or benefit?
Monitor and manage project.	Apply effective and appropriate measures.	Throughout term of program.	Attain all relevant numbers.	Successfully accomplish all goals and objectives.

Objective 1

What will happen?	How will it happen? (Method/Strategy)	Who will do it?	For how many or how much?	With what result or benefit?
Evaluate project.	Formative and summative assessment with quantitative and qualitative measures.	Director and outside evaluator.	All goals and objectives.	Assess formatively to improve ongoing operation; assess summatively to measure success.

Objective 2

What will happen?	How will it happen? (Method/Strategy)	Who will do it?	For how many or how much?	With what result or benefit?
Effectively manage project personnel.	Use effective management techniques.	Director.	All staff.	Consortium members express satisfaction with quality of work of staff.

Objective 3

What will happen?	How will it happen? (Method/Strategy)	Who will do it?	For how many or how much?	With what result or benefit?
Effectively manage funds.	Apply accepted accounting principles.	Director.	All funds and in-kind contributions.	No audit exceptions.

(continues)

EXAMPLE 6.3   *(Continued)*

Goals and Objectives for the Fire and Rescue Project

Objective 4

What will happen?	How will it happen? (Method/Strategy)	Who will do it?	For how many or how much?	With what result or benefit?
Constantly improve project.	Use formative results to assess activities and make changes.	Director.	All goals and objectives.	Project activities improve during course of project.

Objective 5

What will happen?	How will it happen? (Method/Strategy)	Who will do it?	For how many or how much?	With what result or benefit?
Disseminate information about project.	Newsletter, Web site, articles, cable access, present at conferences and clearinghouses.	Director and assistant director.	Community, state, and national peer audiences.	Buy-in from community, replication by peer audience.

Objective 6

What will happen?	How will it happen? (Method/Strategy)	Who will do it?	For how many or how much?	With what result or benefit?
Continue project after term of grant funding.	Using evaluation results and dissemination activities, hold informational meetings with consortium members and stakeholders.	Director.	Approach all stakeholders for appropriate support.	Outreach activities and centralized functions continue after term of grant.

EXAMPLE **6.4**

Goals and Objectives for the
Alcohol and Drug Abuse Program

INNER CITY ALCOHOL AND
DRUG PREVENTION COMMISSION

Goal 1

What will happen?	How will it happen? (Method/Strategy)	When will it happen?	For how many or how much?	With what result or benefit?
Perform project set-up activities.	Hire staff, recruit volunteers, train personnel, obtain materials.	Hiring during project months 1–2; volunteer recruitment begins project month 3; ongoing training and obtaining materials begins during project month 4.	Develop facilities and personnel to accomplish other goals and objectives for 1,250 participants.	Facilities and personnel able to effectively accomplish other goals and objectives.

Goal 2

What will happen?	How will it happen? (Method/Strategy)	When will it happen?	For how many or how much?	With what result or benefit?
Reach young people with anti-substance abuse message.	Educational outreach in schools.	Develop during project months 2–3, implement in project month 4.	Reach 8,000 students in grades K–12.	Student knowledge of substance abuse increases— student ATOD use decreases.

(continues)

EXAMPLE 6.4 *(Continued)*

Goals and Objectives for the Alcohol and Drug Abuse Program

Goal 3

What will happen?	How will it happen? (Method/Strategy)	When will it happen?	For how many or how much?	With what result or benefit?
Provide more comprehensive support and intervention services.	Hotline and 24-hour crisis team.	Develop during project months 2–3, implement in project month 4.	24-hour hotline capable of handling three calls at once — crisis team capable of handling two crises at once.	Drug overdoses decrease, alcohol related crimes decrease.

Goal 4

What will happen?	How will it happen? (Method/Strategy)	When will it happen?	For how many or how much?	With what result or benefit?
Reach community with anti-substance abuse message with impact and urgency.	Develop and implement performance art group.	Develop group during project months 2–4; begin performances in project month 5.	One performance per week for term of project.	Community knowledge about substance abuse problem and solutions increases.

Goal 5

What will happen?	How will it happen? (Method/Strategy)	When will it happen?	For how many or how much?	With what result or benefit?
Effectively monitor and manage project.	Evaluate, disseminate information, continue project, consult advisory board.	Throughout term of program.	Attain all relevant numbers.	Successfully accomplish all goals and objectives.

EXAMPLE 6.4 *(Continued)*

Goals and Objectives for the Alcohol and Drug Abuse Program

Goal 1—and Objectives to Achieve Goal

What will happen?	How will it happen? (Method/Strategy)	When will it happen?	For how many or how much?	With what result or benefit?
Perform project set-up activities.	*Hire staff, recruit volunteers, train personnel, obtain materials.*	*Hiring during project months 1–2; recruitment of volunteers begins project month 3 then ongoing; training begins project month 4 then ongoing.*	*Develop facilities and personnel to accomplish other goals and objectives for 1,250 participants.*	*Facilities and personnel able to effectively accomplish other goals and objectives.*

Objective 1

What will happen?	How will it happen? (Method/Strategy)	Who will do it?	For how many or how much?	With what result or benefit?
Hire project director.	*Commission hiring procedures.*	*Executive director.*	*Project director.*	*Obtain qualified project director.*

Objective 2

What will happen?	How will it happen? (Method/Strategy)	Who will do it?	For how many or how much?	With what result or benefit?
Hire project key personnel.	*Commission hiring procedures.*	*Project director.*	*Outreach coordinator, hotline manager, director of performance art.*	*Obtain qualified key personnel.*

Objective 3

What will happen?	How will it happen? (Method/Strategy)	Who will do it?	For how many or how much?	With what result or benefit?
Hire project personnel.	*Commission hiring procedures.*	*Project director.*	*Assistant director and administrative assistant.*	*Obtain qualified project personnel.*

(continues)

EXAMPLE 6.4 *(Continued)*

Goals and Objectives for the Alcohol and Drug Abuse Program

Objective 4

What will happen?	How will it happen? (Method/Strategy)	Who will do it?	For how many or how much?	With what result or benefit?
Recruit education outreach volunteers.	Commission volunteer recruitment and screening procedures.	Outreach coordinator.	25 outreach volunteers.	Human resources to accomplish outreach activities.

Objective 5

What will happen?	How will it happen? (Method/Strategy)	Who will do it?	For how many or how much?	With what result or benefit?
Recruit hotline and crisis management volunteers.	Commission volunteer recruitment and screening procedures.	Hotline manager.	18 hotline and crisis management team volunteers.	Human resources to accomplish hotline and crisis management.

Objective 6

What will happen?	How will it happen? (Method/Strategy)	Who will do it?	For how many or how much?	With what result or benefit?
Recruit performance artists.	Commission volunteer recruitment and screening procedures.	Director of performance art.	8 performance art volunteers.	Human resources to implement performance art.

Objective 7

What will happen?	How will it happen? (Method/Strategy)	Who will do it?	For how many or how much?	With what result or benefit?
Orient volunteers to organization guidelines and procedures.	3-hour workshop.	Project director.	51 volunteers.	Volunteers understand security, privacy, expectations, and responsibilities.

EXAMPLE 6.4 *(Continued)*

Goals and Objectives for the Alcohol and Drug Abuse Program

Objective 8

What will happen?	How will it happen? (Method/Strategy)	Who will do it?	For how many or how much?	With what result or benefit?
Ready facility for project activities.	Purchase and install materials, supplies, and equipment.	Assistant director and administrative assistant.	Staff, volunteers, and participants.	Facility ready and capable of supporting staff and participants.

Goal 2—and Objectives to Achieve Goal

What will happen?	How will it happen? (Method/Strategy)	When will it happen?	For how many or how much?	With what result or benefit?
Reach young people with anti-substance abuse message.	Educational outreach in schools.	Develop during project months 2–3, implement in project month 4.	Reach 8,000 students in grades K–12.	Student knowledge of substance abuse increases—student ATOD use decreases.

Objective 1

What will happen?	How will it happen? (Method/Strategy)	Who will do it?	For how many or how much?	With what result or benefit?
Choose outreach curricula.	Research existing curriculum and choose effective, grade-appropriate curricula.	Project director, outreach coordinator, committee of school counselors.	Curricula for K–3, 4–5, 6–7, and 8–12 grade groupings.	Proven effective age-appropriate curricula used.

(continues)

EXAMPLE 6.4   *(Continued)*

Goals and Objectives for the
Alcohol and Drug Abuse Program

Objective 2

What will happen?	How will it happen? (Method/Strategy)	Who will do it?	For how many or how much?	With what result or benefit?
Train volunteers in use of curricula.	Classroom instruction and demonstration of mastery.	Outreach coordinator.	25 outreach volunteers.	Outreach volunteers possess skills and knowledge for effective outreach.

Objective 3

What will happen?	How will it happen? (Method/Strategy)	Who will do it?	For how many or how much?	With what result or benefit?
Implement outreach activities in schools.	In-school activities.	Outreach coordinator, outreach volunteers, school counselors.	8,000 students.	ATOD incidents decrease measurably.

Goal 3—and Objectives to Achieve Goal

What will happen?	How will it happen? (Method/Strategy)	When will it happen?	For how many or how much?	With what result or benefit?
Provide more comprehensive support and intervention services.	Hotline and 24-hour crisis team.	Develop during project months 2–3, implement in project month 4.	24-hour hotline capable of handling three calls at once—crisis team capable of two calls at once.	Drug overdoses decrease, alcohol related crimes decrease.

Objective 1

What will happen?	How will it happen? (Method/Strategy)	Who will do it?	For how many or how much?	With what result or benefit?
Develop hotline procedures.	Research existing similar programs and modify for local situation.	Hotline manager.	Hotline procedures manual.	Effective procedures for hotline operation.

EXAMPLE 6.4   *(Continued)*

Goals and Objectives for the
Alcohol and Drug Abuse Program

Objective 2

What will happen?	How will it happen? (Method/Strategy)	Who will do it?	For how many or how much?	With what result or benefit?
Train volunteers on hotline procedures.	Classroom training and demonstration of mastery.	Hotline manager.	18 hotline volunteers.	Hotline volunteers possess knowledge and skills to effectively operate hotline.

Objective 3

What will happen?	How will it happen? (Method/Strategy)	Who will do it?	For how many or how much?	With what result or benefit?
Implement hotline.	Hotline phone staffed at organization office.	Hotline volunteers with oversight by hotline manager.	24-hours, 7-days-a-week.	Hotline available for all ATOD situations on 24-7 basis

Objective 4

What will happen?	How will it happen? (Method/Strategy)	Who will do it?	For how many or how much?	With what result or benefit?
Train crisis teams.	Classroom training and demonstration of mastery.	Consultant and hotline manager.	18 hotline volunteers.	Crisis teams possess knowledge and skills to manage ATOD crises.

Objective 5

What will happen?	How will it happen? (Method/Strategy)	Who will do it?	For how many or how much?	With what result or benefit?
Implement crisis teams.	Hotline operator declares crisis; crisis team members auto-called with team conferencing cell phone system.	Hotline volunteers.	One team on ready, one team on standby to handle two simultaneous crises.	Crisis team available 24-7.

(continues)

EXAMPLE 6.4 *(Continued)*

Goals and Objectives for the Alcohol and Drug Abuse Program

Goal 4—and Objectives to Achieve Goal

What will happen?	How will it happen? (Method/Strategy)	When will it happen?	For how many or how much?	With what result or benefit?
Reach community with anti-substance abuse message with impact and urgency.	Develop and implement performance art group.	Develop group during project months 2–4; begin performances in project month 5.	One performance per week for term of project.	Community knowledge about substance abuse problem and solutions increases.

Objective 1

What will happen?	How will it happen? (Method/Strategy)	Who will do it?	For how many or how much?	With what result or benefit?
Develop performances.	Creative collaboration between director and artists.	Director of performance art and performance artists.	22 performances.	High-impact, dramatic performances ready.

Objective 2

What will happen?	How will it happen? (Method/Strategy)	Who will do it?	For how many or how much?	With what result or benefit?
Give performances.	In public, in unexpected places and at unannounced times (except to media outlets for coverage).	Performance artists.	One weekly (more often if public interest grows).	Public becomes aware of ATOD issues and awareness of commission work rises 100% each project year.

EXAMPLE 6.4 *(Continued)*

Goals and Objectives for the Alcohol and Drug Abuse Program

Goal 5—and Objectives to Achieve Goal

What will happen?	How will it happen? (Method/Strategy)	When will it happen?	For how many or how much?	With what result or benefit?
Effectively monitor and manage project.	Evaluate, disseminate information, continue project, consult advisory board.	Throughout term of program.	Attain all relevant numbers.	Successfully accomplish all goals and objectives.

Objective 1

What will happen?	How will it happen? (Method/Strategy)	Who will do it?	For how many or how much?	With what result or benefit?
Evaluate project.	Formative and summative assessment with quantitative and qualitative measures.	Project director and outside evaluator.	All goals and objectives.	Assess formatively to improve ongoing operation; assess summatively to measure success.

Objective 2

What will happen?	How will it happen? (Method/Strategy)	Who will do it?	For how many or how much?	With what result or benefit?
Effectively manage project personnel, both staff and volunteer.	Use effective management techniques.	Project director.	All staff and volunteers.	Project participants express satisfaction with quality of work of staff and volunteers.

Objective 3

What will happen?	How will it happen? (Method/Strategy)	Who will do it?	For how many or how much?	With what result or benefit?
Effectively manage funds.	Apply accepted accounting principles.	Project director.	All funds and in-kind contributions.	No audit exceptions.

(continues)

EXAMPLE 6.4   *(Continued)*

Goals and Objectives for the
Alcohol and Drug Abuse Program

Objective 4

What will happen?	How will it happen? (Method/Strategy)	Who will do it?	For how many or how much?	With what result or benefit?
Constantly improve project.	Use formative results to assess activities and make changes.	Project director.	All goals and objectives.	Project activities improve during course of project.

Objective 5

What will happen?	How will it happen? (Method/Strategy)	Who will do it?	For how many or how much?	With what result or benefit?
Disseminate information about project.	Newsletter, Web site, articles, cable access, present at conferences and clearinghouses.	Project director.	Community, and state and national peer audiences.	Buy-in from community, replication by peer audience.

Objective 6

What will happen?	How will it happen? (Method/Strategy)	Who will do it?	For how many or how much?	With what result or benefit?
Seek community involvement.	Advisory board.	Mayor, 4 community members, director of ATOD commission, hospital administrator, and project director.	Meets bimonthly.	Community oversight of and input to program.

EXAMPLE **6.4** *(Continued)*

Goals and Objectives for the Alcohol and Drug Abuse Program

Objective 7

What will happen?	How will it happen? (Method/Strategy)	Who will do it?	For how many or how much?	With what result or benefit?
Continue project after term of grant funding.	*Using evaluation results and dissemination activities, hold informational meetings with stakeholders.*	*Project director.*	*Approach all stakeholders for appropriate support.*	*Continue school outreach, hotline, crisis teams, and performance art.*

Chapter 7

Project Description

Description is revelation.
Wallace Stevens[1]

At a Glance

What Else Is It Called?

- Narrative
- Project narrative
- Project explanation

When Is It Used?

Always.

Why Is It Used?

The funder must have as complete a description as possible to choose from among the proposals received. Funders don't just fund good ideas. They fund well-thought out, workable projects. It is critical that the description clearly shows what you intend to do in the project, what resources your organization will contribute, and what role the funder is asked to play.

Key Concepts

- Clear and concise.
- No jargon—you do not know if readers will know your jargon, and it is imperative that the description is clear to readers.

---

[1] Wallace Stevens (1879–1955), U.S. poet.

- Cover major project events.

- Major project events are in logical order.

- If there are any unusual budget requests, clearly show how they are necessary for project success.

- If there are technical issues, be sure that the lay person can understand your description.

- You may include a time chart and project organization chart if there is space.

Formatting Issues

Keep within required space limitations, never cheat. If the funder asks a list of questions about your project, answer them in the order in which the funder listed them. Repeat their question and then answer it. Never, ever leave a question out. Use 12-point type and do not cheat on margins.

Goals and Objectives Can Be Used for Guidance

If goals and objectives are written as we recommend (see Chapter 6), they can be used as an outline for creating the project description. They are the steps to completing your project mission. You should have developed your goals as the major steps to completing your project. You should have developed your objectives as the major steps to completing your goals. You are likely to have goals that involve the following items. Depending on the specific activities involved in your project, you may not have all of them.

- Project set-up, which may include such things as setting up advisory committees, hiring temporary staff, partner meetings, and planning sessions.

- Materials and training, which may include such things as designing training and delivery, setting up a library of materials for use during the project, development of curriculum for students, review of materials to purchase, and development of business, employee, and student manuals.

- Infrastructure set-up, which may include such things as building renovation, purchase of equipment, installation of equipment, and purchase of reference materials.

- Intake activities, which may include such things as creating written procedures for registering participants, scheduling, assigning intake activities to partners, and actually registering participants.

- Project implementation comes next in the scheme of things and may include such things as starting classes, beginning research, allowing participants to access information, beginning a study, opening the doors of a clinic, admitting patients, having a concert, or whatever it takes to launch your project.

- Project evaluation is a critical goal to the funder and should be a separate goal, including such things as surveys and questionnaires, statistical studies, outcomes for every goal and every objective, participant tracking, results of research, and results of tests.

- Project management is important as a goal to inform the funder that you know you have to effectively administer and fiscally manage your project. This goal can include such things as accounting, supervision, administration of tasks, project oversight and auditing.

You may not need all these goal topics for your project, but most projects will follow the general pattern listed above. If you cover all the ground listed in the goal template above, you will cover all the topics in which a funder is interested.

When formulating objectives, think of the steps (tasks or activities) you must take to accomplish each goal, and group like tasks together to form objectives. Keep your objectives in logical order to communicate clearly to the proposal readers, and to facilitate project management.

Cover All Major Project Events in Logical Order

Notice that the goals in the last section are in roughly the order that you would do them to manage your project. Objectives should be also. If two things are being done at the same time, choose one to be listed first. Remember the reader does not know anything about your project—you are communicating with a lay person. We like to say "assume ignorance but not stupidity." The more logical your project plan sounds to the reader, the more the reader will be impressed with it and with your ability to manage the project to a successful ending.

Only cover major project events—do not get into small, nitty-gritty details, or you will confuse the reader. Stick to the main project outline as demonstrated in your goals and objectives. Use clear titles to separate different sections of your description. Make short, concise paragraphs of four to six sentences, and keep the sentences as short as possible to be readable.

If there is space, include a timeline. Some funders require a timeline in another section. If it is not required, it is a good idea to include it to clarify the work flow for the reader. Keep to the major benchmarks for the timeline. Nothing is worse than seeing a timeline that is so busy that it is impossible to read. Exhibit 7.1 presents a simple one that is made using the table function of a word processor. Other timelines will appear in other sections of this book.

Also, if there is space included, it is a good idea to include an organization chart. Again, do not show every aspect of your organization—just the parts of it that are important to the project. Be sure to show the project as integral to the organization by connecting it to a top manager, as we discuss under the chapter on continuation (Chapter 12). Exhibit 7.2 is a simple organization chart. Other organization charts will be illustrated in various sections of this book.

Cover All Hot Buttons

Each funder has certain things that are important to them. Sometimes they state those things outright, and sometimes you have to read between the lines. You must always research the funder and read all available material to uncover the hot buttons, and insure your project matches what they want to fund. Take an example from the Ford Foundation's Web site.

> ### Family Crisis, Community Response
>
> *AIDS continues to devastate African societies, but in Kenya and Tanzania, community organizations are making a difference with programs that combine care, health, education, neighborhood activism and efforts to expand employment options for the poor. "Economic opportunity will reduce the transmission of AIDS" explains one expert, pointing to women who have used small loans to escape prostitution by selling produce or opening beauty salons and handicraft shops.*

EXHIBIT 7.1

Project Year One Major Activities Timeline

Jan	Feb	Mar	Apr	May	June	July	Aug	Sept	Oct	Nov	Dec
Train staff, write	Purchase and install	Screen potential	Enroll participants	Begin administering	Track participant	Evaluate one month	Review response to	Analyze results from	Adjust hours of	Administer revised	Evaluate seven month

EXHIBIT 7.2

Project Organization Chart

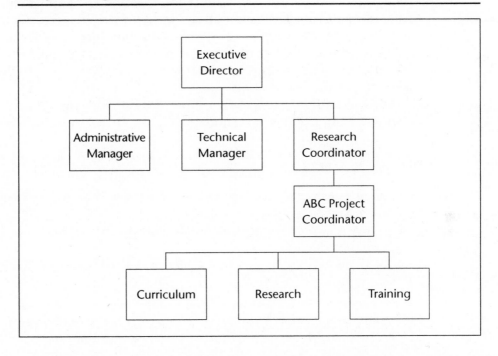

Judging from this brief statement, what do you think are Ford's hot buttons? Ford wants to see projects that have partners—specifically from health, education, community activism groups, and small business. If your project does not combine most of those elements, it has little chance for funding.

Let's look at another example from the W. K. Kellogg Foundation under its Youth and Higher Education funding category.

The W.K. Kellogg Foundation has a long history of supporting the education and development of young people. From 2001 through 2008, key Youth and Education programs will focus on improving learning for young people—especially those most vulnerable to poor achievement—so children can enter school ready to learn, more adolescents are able to achieve, and young adults are prepared for meaningful work or further education.

The Kellogg Foundation will employ a number of approaches in addressing this theme. One major approach will develop a more seamless educational pipeline, especially engaging post-secondary education institutions with communities to achieve mutually beneficial goals. Other programs will support partnerships among families, communities, and institutions—including schools and state agencies—so that they will work together for children.

What would you have to have in your project to attract Kellogg as a funder? First, your postsecondary institution would have to show that it has heavily involved the community in designing and supporting its programs. Second, your institution should involved families of at-risk children, community partnerships and other institutions including K–12 schools and state agencies, all partnering in some way to support the most vulnerable children in the community. Without partnerships, your project would have little chance of funding.

We will look at one more example. This is from the Charles Stewart Mott Foundation under its funding category Pathways Out of Poverty.

> *When Charles Stewart Mott established the Foundation that bears his name, it was with the belief that:*
>
> - *an individual's well-being is inextricably linked to the well-being of the community;*
> - *individuals are essentially in an informal partnership with their community; and*
> - *by working together, individuals can make a difference in our society and our world.*
>
> *Those beliefs are perhaps no more readily apparent than in our grant-making to address poverty in the United States. We have consistently supported efforts to help ordinary citizens come together to strengthen their communities, grow through their participation in educational opportunities and attain economic self-sufficiency by engaging more fully in our economy.*
>
> *Increasingly, we have come to see community organizing, education, and economic opportunity as critical to moving low-income Americans toward greater prosperity. In fact, those three areas have become the pillars for the Foundation's grantmaking plan for addressing poverty in the United States.*

A project that brings people in poverty together to impact supports services, with the support of community organizations, would be an attractive project to the Charles Stewart Mott Foundation. One would not have to combine community organizing, education, and economic opportunity, all three, in a project to be successful, but one will have to, at least, center the project on one of the three.

Before you develop a proposal, follow these three steps:

1. Develop a good project profile (remember a project solves a problem).
2. Find funders that, on the surface, look like they have the same interest in solving the problem that interests you.
3. Research those funders thoroughly to insure you have a match.

Meet Any Special Considerations Listed

Some funders have special considerations for grant projects. These considerations can be that grantees serve people that are in poverty, that projects come from certain states or regions of the country, are limited to special organizations, are limited to parts of the country having a special designation, and are limited to certain types of partnerships. You do not want to go to the trouble of writing and submitting a proposal if you do not meet all of the requirements.

Let's look at a few examples. First, from the U.S. Department of Education.

CFDA#: 84.359A and 84.359B

Program Name: Early Reading First Program

Closing Date: July 15, 2002 (preapplication); October 11, 2002 (application)

Program Description: The purpose of the Early Reading First Program is to create preschool centers of excellence by improving the instruction and classroom environment of early childhood programs that are located in urban or rural high-poverty communities and that serve primarily children from low-income families.

Your school would have to serve primarily children from low-income families to fit this funder.

The next example is from the U.S. Department of Justice.

Drug Courts

Violent Crime Control and Law Enforcement Act of 1994,

Pub.L. 103-322, § 50001, [42 U.S.C. § 3796ii]

States (including Guam, American Samoa, Northern Mariana Islands, Puerto Rico, U.S. Virgin Islands, and the District of Columbia), state courts, local courts, units of local government, and Indian tribal governments may apply for funding. Preference will be given to jurisdictions that are also Empowerment Zones or Economic Communities.

Your organization should be in an Empowerment Zone or have an Economic Communities designation to have a good chance for funding.

The third example is from the U.S. Department of Health and Human Services.

Department of Health and Human Services

Administration on Aging

Program Announcement No. AoA-02-09

Agency: Administration on Aging, HHS.

Action: Announcement of availability of funds and request for applications. Eligibility for grant awards and other requirements: For both competitions under this Announcement eligibility is limited to State Agencies on Aging. Grantees are required to provide a 25% non-federal match.

You need to be a state agency on aging to have a chance for funding. Moreover, if you are a state agency on aging, you will have to come up with 25% of the budget from nonfederal funds.

> It is very important to read *everything* the funder publishes to be sure your project and your organization match the funder's preferences and requirements.

Special Budget Requests

If you have a large budget item, be sure that you connect it securely to the project in the project description. Do not let the funder simply find it in the budget and wonder how it fits. Suppose one of your requests is a lease arrangement for buses for transportation. Show how transportation is a critical part of your project in the project description.

If you have an unusual request—some budget item for which the purpose is not obvious, carefully connect it to a goal in the project description. Do not assume the reason for your budget item is intuitive. What if you have a budget item for a tent? It would be good to inform the reader that in the Pacific Northwest it rains a lot, and it is necessary for your outdoor concert series to be prepared for all eventualities.

Be Clear on Technical Issues

Some projects have a technical bent or component. It is important that you clearly explain the technicalities, so that any reader can understand what you are trying to do. You cannot assume that the readers are all going to be well-versed in your area of expertise. Sometimes it only takes one reader giving your proposal a poor score for you to lose an award. As we said before, assume ignorance, not stupidity. Illustrate your technical issue with charts or other graphics when there is space. Otherwise have a colleague in another area of expertise read your description and see if the colleague can understand it.

Checklist—Project Description[2]

 ✔ Follow grant maker's order.
 ✔ Use grant maker's names for parts.
 ✔ Avoid acronyms.
 ✔ Avoid jargon.
 ✔ Maintain consistency with names and titles.
 ✔ Preempt possible objections.
 ✔ Eliminate possible confusion.
 ✔ Explain unusual activities, situations, or circumstances.

Last Words

Develop goals and objectives before writing the project narrative. An outline is a writer's best friend, and the goals and objectives are, for all practical purposes, an outline of the project. Using our method, goals and objectives can be fully developed without writing paragraphs of text. Simply fill in the boxes. Once the goals and objectives are done, writing a project narrative becomes much easier, just as writing an article, a paper, or a book is facilitated by working from an outline.

Next, use the grant maker's proposal evaluation guidelines (the grant reader's assessment guidelines) to create an empty document with all the headings, and the actual requirements for all the sections in the narrative. You have now created a mock-up of the project narrative.

With these two items—the completed goals and objectives, and the narrative mock-up, you are ready to begin work. Simply respond to what each narrative section requests. Answer the questions. As you write each section, delete the grant maker's grading guidelines, leaving only the headings. Once you work your way completely through the grant maker's evaluation guidelines, simply answering the questions and responding to the requirement, you will have completed the project narrative.

Over the past few years, project narratives have become shorter and shorter. It is not at all unusual to apply for over a million dollars a year from a federal agency with a twenty-page, double-spaced narrative. The double-spacing means that the narrative is actually around ten pages of text. This means it won't take long to finish the project narrative.

---

[2] Remember that a grant maker's directions (instructions/guidelines) take precedence over any and all other considerations. You must absolutely, positively follow the grant maker's directions exactly, precisely, and painstakingly.

Don't lose track of the fact that what you are writing is a sales piece. A grant proposal is not an academic paper. It is a sales pitch. A basic of sales training is teaching how to overcome objections. Sales people are taught that objections are predictable and that presenting a reasonable solution to each objection as it is raised will lead to an eventual sale.

A proposal writer, however, is not involved in a dialogue with the reader. The proposal writer does not have the luxury of hearing objections and mounting arguments to overcome them. A grant proposal is a monologue, a one-way sales pitch, with no opportunity to hear and overcome objections.

Possible objections must be understood in advance. This means looking at the project with new eyes, with critical eyes. Look at the project as though for the first time. This may take outside help. When an outside reader misunderstands something or is confused by an aspect of the project, it is not the fault of the outside reader. It is the proposal writer's fault.

Foresee objections and preempt them. Remove the possibility of confusion and disagreement in advance. It is the only chance you will have.

An interesting source of reader confusion is lack of consistency with names and titles. If the person who will lead the project is called the director in one place, do not call that person the coordinator in another place. Do not mention counselors in one place and social workers in another while referring to the same position. Settle on names and titles and stick with them. If computer installations are called neighborhood work stations in one place and community access points in another, how will the reader know for sure whether they are the same thing or different? Emerson may have been correct in saying "Mindless consistency is the hobgoblin of little minds." But, in a grant proposal, absolute consistency is a cardinal virtue.

Examples of Project Descriptions for Four Projects

The following four examples (7.1 to 7.4) are examples of project descriptions for each of the four diverse organizations profiled in this book. The specific elements highlighted in this chapter are reflected in each example.

EXAMPLE 7.1

After School Program—Project Description

Sunnyvale School District

Introduction

The mission of the After School Program for Middle School students is to improve academic performance, reduce the incidence of behavioral problems, increase recreational and social opportunities, and promote positive parental involvement.

The program is for middle school students and will run at the five middle schools and have a maximum of 1,200 total participants.

The after school program can be described fully by using nine topics:

1. Set-up
2. Training
3. Supplemental academic activities
4. Applied learning activities
5. Recreational activities
6. Social/health services and activities
7. Parental involvement activities
8. Evaluation
9. Management and communication

Topics 1–7 are discussed below, each under its own heading. Topic 8, evaluation, is discussed in a separate section elsewhere in the proposal. Topic 9 includes the subjects of dissemination and continuation along with the management plan. Each of these subjects is discussed in a separate section elsewhere in this proposal.

To simplify the discussion of the seven separate topics, those features of the program that all the topics have in common—mainly, scheduling and transportation—will be discussed under their own headings below.

Scheduling

The program will operate five days a week, Monday through Friday, during the school year (August 15 through June 12). The program will close only for school holidays as published in the official school calendar. The program will operate on those Fridays designated as "Teacher Work

(continues)

EXAMPLE 7.1 *(Continued)*

After School Program— Project Description, page 2

Days" on the school calendar. The program will not operate on days that schools are closed due to inclement weather (snow days) but will operate on days designated as "snow make-up days."

The normal hours of operation of the program are from 3:00 to 7:30 P.M. Student activities run from the end of the school day (approximately 3:00 P.M.) until 6:00 P.M. Adult activities are scheduled from 5:30 to 7:30 P.M. The one exception to the normal schedule is that the program is open from 7:00 A.M. until 7:30 P.M. on scheduled "teacher workdays."

The first after school program activity each day is a snack scheduled from 3:00 to 3:15. The snack consists of a serving of fruit (apple, banana, etc.), a starch (crackers, cookie, etc.), or a dairy-based item (cheese, yogurt, etc.), and a beverage (milk, juice, etc.). The snack conforms to the nutrition standards set by the state for school-based food service. Snack menus are set by consultation between the site director, the cafeteria supervisor, and the district nutritionist.

A snack coordinator at each program site, with oversight from the supervisor of the school cafeteria and the site director, is responsible for preparing and serving the snack and cleaning up afterwards. The position of snack coordinator is part-time running from approximately 1:00 to 4:00 in the afternoon.

Supervised homework time is scheduled after the snack. All students in the after school program participate in supervised homework. Tutors, teachers, and other program staff provide supervision. The ratio of staff to students is maintained at a maximum of 1:10. The length of time spent in supervised homework depends on a student's academic situation. Regardless, supervised homework is over for all students at 4:15.

Part of the Individual Academic Plan (IAP) developed for each participant is a determination of the amount of time spent in supervised homework. This is also a time during which students can receive tutoring. Tutoring can be one-on-one or take place in groups of up to five students, depending on the student's need. Another part of the IAP is the determination that tutoring is needed. Tutors can be either adults or high school students. In either case, a tutor must undergo the district's screening process and successfully complete the course of training.

EXAMPLE 7.1 *(Continued)*

After School Program— Project Description, page 3

After supervised homework time, students break into small groups for a variety of activities based on the individual student's academic needs and personal preferences. After 3:45 for some students and 4:15 for all students, the remainder of the afternoon is divided into two or three blocks depending on the activities. These blocks may be spent on academic supplementation, applied learning, or recreation, social, or health activities. Students with special needs may be placed in certain activities targeted at the need. An example of this would be anger management. Students who are academically successful may choose their activities for all the blocks. Regardless of their academic situations, all students have one block reserved for their personal choice of activity.

Pick up of students by parents begins at 5:00. All students must be picked up by 6:00. Activities end at 5:15 for students riding a bus. The buses leave at 5:30. All bus riders should be home by 6:45.

Classes for parents begin at 5:30. The lengths of the classes vary based on content. Generally, hands-on subjects such as the various computer classes last an hour, with other subjects lasting only 30 minutes.

> **Special Note.** In this proposal, reference is made numerous times to a "parent" or to "parents." The term "parent" does not convey the complete picture. Complete accuracy would require a phrase such as "custodial parent or legal guardian." For simplicity, we use the term "parent" to refer to the person who is entrusted by law with the care of the child or student in question. This person may be neither the biological nor the adoptive parent but another person who has legal standing as custodian or guardian.

Transportation

Each middle school houses an after school program. Middle school students who participate remain in the same school. Therefore, no transportation of students is necessary at the beginning of the after school program. On teacher workdays when schools are closed for students, it is the parents' responsibility to transport their children at the start of the school day.

Student pick-up begins at 5:00 P.M., and all students must be picked up by 6:00 P.M. The normal school requirements concerning persons

(continues)

EXAMPLE **7.1** *(Continued)*

After School Program—
Project Description, page 4

authorized to pick up children are in effect. Bus transportation will be provided for students whose parents or guardians, due to work schedules, cannot pick up their children during the hour between 5:00 and 6:00. Parents will be required to attend a conference with after school program staff to arrange bus transportation. Bus drivers are hired from the existing pool of district bus drivers

Set-up

Set-up includes hiring program staff, recruiting tutors, completing agreements with private contractors, and preparing the physical facilities. The first position to be filled is the program director, the person with responsibility for the entire five-site after school program. The program director works out of the district office and reports directly to the district superintendent. This puts the director of the after school program at an equal organizational level with the four assistant superintendents for curriculum, student affairs, operations, and personnel. Dr. Christopher Allen, now principal of Ripley Middle School, has agreed to assume the position of director of the after school program. Dr. Allen's preeminent qualifications for the position of director can be seen in his biographical sketch in the key personnel section of the proposal. The availability of Dr. Allen to fill the director's position as soon as funding is approved means that there will be no time lag in beginning the other start-up activities.

Using the district's hiring procedures and coordinating with the assistant superintendent of personnel, the director will fill the remaining program staff positions. The director will hire directly the two people who will work at the district office: the assistant program director and the administrative assistant. The program director also will directly hire the five full-time site directors. The position requirements for site director can be seen in the key personnel section of this proposal.

It is important to note that the five middle school principals, though they do not occupy positions on the program organizational chart, are an important part of the program's management team. During planning and project development for the after school program and this application package, the school principals raised serious concerns about having activities occur in their schools which they would have no control over but would be held responsible for. These concerns were addressed in the

EXAMPLE 7.1 *(Continued)*

After School Program—
Project Description, page 5

form of a directive added to the district's policy and procedures manual with the necessary approval of the school board. The policy directs that no activities may be held in a school or on its grounds without consultation and coordination with, and the approval of, the principal. This policy makes each middle school principal an integral part of the management team. It is also important to note that each middle school principal has enthusiastically endorsed housing an after school program. One further note on this subject is that the school board approved a change to the middle school principal job description that includes oversight and collaboration on an after school program. The import of this discussion is that the middle school principals are involved in decisions about the after school program in their school. That point is not made every time a decision is discussed below, but it remains true.

Each site director, coordinating with the program director and the assistant superintendent of personnel, will hire a full-time assistant site director, a part-time snack coordinator, and five part-time certified teachers. Each site director, in accordance with district policy and procedures, will recruit and screen 30 qualified tutors.

A number of contractors will be hired to provide leadership or instruction in applied learning, recreational, social, and health activities. Examples of activities that might be included are dance, karate, cooking, and cake decorating. The authority to enter into the contractual agreements resides with the program director. An activity committee of the five site directors, chaired by the program director will make the choices of activities and contractors. The decisions of the activity committee will be guided by the project planning focus group results and input from the advisory committee but will also adhere to the district's extracurricular activity policy. In keeping with district policy, approved written agreements must be executed with each contractor.

The final step in the set-up phase of the after school program is to physically prepare each middle school facility. The site director and the school principal will work through the physical requirements of the after school program and ensure that the facility is prepared to accommodate the activities. For example, if the chairs in the cafeteria are normally placed on the tables for floor cleaning during the time immediately after school, the schedule for floor cleaning must be changed to

(continues)

EXAMPLE 7.1 *(Continued)*

After School Program—
Project Description, page 6

accommodate the after school snack and supervised homework time. It is the responsibility of the site director and the site principal to ensure that the facility is ready to handle the number of expected participants. This number is different for each site but averages 240 participants.

Train Program Personnel

No person may interact with after school participants in any capacity until successfully completing the three-hour orientation training. This restriction applies to everyone—hired staff, certified teachers, volunteers, and contractors. The orientation training explains how persons representing the school district must comport themselves and the standards and expectations for all interactions with students and their parents. This training is done by district training personnel. Obviously, this training is ongoing, since any staff added as the school year progresses must complete the training before beginning work with students. District training personnel offer the training weekly, because the policy applies to all district personnel. Tutors and the snack coordinators must complete this training.

The persons qualified by the screening process to become tutors must successfully complete the self-paced, online tutor tutorial. They must also pass the subject matter mastery test. It is the responsibility of each site director to ensure that no person tutors students until successful completion of the tutor tutorial and the appropriate subject matter mastery test.

A participant's after school activities do not stand alone, unconnected to the rest of the student's experiences. The ultimate purpose of an after school program is to improve academic performance, reduce behavioral problems, increase recreational and social opportunities, and promote positive parental involvement. For after school activities to have a positive impact in these areas, they must be targeted with careful purpose. For this reason, school personnel—classroom teachers, counselors, coaches, librarians, and specialists (in short, anyone who interacts with the student)—are the sources of the information that forms a student's after school experience.

The program director, working with the site directors and school principals, must explain to school personnel the pivotal role they play

EXAMPLE 7.1 *(Continued)*

After School Program— Project Description, page 7

in the success of students in the after school program. In general terms, school personnel are expected to provide the information from which a student's Individual Academic Plan will be developed. Teachers also participate in a homework information loop, the purpose of which is to ensure that the supervised homework time is as productive as possible, perhaps including tutoring. Ongoing information feedback loops ensure that after school activities are aligned to the needs of the student and that both ends of the loop have sufficient information to change activities to meet changing circumstances.

Supplemental Academic Activities

Participation in after school activities will benefit any and all students, but the real targets of this program are those students having academic difficulties. That is why the topic of recruiting students to participate in the after school program is discussed here under academic activities. It must be made abundantly clear that the program does not limit participation on any basis whatever—not race, nor gender, nor religion, nor disability, nor non-English speaking, nor academic standing, nor even past behavioral problems. It is true that certain negative behaviors can lead to expulsion from the program, but all students start in the after school program with a clean slate.

The program will be publicized to all parents with the intention of accomplishing three separate "hits" for each middle school student. Because of the time involved in the set-up phase for the first project year, two report card periods will occur before the program begins operation. A flyer will be sent home with the first two report cards. The third "hit" will be a direct mailing to all middle school parents.

Extra effort will be made to recruit those students most in need of academic supplementation into the program. Teachers will discuss the academic opportunities available in the after school activities during the year's first parent-teacher conferences. In addition, teachers will make follow-up telephone calls to ensure that parents who want their children to participate get the chance. The goal is to recruit about 240 participants per middle school.

Once parents have signed the informed consent forms, the process begins of developing an Individual Academic Plan (IAP) for each participating

(continues)

EXAMPLE 7.1   *(Continued)*

After School Program—
Project Description, page 8

student. The site director and assistant lead this effort. The process begins with teachers completing an academic progress questionnaire on each student. In many cases, this will provide all the information that the after school staff need to complete the IAP. When additional information is needed, a conference between school day and after school staff will be scheduled through the auspices of the school principal.

As has been discussed already, each participant will spend time in supervised homework. When deemed appropriate during the IAP process, students will work with a tutor. Finally, those students most in need of help will be scheduled for academic supplementation classes taught by certified teachers during the after school program. For the first two program years, academic supplementation will be offered in language arts and mathematics. Additional subject areas may be added beginning in program year three if the need is great enough and the resources exist.

Applied Learning Activities

Applied learning refers to activities that while not classically academic in nature still teach valuable skills. Examples include cooking, sewing, carpentry, and landscaping.

The first few applied learning topics were determined by results of the planning focus groups. It is the responsibility of site directors and their assistants to canvas participants for additional topics for applied learning activities. After a topic is identified, it must be determined to be acceptable under the district's guidelines on extracurricular activities and it must be approved by the school principal and the program director.

Once an applied learning activity is approved, the site director must recruit a provider. If the provider must be paid, negotiations are turned over to the program director for completion of a contract. Each site will begin the first program year with the four applied learning activities listed above. It is the responsibility of each site director to add one applied learning topic each semester (two per school year). Using a site-based identification process for new applied learning topics allows each site, over time, to develop its own distinct culture.

EXAMPLE 7.1   *(Continued)*

After School Program—
Project Description, page 9

Recreational Activities

Outside recreation refers, generally though not always, to physical activity in a game or competitive format. Examples include volleyball, soccer, softball, and flag football. The policy of the after school program is that, normally, each student should participate in at least one block of outside recreational activities. For days when outside activity is not practical, indoor activities will be used. Examples include chess and checkers, miscellaneous board games, and "party" type participatory games such as charades.

Inside recreation refers to games such as those listed just above and also to creative pursuits such as drawing, painting, and sculpture. Dance can also be a considered a recreation activity.

As with applied learning, additional recreational opportunities are to be researched and added as the program moves forward. Student preference is the prime source of new recreational activities, though suggestions from parents will be entertained.

Social/Health Services and Activities

For the purposes of the after school program, a social activity is generally one that involves significant interaction between individuals but does not involve competition. Many of the after school social activities involve learning or improving social skills such as interview techniques, telephone etiquette, conversation skills, and conflict management. These activities obviously have a great deal in common with applied learning. Other social activities overlap almost completely with recreation. Dance is the prime example. This overlap of common features is to be expected. The category into which a particular activity is placed is based more on the overall impact than on an inventory of features.

For our purposes, health services deal with issues that affect a child's physical or mental well being. The most common examples are violence and the use of alcohol, tobacco, and other drugs. Other situations may involve people other than the child (usually the parents) and such issues as personal hygiene, nutrition, abuse, or neglect. In such cases, involvement by outside agencies such as social services or child protective services may be warranted.

(continues)

EXAMPLE 7.1 *(Continued)*

After School Program— Project Description, page 10

As with applied learning and recreation, it is the responsibility of the site directors to expand the offerings of social activities and health services to meet the needs and interests of the students.

Parental Involvement Activities

Each site director is responsible for implementing a number and variety of parent involvement opportunities. Examples include workshops, open house, group meetings, individual meetings, a Web site, and direct mail.

Another important opportunity to involve parents is by offering classes on topics of interest to the parents. The results of the planning process focus groups identified computer skills as the topic with the most interest. The after school program will use the computer labs at the middle schools to hold a variety of computer skills classes including basic computer literacy, using email, using the Internet, word processing basics, database basics, and graphics basics.

Additional topics for parent classes revolve around teaching parents how to help their children succeed in school. It is the responsibility of the site directors to constantly canvas parents to identify new parent involvement activities to meet the needs and interests of participant's parents.

EXAMPLE 7.2

Senior Citizen Wellness Center— Project Description

The Senior Citizen Wellness Center

The mission of the Senior Citizen Center Project is to enhance health, wellness, and social activity, and to provide a single point of entry into the world of services for the elderly.

Most of the activities of the project fall into three main areas: (1) health and wellness services enhancements, (2) social enrichment activities enhancement, and (3) a single point of entry to services for the elderly. These three areas correspond respectively to Project Goals 2, 3, and 4.

Through the life of the senior citizen center, the facility and the services provided have improved and expanded steadily, but the progress and outcome have turned out much like Topsy—they "just grew." Up to now, there has been no overall strategic plan. Intentions always have been good, even grand, but specific methods and activities specifically designed to move purposefully toward the good intentions have been lacking.

Over the past two years, the senior citizen center has led an extensive consortium of the city's public and private service organizations in a comprehensive inventory and assessment of the needs of our senior citizens, the available services for the elderly, and the connection or lack thereof between the two. The project described in this proposal is one of the more significant outcomes of that effort. Specific activities in the project are included specifically in response to identified needs of our community's elderly and concomitant lack of sufficient existing services.

The inventory and assessment consortium consisted of a relatively small number of primary members that worked together through the entire process along with a much larger number of secondary members actively involved only when appropriate to their specific interests. The primary members of the consortium include the following organizations:

- Senior citizen center
- City government
- County government
- Council on aging

(continues)

EXAMPLE 7.2 *(Continued)*

Senior Citizen Wellness Center—
Project Description, page 2

- Memorial hospital
- Department of public health
- State department of social services

The secondary members of the consortium include but are not limited to the following organizations:

- ATOD commission
- School district
- YMCA
- YWCA
- Lila Jones Memorial Water Sport Park (swimming pool)
- Privately managed extended care facilities (12 of the 14 in the city and county)
- Office of mental health of the department of public health
- City department of parks and recreation
- County department of parks and recreation
- Lion's Club
- Rotary
- Chamber of Commerce
- Junior Chamber of Commerce
- Department of Consumer Affairs, state attorney general's office
- City transit service (bus)
- Fire department
- City police department
- Sheriff's department
- Emergency services
- Social security administration
- Department of medicare, health and human services
- Department of veterans affairs
- County library system
- Red Cross
- Salvation Army
- Goodwill Industries

EXAMPLE 7.2 *(Continued)*

Senior Citizen Wellness Center— Project Description, page 3

- Catholic Charities
- Ministerial association

On concluding the two-year process of inventory and assessment, the consortium reconstituted itself as the Oversight Committee for Senior Affairs (OCSA), giving itself the mission of facilitating solutions for the problems of senior citizens. Working with the senior citizen center as the lead agency, the first substantive action of the advisory board was to develop fully the plan for a comprehensive program of services for the elderly—a road map into the future with strategic directions, timelines, and benchmarks. The project described in this proposal is comprised of a number of the master program's activities that address the most pressing needs of our community's elderly.

The senior citizen center ("the center") has always provided a few health and wellness services and a couple social enrichment activities. Until now, decisions about which activities to undertake were not guided by a strategic vision or plan. The activities included below, however, are the first phase of a fully planned strategic approach to a "big picture" approach to the welfare of our community's senior citizens.

Health and Wellness Services Enhancements

The health services we intend to enhance include but are not limited to the screening and appropriate referral for the following conditions:

- Heart disease
- Diabetes
- Arthritis
- Hypoglycemia
- Elevated blood pressure
- Bone density
- Skin cancers
- Kidney function
- Liver function
- Glaucoma
- Obesity
- Depression
- Muscle weakness

(continues)

EXAMPLE 7.2 *(Continued)*

Senior Citizen Wellness Center— Project Description, page 4

Partnering to make these screenings and referrals possible are Memorial Hospital, Public Health, and various private-sector health care professionals.

The wellness services we intend to enhance include but are not limited to the following supervised activities:

- Exercise programs (open air and pool)
- Weight room
- Dance lessons and opportunities
- Swimming lessons and opportunities
- Walking path
- Jogging track

Partners helping with these wellness activities include the YMCA, YWCA, Lila Jones Memorial Water Sport Park, city and county departments of parks and recreation, and various private-sector companies and individuals.

Important additional wellness services are provided by cooking classes. Participants learn food preparation techniques for the specialized diets needed for treatment of conditions that include but are not limited to the following:

- Diabetes
- High blood pressure
- Heart disease
- Obesity

Help with planning and implementing these classes has been obtained from Public Health Nutrition Services and from the vocational education center and the home economics department of our school district.

Social Enrichment Activities Enhancement

The social enrichment activities we intend to enhance include but are not limited to the following:

- Communal meals
- Game room
- Dances

EXAMPLE 7.2 *(Continued)*

Senior Citizen Wellness Center— Project Description, page 5

- Seasonal events
- Holiday parties
- Foster grandparent program

The foster grandparent program is a self-contained project that includes the activities of recruitment, screening, training, oversight, and assessment. We have entered into relations with the national organization of the foster grandparent program. Our program will follow the guidelines published by the national organization, and our program will participate fully in the national and state programs.

Combination Activities

Support groups help improve health and wellness as well as promote social enrichment. The support groups we intend to enhance include but are not limited to the following:

- Caregiver's stress
- Grief (loss of a loved one)
- Depression
- Substance abuse

The support groups will be run in partnerships with a number of agencies, people, and organizations. Partners include the Office of Mental Health, Memorial Hospital, various private practice mental health professionals, ATOD commission, and clergy and lay leaders of various religious groups.

One of the findings from the two-year inventory and assessment was that the elderly overwhelmingly cited religion as an important part of their lives. This was an important reason for choosing the private-sector senior citizen center as the lead agency for the single point of entry. Having the SPE work from the private sector amplified our ability to include faith-based aspects.

To help with support groups as well as other functions, we have established working relations with clergy and lay leaders of all the major faiths represented in our community. These include Jewish, Roman Catholic, Greek Orthodox, various denominations of Protestant Christian, Hindu, Moslem, and Buddhist. We remain open to relations with additional faiths.

(continues)

EXAMPLE 7.2 *(Continued)*

Senior Citizen Wellness Center— Project Description, page 6

Single Point of Entry

In summary, the purpose of the single point of entry is to provide an elderly person with a single place/person through which to access all the various available services, both public and private. Single point of entry may be accessed three ways: walk-in counselor-aided assistance, walk-in self-service assistance, and home counselor visit.

Discussions among service providers began during the inventory and assessment process and continued during project development and preparation of this proposal. Obstacles remain to the implementation of the single point of entry system, mostly in the areas of information security, privacy issues, and communication protocols. We have letters of commitment from each of our 23 partnering service providers in which they agree to a good faith effort to overcome the barriers to cooperation.

Because of the need for a great deal of collaboration and flexibility, the choice of the person to lead this project is especially important. Our choice of Dr. Aaron Hoyt for project director (please see key person bio sketch) was made specifically to overcome the initial setup difficulties. Dr. Hoyt is one of the most well-known and most highly respected leaders in our community. He brings to this project the proven ability to bring disparate organizations together to work toward common goals.

While Dr. Hoyt brings tremendous people skills to the project, management of the single point of entry (SPE) also requires a high degree of technical expertise to establish and maintain the necessary communication and database systems. Our choice for SPE coordinator, April Foot, was made for just that reason. Ms. Foote brings extensive experience, not only with the organization and management of collaborative service-oriented efforts but also with computers, software, and communications networks. Please see Ms. Foote's key person bio sketch for more detail about her qualifications.

The first major responsibility of the SPE management team will be resolving the issues of information security, privacy, and secure, convenient, and reliable communications between and among the many partners. To facilitate the process of keeping government agencies focused on solving problems instead of protecting turf and walking away, we have gained commitment from our city mayor, our state

EXAMPLE 7.2 *(Continued)*

Senior Citizen Wellness Center— Project Description, page 7

governor, and our senior U.S. senator. They have agreed to exert influence when necessary at the city, state, and federal levels, respectively, to keep the process moving forward.

For the SPE to be worthwhile, senior citizens will need to know it exists and what it does. A major publicity campaign is planned, including the use of radio, television, direct mail, inserts in utility billings, and presentations wherever groups of senior citizens can be found.

Once fully implemented, the SPE will accommodate senior citizens on both a walk-in and at-home basis. Users of SPE can visit the senior citizen center and be individually helped by an SPE guide, or they can, on their own, directly access the system from a computer terminal. For stay-at-home use, an SPE guide can visit or the SPE system can be accessed via the Internet.

The different methods of access to the SPE will implement on a phased basis. First available will be walk-in/guided access at the senior citizen center. Implemented next will be home visit/guided access. Later, the first capacity to use computer access will be implemented at the senior citizen center. Internet access to the SPE will be the last method implemented. We plan to provide walk-in/guided access beginning in project month 5. Access via the Internet will be available at the start of project year 3. Home visit/guided access will be implemented at the start of project year 2. Walk-in computer access will come online midway through project year 2.

EXAMPLE 7.3

Fire and Rescue Project—
Project Description

Quad-County Fire and Rescue Association

Fire, flood, tornado, hurricane, earthquake—disasters all of the first order destroying lives, property, and dreams with one huge difference: Fire is preventable.

The first and best line of defense against the devastation of an out-of-control fire is an informed and vigilant populace. Moms and grandmas, dads and grandpas, brothers and sisters, in-laws and out-laws, whether homemakers, business owners, teachers, or truckers, the individual day-to-day decisions and actions made by us all, at times singly and at times in concert, determine our likelihood of a visit from the ruin and loss of fire.

When prevention fails and a destroying fire rages out of control, the next line of defense is the firefighter—equipped, trained, and ready to roll.

Contained in these simple concepts are the difficult realities behind a fire department's ultimate purpose of preserving life and property. Reality number one is that the public must be educated and brought on board as fully functioning fire prevention partners. Reality number two is that motivated people must be recruited and retained as fire fighters. Third, firefighters must be properly and thoroughly trained, not only to preserve life and property but also to ensure their own safety. Fourth and finally, no firefighter can be effective without the right equipment. Firefighters' success and survival depend on their gear—the tools, the outfit, and the machinery they use to battle their ravenous and relentless foe.

In the four-county area of the state that is the subject of this proposal, fire departments are staffed by volunteer firefighters. In the past, volunteer fire departments worked individually, drawing their financial support from fundraising efforts in their communities and miscellaneous fees for service. This method of operation has become less and less sustainable. The main reason is the expansion of responsibility for threats such as the release of hazardous materials as well as the terrorist threats of nuclear, chemical, and biological attacks. These additional responsibilities greatly increase the amount

EXAMPLE **7.3** *(Continued)*

Fire and Rescue Project—
Project Description, page 2

of training and equipment now necessary. In addition, the complexity of today's firefighting environment necessitates a great deal more sophistication in recordkeeping and reporting, which makes working effectively with computers and communications networks an additional necessity.

In response to today's challenges, the 47 volunteer fire departments of our four-county area began working together, pooling resources for the improvement of all. To formalize the alliance and provide a legal entity from which to carry out its efforts, the Quad-County Fire & Rescue Association ("the association") incorporated as a nonprofit organization. The association sought and obtained its 501(c)(3) tax-exempt status from the IRS.

Financial support for the association comes from allocations from each member fire department. The purpose of this proposal is to obtain a one-time infusion of funding to cover the expenses of the set-up of the association. The member fire departments can support the association once it is up and running. We believe that funds invested in the association will show the way—provide a model—for the survival of thousands of volunteer fire departments across the country. The stand-alone model no longer works. It needs to be shown that a new collaborative model will work. We are in a position to demonstrate that this approach will work.

The funding we are requesting is to renovate and equip a donated building to serve as office space for the association. The director and her administrative assistant have been hired and are on the job, working in temporary space created at a centrally located fire department by parking a truck outside. Once we are able to move into a permanent facility, an assistant director, training coordinator, and shipping and receiving clerk will be hired, all with association funds.

The overall purpose of the association is to serve as a central information hub and service provider. The community outreach program is a good example of how the association will function. All 47 fire departments have community outreach programs, but the programs often are hindered in their effectiveness due to lack of time

(continues)

EXAMPLE 7.3 *(Continued)*

Fire and Rescue Project—
Project Description, page 3

and resources at the local departments. The association will provide research, literature procurement or development, training, organization, database management, printing, mailing, and other tasks and activities that local departments lack the personpower or expertise to accomplish.

The association will serve three other very important functions: centralized recruiting, training, and purchasing. The effort to recruit firefighters is an ongoing struggle for local departments. Generally, people choose to become volunteer firefighters to fight fires, not become involved in planning, paperwork, and outside projects, regardless of the importance of such tasks. By placing much of the administrative detail of recruiting, training, and purchasing in a central location, local departments can focus on their central responsibilities.

Centralizing the training will cut the cost and increase the availability of advanced training. Centralizing purchasing will eliminate duplication of effort, allow economies of scale, and shift resources among departments, meeting the needs of one department with the excess from another. The financial and legal requirements for such transfers were perhaps the most difficult aspect of the agreement that had to be reached among departments.

EXAMPLE 7.4

Alcohol and Drug Abuse Program— Project Description

INNER CITY ALCOHOL AND DRUG PREVENTION COMMISSION

The mission of the ATOD Prevention Project is to reduce ATOD abuse among school students, provide intervention services, and effectively take the ATOD prevention message to the community.

Once funded, a series of set-up activities will be accomplished. After completion of the set-up activities, the project will operate on three tracks corresponding to Project Goals 2, 3, and 4. One track is educational outreach in our community's schools. Another track is the operation of a hotline and a crisis team. The final track is community education and outreach through the medium of performance art.

Set-Up Activities

The executive director of our community ATOD commission has the responsibility of hiring the project director. The choice for project director is Dr. Kathryn Brandon, as described in the management plan. Dr. Brandon has agreed to serve in the position; therefore, the project director position can be filled quickly.

Once the project director is on board, her first tasks will be to hire the outreach coordinator, the hotline manager, the director of performance art, her assistant (assistant project director), and her administrative assistant. Although the project director has authority to make hiring decisions for project personnel, the executive director of the ATOD commission will be consulted and will provide guidance. The advertisement, interview, and decision-making process in place within the ATOD commission will be used for all personnel hiring.

The ATOD commission is providing office space for the project. It will be the responsibility of the assistant project director and administrative assistant to make the office space into a prepared facility for implementation of the project. This entails purchase, installation, and stocking of the materials, supplies, and equipment necessary for efficient operation of the project.

Educational Outreach

The responsibilities of the outreach coordinator fall into four main areas: (1) recruiting outreach volunteers, (2) choosing the outreach

(continues)

EXAMPLE 7.4 *(Continued)*

Alcohol and Drug Abuse Program— Project Description, page 2

curriculum, (3) training the volunteers to use the outreach curriculum, and (4) implementing and managing the outreach program in the schools.

As part of our state's youth drug prevention efforts, class time for drug prevention activities is mandated by state regulation. In addition, the school district receives state funds allocated for drug prevention. In an agreement reached between the school district and the ATOD commission, a team of outreach volunteers will work in each school in partnership with teachers and school staff, using mandated time and the state funding to implement an ATOD prevention program.

The outreach coordinator will use the ATOD commission procedure for recruiting and screening volunteers. In tandem, each volunteer must undergo the school district's requirements for screening volunteer workers. The school district has given the assistant principal in each school the responsibility as the single point of contact between the school and the project as well as oversight responsibility for ATOD prevention activities within the school.

A research committee has been established, comprising the project director, the outreach coordinator, and one school guidance counselor assigned by the school district from each of the four class groupings (K–3, 4–5, 6–8, and 9–12). The purpose of the research committee is to identify ATOD prevention curriculums that have proven effective and then to choose grade-appropriate curricula for our use. The outreach coordinator will enter into the necessary financial and contractual arrangements with the providers of the chosen curricula.

A cadre of volunteers and school personnel will be trained as trainers of the ATOD prevention curricula. The trainers may need to travel for training or consultants may travel to us. The method depends on the provider of the curriculum. Once the trainers are trained, they will, in turn, train the remaining outreach volunteers and school personnel.

The ATOD prevention activities will be implemented in the schools as outreach volunteers and school personnel become trained. We will not withhold implementation until all personnel are trained but rather will implement in each school as soon as that school's volunteers and staff are ready.

EXAMPLE 7.4 *(Continued)*

Alcohol and Drug Abuse Program— Project Description, page 3

Hotline and Crisis Team

The responsibilities of the hotline manager fall into three main areas: (1) recruiting hotline and crisis team volunteers, (2) training the volunteers in hotline and crisis team procedures, and (3) implementing and managing the hotline and crisis teams.

The hotline manager, working with the project director, will research hotline programs and develop a procedures manual for the hotline based on proven effectiveness. Once volunteers are recruited and screened using ATOD commission guidelines, they will be trained in the hotline procedures. Consultants will be used to both train hotline volunteers and perform practice phone calls, putting the hotline operators into the most realistic situations possible.

Once sufficient hotline volunteers have been trained, the use of the hotline will be started slowly with a phased approach to publicizing the service. Originally, the hotline will be publicized only in a newspaper article, which our local newspaper has agreed to publish on the appropriate date. Once the hotline volunteers have become acclimated to real-time situations, publicizing of the hotline will accelerate, using all available means to reach members of our community. Such means include teaming with educational outreach program, featuring the service on appropriate Web sites, partnering with local health care providers, notifying all mental health care providers in our community, and partnering with local lodging, dining, and entertainment providers. One of the hotline manager's main responsibilities will be to continue and expand publicity about the hotline.

The hotline manager will also recruit, screen, and train crisis team volunteers. The agreements and relations we established during project development activities will be finalized with community fire and rescue departments, hospitals, mental health care providers, and other people and organizations necessary to the effective and efficient working of the crisis teams.

When a hotline operator encounters a crisis situation, the on-call crisis team will be notified and appropriate action taken based on the particular need. The crisis team leader will call on those people and organizations necessary for a resolution of the crisis and coordinate the activities. *(continues)*

EXAMPLE 7.4 *(Continued)*

Alcohol and Drug Abuse Program— Project Description, page 4

Performance Art

The primary purpose of the performance art group is to publicize to the community the dangers and consequences of alcohol, tobacco, and other drugs, and secondarily to publicize the hotline and the crisis teams.

The responsibilities of the director of performance art fall into three main areas: (1) recruiting performance art volunteers, (2) developing performances, and (3) directing the performances.

Once performance artists have been recruited and screened, the director of performance art and the performers form a creative collaboration to develop dramatic, high-impact performances capable of both holding public interest and delivering the ATOD message. Once the initial period of start-up is past, we will stage a weekly performance somewhere in the community.

The mode of operation is guerilla theater—taking performances to the sidewalk, the workplace, and the public square.

Chapter 8

Project Management Plan

The conventional definition of management is getting work done through people, but real management is developing people through work.

Agha Hasan Abedi[1]

At a Glance

What Else Is It Called?

- Project administration

When Is It Used?

There should be statements throughout your project description, and in many parts of the proposal that address project management. Few funders require a full management plan. Even if the management plan is not required, all the elements of it should be addressed in your proposal.

Why Is It Used?

No project will be successful without good management. The funder must be assured that your organization is capable of handling the project, that key personnel are qualified to supervise and manage the project, and that your fiscal management is above reproach. Remember the funder is looking for a good investment, not just a good idea. Many things covered in overview in the management plan will be covered in complete sections in the proposal. Duplication is inherent in proposal writing. The reader who is interested in the management plan may not read the other sections.

---

[1] *Leaders,* July 1984.

Key Concepts

- Devise an organization chart clearly showing that the project is highly connected in your management structure and is integral in your infrastructure.

- If you have had other successful grants, briefly describe them—hopefully you can state that there were no audit exceptions.

- State how your project will be fiscally managed and audited.

- Indicate the level of expertise in the subject matter of key personnel—you will include biographical data elsewhere in the proposal.

- Briefly give an overview of how the project will be evaluated—you should include a complete evaluation plan in the proposal.

- Briefly give an overview of how the project will be documented, and where the files will reside.

Formatting Issues

Use standard margins and 12-point type, being sure to stay within the funder's space requirements.

Organization Chart

As stated in the section on project description (Chapter 7), the organization chart can go many places in the proposal. For a simple proposal such as a letter proposal, an organization chart is not necessary. However, it is necessary to strongly connect your project to upper management and to show clearly how important it is to your organization. The funder wants to make a good investment in a project that the grantee will manage effectively and continue after grant funding ceases. The funder wants to fund projects that are important to the grantee organization. An organization chart is a way of showing that in a graphic. Exhibit 8.1 is an example of an organization chart.

Discuss the Responsibilities of Key Personnel

Most funders want biographical sketches of key personnel (see Chapter 13 for a full description). In the project management plan, you have the opportunity to provide an overview of the relevant credentials for your key personnel. By key personnel, we mean the project coordinator and any critical staff members who provide leadership of various project components. By relevant, we mean credentials that relate to the topic and scope of your project. It is important to keep this discussion to a bare minimum while

EXHIBIT 8.1

Organization Chart

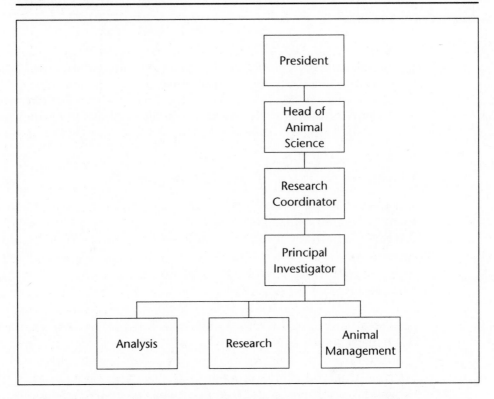

impressing the funder with the fact that the people you have chosen for your project have the skills needed to insure its success. You do not have a lot of space for this discussion, so it is important to be concise. The following is an example.

> *Dr. Noah Brandon, the project coordinator has ten years' experience leading successful research grant projects. He holds a doctorate in chemical engineering and his medical degree in forensic science. Lydia Stevens, is the documentation coordinator. She has seven years' experience in documentation of research projects and a masters degree in chemical laboratory management. Dr. Zelda Fitzsimmons, the project analyst, has been chief coordinator on seven successful research projects. Her doctorate is in chemical engineering. Biographical sketches of all key staff can be found on Page 32, in the key personnel section.*

Discuss Loaned or Volunteer Staff

It is important to show any partners' contributions to the project. Funders like partnerships because the more partners there are, the more secure the project is as an investment. The more stakeholders, the more likely the project will succeed and continue. If there are loaned staff or volunteers, tell the funder what roles they play and how they are supervised. The following is an example.

> *Intake personnel are provided by the North Carolina State Department of Health and Human Services and are paid by the department. In addition, the local Association of Family Counselors will screen volunteer mentors for the participating students. Both intake personnel and mentors will be supervised by the project coordinator. The project coordinator, with oversight of the advisory committee, has final approval over both intake staff and volunteer mentors.*

Provide an Overview of Fiscal Management

If you have experience with grants management, provide a very brief statement about your experience managing grant funds. As you work with grants, it is important that you are meticulous with the funds. They should be kept separate from your other organization funds, and a paper trail kept on all expenditures. If you have a budget problem, you must contact the funder and get approval for any changes you need to make. Always get approval in writing. It is important to be able to tell potential funders that you have managed your grants with no audit exceptions. The first grant is always the hardest to get. After you have a proven track record, it is much easier.

If you have not had experience with grants, choose other similar projects for which you have provided fiscal management. You are trying to assure the potential funder that you have the experience and stability to handle their investment effectively.

Discuss who within your organization will manage the funds. Tell the potential funder that a separate account will be set up for the grant funds. Discuss who will be authorized to expend grant funds, and who will provide oversight. If the potential grant is a large one, discuss how the funds will be audited. The following is an example:

> *Though this is our first experience with grant funds, we have a great deal of experience running projects and effectively managing funds. A year ago, we established a community counseling program that has an annual budget of more than $350,000. Our advisory committee for that project reviewed all the documentation and reported that our handling of every aspect of the project was superb. Outside auditors approved every aspect of our fiscal management. We are very experienced with projects similar to the one for which we are applying to your organization. If you wish, we will be glad to share our audit records and reports of advisory committees.*
>
> *For the ABC Project, only the project coordinator will be authorized to sign off on expenditures. A separate bank account will be set up to handle*

project funds. The advisory committee will provide oversight as will our executive director. A quarterly report of expenditures will be provided. An annual audit will be performed using an outside auditor. Our records will be open to your organization any time you wish to review them.

Evaluation

Provide a statement about the manner in which you intend to evaluate the project. You should include a complete evaluation plan (see Chapter 10) in the proposal. Accountability is a key element to any funder. Evaluation is how you show accountability in the proposal.

Discuss any advisory committees and the chain of command for accountability. If your project is a research project, discuss how the research will be monitored and how the analyses will be done.

If your project is not a research project, each goal and objective should have outcomes. Those outcomes should be concrete and measurable. You then discuss expected outcomes of the project. Keep in mind that this is an overview, because you will include a complete evaluation plan in the proposal.

A full evaluation plan is included in this proposal on pages 34–40. The ABC Counseling Project expects that 65% of the people counseled will quit smoking. Of the 65%, three-quarters will still be nonsmokers after six months. If the remaining participants stay in the program for an additional six months, half will quit smoking and will still be nonsmokers after six months.

Documentation

In the management plan, you simply provide an overview of how the program will be documented, where records are kept, and what documents will be available for others who want to duplicate your project. There is a documentation and dissemination plan in a full proposal—some funders require this section. Here you will simply provide an overview of your documentation plan.

Why does the funder want to know about documentation? Funders do not have enough money to solve the problems in which they are interested. Therefore, they fund good projects and publish information about them in the hope that other groups will duplicate the successful ones, and thus multiply their investment. If the project is not documented, then others will not be able to replicate the project. The following is an example.

The ABC Curriculum Development Project will publish the curriculums as they are developed on the university Web site for other colleges and universities to use. In addition, a summary of results of student participation will be posted on a quarterly basis. A list of course materials, lab kit contents, and reference materials and Internet sites will also be posted on the Web site.

Checklist—Management Plan[2]

✔ To whom does the project director report?

✔ Clear lines of responsibility for all project personnel.

✔ Screening, training, and monitoring of volunteers.

✔ Consent and privacy issues.

✔ Security of people and things.

✔ Target population activity documentation.

✔ Financial transaction documentation.

✔ Insurance and liability issues.

✔ Transportation.

Last Words

The management plan is the place that an applicant demonstrates an understanding of the work involved in running the project. Large projects can require management of people, money, paperwork, travel, transportation, purchasing, shipping, receiving, installation, renovation, training, security, maintenance, repair, publicity, public relations, testing, volunteers, contracts and contractors, facilities, and fund raising.

Grant makers do not expect detailed policies and procedures. Grant makers simply want assurance that an applicant understands the work involved behind the scenes. Working with the target population gets all the publicity and generates the enthusiasm, but it is the plodding, boring, behind-the-scenes stuff that makes working with the target population possible.

The two key questions to answer about any proposal section are always: (1) what is the grant maker trying to learn and (2) does the section explain what the grant maker wants to know? Reading with comprehension is perhaps the most important skill a proposal writer can possess—the ability

---

[2] Remember that a grant maker's directions (instructions/guidelines) take precedence over any and all other considerations. You must absolutely, positively follow the grant maker's directions exactly, precisely, and painstakingly.

to read and understand application guidelines, and the ability to read and understand what the proposal actually says.

Nowhere is this more important than with the management plan. Invariably, the grant maker has concerns about only a few specific activities. Identify the grant maker's concerns and address them directly.

Examples of Management Plan for Four Projects

The following four examples (8.1 to 8.4) are examples of project descriptions for each of the four diverse organizations profiled in this book. The specific elements highlighted in this chapter are reflected in each exhibit.

Example 8.1

After School Program—
Management Plan

Sunnyvale School District

The After School Program (program) will be supervised directly by the superintendent. The Program is considered a critical element in the district's efforts to provide a quality education for our students. Following is the program's organization chart.

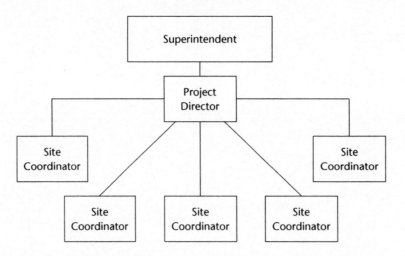

Our district has a sizeable Title I program due to the large number of low income families in our community. Our Title I program has never had an audit or evaluation exception. In addition, our district was awarded a Kellogg Foundation grant to work within our poorest neighborhoods through vocational and general education. The program was deemed a success and again there were no audit or evaluation exceptions. A five-year technology improvement grant was awarded by the National Technology Agency to install an infrastructure and at least one computer per classroom, along with a lab at each school. The grant was a supplement to the district and state's effort to level the playing field for our low-income students. Again, there were no audit or evaluation exceptions. The district has also received numerous small grants, all of which have been completed successfully.

EXAMPLE 8.1 *(Continued)*

After School Program— Management Plan, page 2

Fiscal management will be handled through the office of our financial manager. A separate account will be created and audited for the grant. We have an internal audit on a quarterly basis, and we hire external auditors annually. We change external audit firms every three years to insure objectivity.

Dr. Christopher Allen is our choice for project director. He has fifteen years of experience being a principal. He has an excellent record for supervising special projects. He has been placed in schools that were underachieving and has repeatedly managed those schools to become among the best in the district. His schools have won awards for improvement. He is a mentor trainer, a fact that will add significantly to his work with community members, students and faculty alike.

Our site coordinators must each have experience working with parents and must be computer literate. They must have supervisory experience and 10 years of experience in education. Each must at least have a master's degree in education and be a master teacher.

An advisory board made up of our most experienced educators and subject area coordinators will evaluate the program. In addition, we will hire outside evaluators to do regular observations and to compile data for reports. As can be seen in the goals and objectives section of this proposal, every goal and every objective has an outcome or result. We will use the goals and objectives for guidance in our evaluation. For more details, please review the evaluation plan in this proposal.

Documents will be kept primarily in the project director's office with some site records kept in the principal's office of participating schools. All evaluation documents will be kept in the office of the superintendent. Fiscal reports will be kept both in the office of the superintendent and also in the office of the financial manager.

EXAMPLE 8.2

Senior Citizens Wellness Center— Management Plan

The Senior Citizen Wellness Center

All major partners coming together to form the Senior Citizens Center Project (Project) have worked with grants. In no case has there been a problem with their management of grants. Major partners are the AnyTown Memorial Hospital, the public health department, and the ATOD Commission. Grant funding has been used appropriately by each agency. Books are open and audited annually. All partners have had positive, effective experience with grants management.

The project director will report directly to the executive director of the ATOD Council. This was a decision of the partnership based on the stature of the ATOD Council in the community and the ability to do fundraising which the hospital and public health department cannot so easily manage. The project director will supervise all project operations including the single point of entry coordinator, social workers, and volunteers. The advisory board of the ATOD Council will provide additional support and guidance because it is made up of three doctors—two in family practice and one internal specialist. The other members are two psychologists, one M.D. psychiatrist, and two master social work managers. It was decided that this board with its professional practitioners was the most appropriate for guidance.

The following is the organizational chart of the project.

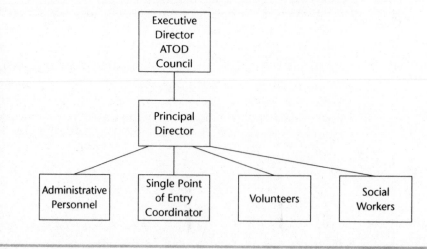

EXAMPLE 8.2 *(Continued)*

Senior Citizens Wellness Center— Management Plan, page 2

The funding for the Project will be managed by the ATOD Council chief financial officer who will set up a separate account at a separate bank from the one holding ATOD funds. There has never been an audit exception for any ATOD project. The ATOD Council effectively manages over $3.5 million in grant funds annually. There will be an internal audit and external audit annually. Oversight will be accomplished by the ATOD Council board.

Dr. Aaron Hoyt has superior experience running projects similar to this one. He literally built our local YMCA from the ground up—it now serves 800 people a week. He was manager of a town of 20,000 through a growth of 20%. He has managed budgets of over $8 million annually. He prefers to initiate new projects, and that is one reason he is perfect for the job of project director.

April Foote, as single point of entry coordinator, was carefully chosen for her experience in bringing together community resources to work together on a project. Her department has won awards for efficiency. She has a great deal of experience and training in working with computers—a critical skill for this project.

Goals and objectives each have outcomes (results). Those results are measurable. Evaluation will be guided by the stated outcomes. There will be an internal evaluation accomplished by the members of each partner. One group of medical professionals will monitor the medical and psychological parts of the program. Another team will look at the social and recreational aspects. Outside evaluators will be also hired to create comprehensive reports of findings.

Documents will be housed in the offices of the project director and single point of entry coordinator. All participant files will be kept in a safe room under lock and key with only the executive director of the ATOD Council and project director having access. There is a comprehensive documentation plan in this proposal.

EXAMPLE 8.3

Fire and Rescue Project— Management Plan

Quad-County Fire and Rescue Association

Eight of the 47 volunteer fire departments have had grants through the Federal Emergency Management Agency. All of the 47 volunteer fire departments have managed local and state funds effectively. None of the 47 fire departments have mismanaged or otherwise mishandled funding. All have annual audits.

Centralized purchasing will be housed at the most central of the 47 fire departments. During the term of the grant, purchasing procedures will be developed, and training will be done with each fire department so that consortium purchasing is understood. Funds will remain with each fire department, and the department will be billed on a monthly basis for goods purchased. The consortium director will handle questions and troubleshooting.

Recruitment and training procedures and operations manuals will be developed during the term of the grant. All fire departments will have copies of these manuals and will be trained in their use. The state fire agency will approve the manuals to insure they are in line with best practices. Recruitment and training will be organized by the consortium director with oversight of a board of advisors made up of representatives from a third of the fire departments. Every two years a third of the board of advisors will be replaced by a representative from a fire department that was not represented the previous two years.

The junior fire marshal program will be supervised by the consortium director with the guidance of the advisory board and school officials. Once the term of the grant is over, a new guidance board will be chosen with half fire department officials and half school officials.

Fiscal management will be done through the central purchasing department. A separate bank account will be set up to handle grant funds. An independent certified public accountant in private practice will oversee finances. There will be an annual audit with an outside auditor.

EXAMPLE 8.3 *(Continued)*

Fire and Rescue Project— Management Plan, page 2

With his experience coordinating emergency medical services in our community, Mr. Swift has the organizational and supervisory experience needed for consortium director. He has been trained as a volunteer firefighter, serving 12 years. He has experience organizing and managing community-wide efforts and has the respect of community agencies and organizations. He holds a masters degree in public administration.

The advisory board will evaluate the project following outcomes of goals and objectives. All records will be housed in the office of the consortium director. Annually there will also be an evaluation by an outside evaluator.

Progress toward goals and objectives will be thoroughly documented. Documentation will include all procedures and operations manuals. Copies of all public relations brochures, flyers, and posters will be filed to show implementation. All documents will be kept in the office of the consortium director.

EXAMPLE 8.4

Alcohol and Drug Abuse Program— Management Plan

INNER CITY ALCOHOL AND DRUG PREVENTION COMMISSION

The Project will be located within the area ATOD Commission. The executive director of the ATOD Commission will personally supervise the project with the assistance and guidance of the ATOD Advisory Board. The project director reports and is evaluated by the executive director of the ATOD Council. The hotline manager, outreach coordinator and performance arts director will all report to the project director. An organizational chart follows.

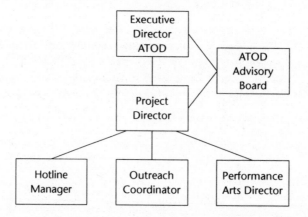

The ATOD Commission has managed grants averaging $3 million a year for over 20 years. Grants have been federal, state, and local. They have been from government agencies, foundations, and corporations. Our chief financial officer works with a certified public accountant in private practice and outside auditors to manage our fiscal resources. In our history there has never been an audit exception. Fiscally, the ATOD Council has had sound, efficient, effective management. Every grant has its own separate account—no funds are mixed with operational funds. This grant will have its own account and will be under the oversight of a certified public accountant in private practice. The grant account will be audited annually, or more frequently, depending on funder requirements.

EXAMPLE 8.4   *(Continued)*

Alcohol and Drug Abuse Program— Management Plan, page 2

Our choice for project director is Dr. Kathryn Brandon, a clinical psychologist with fifteen years of experience working in our community to stop substance abuse by our citizens. She works well with our community resources to pull them together for a unified effort. She initiated a committee of physicians, psychologists, psychiatrists and social work professionals to review cases of substance abuse and make recommendations for treatment and rehabilitation. Our choice for outreach coordinator, Laura Merrell, has successfully managed outreach services for the Department of Health and Human Services. She is highly qualified and has the respect of the service sector to be effective as outreach coordinator.

A team from the University of Anystate Medical and Psychological Colleges will evaluate the project. This team has evaluated a number of other related projects in the state and nationally. There will be a longitudinal study to see what the long-term impact of the project is. In addition, the advisory board will use the outcomes of each goal and objective to do an internal evaluation.

Participant records will be kept in a safe room under lock and key with only the executive director and project director having access. Otherwise documents will be kept in the office of the project director with evaluation records being kept both at the university and in the office of the project director. Documentation will be scientific and thorough under the guidance of national substance abuse program standards.

Chapter 9

Documentation Plan

**There is no surer way to misread any document
than to read it literally.**

Learned Hand[1]

At a Glance

What Else Is It Called?

• Publications

When Is It Used?

Almost always with federal funders—not so frequently for foundations and corporations.

Why Is It Used?

The first reason for documentation has to do with accountability. Documentation includes reports of results, fiscal documentation and details of project set-up, implementation and management. If your project is a research project, the need for documentation is obvious. But, there is another important reason for documentation. Grant funders do not have the funds to completely solve the problem in which they are interested. Therefore, they invest their money in good projects that have a chance of providing at least a partial solution to the problem. If the project is successful, the funder wants other organizations to adopt the project to replicate the good result. For this to work, the project needs to be documented so there is an adequate record to follow. Most times, the funder will request that a certain amount of documentation be made available for others interested in duplicating the project.

---

[1] Learned Hand, 1872–1961, American jurist. *The World: Law: Attorneys & the Practice of Law.*

Key Concepts

- When in doubt, document.
- Plan what you will share with other organizations, and write that into proposal.
- Decide how you will distribute information, and if there will be a charge for duplication.
- Describe in the proposal what you will document, and what will be sent to the funder.

Formatting Issues

Use standard margins and 12-point type.

Project Planning

Every project has a planning phase. This is usually marked with meetings and strategy sessions. It may involve setting up advisory committees or getting expert advice from consultants. What is adequate documentation? For meetings, keep minutes. These can either be on tape or written. For strategy sessions, there should be a recorder and a report of results. For advisory committee meetings, keep minutes and sign-in sheets. If you have a consultant, have the consultant create a report for you. There are planning grants. If you have a planning grant, you will need to share all this information with the funder. Project planning can include documents such as:

- Minutes of meetings (in writing or on tape).
- Sign-in sheets.
- Reports of strategy sessions.
- Advisory committee membership records.
- Charts and graphs from planning sessions.
- Reports of decisions about project set-up, implementation and management.

Project Set-up

There is always a set-up period with a project. You should always include set-up in your proposed project. Not only will the grant funders fund it, but you have to do it regardless. What is project set-up? It is all the things you have to do before you actually implement the project. Project planning can be included to a certain degree, as long as your proposed project is well thought-out, and planning is just incidental to get things on a firm foundation. You should have a thoroughly planned project before you ever write the first word of a proposal. But, there are planning activities that must be done throughout the project set-up and implementation. One example is setting up advisory committees and initiating meetings.

Other set-up tasks are hiring temporary staff and holding meetings with partners. Training can be a set-up activity for a project that is not purely a training project. Review of materials to purchase for reference is a valid set-up activity. Development of procedures and staff and student manuals is a set-up task.

Then, there is the matter of infrastructure. If your project involves technology, there are equipment reviews and purchase. But it does not stop there—the equipment must be installed before you begin your project. This might involve building renovation.

For a research project, you might include patient or participant intake as a set-up activity. Certainly equipment set-up and calibration will be a part of your set-up. Animal purchase and housing may be a part of your set-up.

So how do you document set-up? What do you promise in the proposed documentation plan? The following list should help.

- Planning reports.
- Contracts with consultants and consultant reports.
- Lists of advisory committee members and credentials.
- Advisory committee minutes and sign-in sheets.
- Temporary staff resumes and interview records.
- Minutes of partner meetings and reports of decisions.
- Training materials, rosters and evaluations.
- Minutes of review committee meetings and lists of considered materials along with final decisions.
- Minutes of review committee meetings and list of considered equipment along with final decisions.
- Procedures manuals.
- Staff and student manuals.
- Contracts for purchased materials and equipment and purchase orders.
- Contracts for building renovation and blueprints or drawings.
- Patient or participant intake procedures and records would document a research project.
- Equipment tests and calibration records for a research project.
- Animal purchase and housing plans might be a research project set-up activity.

Implementation

Project implementation includes all the activities you will do to launch the project. For a research project, you might have pretesting as an implementation task. If you are testing medication, you would start administering drugs and placebos, and tracking patients. You might have an animal project where you administer tests and medication to animals. You may be combining chemicals for testing, or you might be using computers to simulate a trip to Mars. The possibilities are almost endless. Virtually everything is documented in a research project—tell the funder who will keep records, and what to expect by what project month for documentation.

If you have a curriculum project, you will start either developing the curriculum, or offering it to the first students. You might be pretesting and posttesting. Professor or teacher records provide documentation. Certainly all curriculum materials and lists of reference texts, as well as records of research done through the Internet, are valid documents to keep. Records of students taking courses, and their activities, are necessary for documentation.

What if you had a project to feed the hungry in Africa? You would keep records of the numbers of people fed. Records of raw products and food served would be valid documentation. Volunteer names and associated costs would be documented. Transportation to get the food to the field would be needed, and records involving gasoline, lease, purchase, insurance, shipping costs, and maintenance would be kept. You would be likely to have records required by the governments of the countries you serve as well.

In summary, think through what records are logical for your project, and very briefly describe or list the documents that you will keep. Indicate where records will be kept, and who will be responsible. Specify what reports will be sent to the funder.

Results or Outcomes

This is the most critical part of the documentation plan. You will cover this more completely in the evaluation plan (discussed in Chapter 10). Here, you will simply tell the funder what documentation you will keep of project outcomes.

If you have a research project, list the reports and documents that you will keep to track your project. The documentation might include:

- Charts and graphs of progress.
- Patient or animal dosage records and tracking.
- Pretests and posttests along with analysis.

- Makeup of control groups and test groups.
- Random sampling procedures.
- Reports and analyses.
- Testing procedures.
- Computer records of simulations and experiments.
- Final report of findings.

If you have a nonresearch project, use your goals and objectives for guidance on outcomes. Every goal and objective should have a concrete and measurable outcome. It is a good idea to organize the documentation plan by goal. Write a sentence in overview for each goal and then list documentation of the results. The following is an example.

> **Goal 1:** *Develop science and math units for middle school students using subject matter experts to serve 3,213 students. Outcomes will be: Increased student motivation and interest especially in the areas of science and math, increased parent involvement in child's projects, increased knowledge and skill for all children, and improvement of children's scores and attitudes. Documents for outcomes will be kept by the project coordinator and will include:*
>
> - *Science and math units.*
> - *Student questionnaire results precourse and postcourse.*
> - *Student grades and test results compared to state, nation and past classes.*
> - *Results of state achievement tests as compared to state, nation and past classes.*
> - *Results of parent questionnaires precourse and postcourse.*
> - *Parent involvement as measured against the STAR scale.*
> - *A longitudinal study will follow a random sampling of students through high school in science and math.*

If you organize by measurable goals, you will cover all the ground the funder wants to see in a good documentation plan.

Planning What to Share

It is important to plan what you will share with others who want to replicate the project. Funders cannot fund this effort and will require the grantee to share pertinent information and data. You will need to carefully think through what the materials will look like and publishing costs, so that your organization will not lose money trying to provide documents to those who seek them. Then, tell the funder with whom you are willing to share, and what the costs are for copies of the documents.

Checklist—Documentation Plan[2]

✓ Staff activities.

✓ Volunteer activities.

✓ Partner activities.

✓ Target population activities.

✓ Financial activities.

✓ Training activities.

✓ Testing activities.

✓ Treatment activities.

✓ Evaluation and assessment activities.

✓ Create necessary information (data) capture documents.

Last Words

This probably is the simplest section of a grant proposal. The entire point is to document everything that happens. If a document trail does not naturally occur, create one with a meeting report, a weekly report, an incident report, or some other such documentation. The accumulated documentation provides the information used during dissemination, evaluation, and continuation activities. It is always better to save documentation and later not need it, than to need it and not have it. Save everything

Keep in mind that documentation is not necessarily on paper. Documentation can be in the form of computer files, computer media, video, audio, or even artifacts. The type of media is not relevant. The point is to save information (data).

Examples of Documentation Plan for Four Projects

The following four examples (9.1 to 9.4) are examples of documentation plans for each of the four organizations profiled in this book. The specific elements described in this chapter are incorporated in each example.

---

[2] Remember that a grant maker's directions (instructions/guidelines) take precedence over any and all other considerations. You must absolutely, positively follow the grant maker's directions exactly, precisely, and painstakingly.

EXAMPLE 9.1

After School Program—Documentation Plan

Sunnyvale School District

Goal 1—*Develop necessary infrastructure including facilities, staff, volunteers and contractors to accommodate 1,200 students at 5 sites.*

Documentation for Goal 1 will include:

- Advertising for staff.
- Staff qualifications and hiring records.
- Plans for facilities use and renovation.
- Advertising for volunteers.
- Screening process and procedures for volunteers.
- Volunteer rosters.
- Contractor plans and agreements.
- Site plans and schedules.
- Staff and volunteer operations manuals.
- Supervisory observation reports.
- Evaluation reports.

Goal 2—*Train program personnel in classroom, online and through self-study so they are sufficiently trained to effectively handle all aspects of activities.*

Documentation for Goal 2 will include:

- Trainer qualifications, training manuals and rosters.
- Online course syllabi, materials and rosters.
- Self-study manuals, tracking reports and rosters.
- Skill tests and experiential assessments.
- Contractual agreements.
- Supervisory observation reports.
- Evaluation reports.

(continues)

EXAMPLE 9.1 *(Continued)*

After School Program— Documentation Plan, page 2

Goal 3—*Provide supplemental academic activities*—*supervised homework for 1,200, tutoring for 600 and additional activities for 600*—*so that all participants complete homework and participants grades rise one letter grade.*

Documentation for Goal 3 will include:

- Schedules and rosters of students.
- Volunteer schedules and assignments.
- Teacher questionnaire about homework.
- Pre-project grades and grade tracking throughout project.
- Tutor schedules and student assignments.
- Individual student plans.
- List of additional supplemental activities and student assignments.
- Web site records of homework assignments.
- Supervisory observation reports.
- Evaluation reports.

Goal 4—*Provide applied learning activities in partnership with 4-H, home economics and vocational education for 400 participants so that participants become proficient in applied life skills.*

Documentation for Goal 4 will include:

- 4-H applied learning activities, schedules, and student rosters.
- 4-H learning materials and student assignments.
- Home economics applied learning activities, schedules, and student rosters.
- Home economics materials and student assignments.
- Vocational education applied learning activities, schedules, and student rosters.
- Vocational education materials and student assignments.
- Pre-assessments and post-assessments.
- Supervisory observation reports.
- Evaluation reports.

EXAMPLE 9.1 *(Continued)*

After School Program— Documentation Plan, page 3

Goal 5—*Provide recreational activities in partnership with parks and recreation and private providers for all 1,200 participants so that participants have daily opportunity to participate in choice of activity.*

Documentation for Goal 5 will include:

- List of recreational activities.
- Agreements with parks and recreation.
- Agreements with private providers.
- Student schedules.
- List of equipment and games.
- Purchasing records of equipment and games.
- Supervisory observation reports.
- Evaluation reports.

Goal 6—*Provide social and health services and activities in partnership with public health, ATOD, violence prevention project and hospital for 600 participants with incidents of substance abuse and violence decreasing by 50% and health issues resolved.*

Documentation for Goal 6 will include:

- List of social and health services by partners.
- Schedules of events.
- Example materials and education information.
- Counseling session reports.
- Court advisories.
- Numbers of students counseled in groups or individually.
- Incident reports.
- Crime reports and substance abuse reports.
- Statistical data.
- Supervisory observation reports.
- Evaluation reports.
- Longitudinal study reports.

(continues)

EXAMPLE 9.1 *(Continued)*

After School Program— Documentation Plan, page 4

Goal 7—*Provide parent involvement activities*—*workshops, open houses, meetings, Web site, and direct mail*—*for all 1,200 students' families with positive parent involvement increasing 100%.*

Documentation for Goal 7 will include:

- Plans, schedules, materials, and rosters of workshops.
- Plans, schedules, materials, and rosters of open houses.
- Plans, schedules, materials, and rosters of meetings.
- Web sites operational and with appropriate content.
- Direct mail pieces and schedules of delivery.
- "I care" parent involvement reports.
- Parent survey results.
- Teacher survey results.
- Student survey results.
- Comparisons of survey results.
- Anecdotal incident reports.
- Supervisory observation reports.
- Evaluation reports.
- Longitudinal study reports.

Goal 8—*Evaluate effectiveness of activities through quantitative, qualitative, formative and summative measures to improve the project and report to stakeholders.*

Documentation for Goal 8 will include:

- Quantitative tracking and final reports.
- Qualitative tracking and final reports.
- Formative tracking and final reports.
- Summative tracking and final reports.
- Results of surveys and questionnaires.
- Results of longitudinal and cohort studies.
- Supervisory observation reports.
- Evaluators observation reports.
- Database reports to funder.
- Goal and objective tracking and results.

EXAMPLE 9.1 *(Continued)*

After School Program— Documentation Plan, page 5

***Goal 9**—Effectively manage the After School Program to successfully accomplish all goals and objectives.*

Documentation for Goal 9 will include:

- Fiscal reports and audits.
- Supervisory reports.
- Purchasing reports.
- Schedules and timelines.
- Student rosters at all sites.
- Goals and objectives tracking and results.
- Evaluation reports.
- Records of staff qualifications and hiring.
- Training records and reports.
- Minutes of meetings.
- Planning reports.
- Counseling reports.
- Partner reports.
- Event reports.
- Grades and behavior reports on students.
- Reports of surveys and questionnaires.

EXAMPLE 9.2

Senior Citizen Wellness Center—
Documentation Plan

The Senior Citizen Wellness Center

Goal 1—*Perform all preparatory activities—hire staff, recruit volunteers, train personnel and obtain materials—to support 1,250 participants such that the foundation is laid to effectively accomplish goals.*

Our plans for documentation include gathering together in the office of the project director: staff hiring records; recruitment, screening and procedures for volunteers; training materials, rosters, evaluations and contracts for training; and reference, guidance, individual support and other materials to support the Project; and purchasing records for materials.

Goal 2—*Develop and implement wellness services and enhancements for 1,250 participants in partnership with the hospital, public health and ATOD Commission to improve wellness of participants as measured on Seniors Scale.*

Our plans for documentation include gathering in the office of the project director: lists of services provided by each partner; schedules and appointment records; individual participant records; referral records; individual development plans; participant tracking records; all reports; meeting minutes; partner agreements; planning session records; all communications among partners.

Goal 3—*Develop and implement social enrichment activities and enhancements for 1,250 participants in partnership with public and private community organizations so that there is improvement in quality of life.*

Our plans for documentation include gathering in the office of the project director: lists of social enrichment activities and enhancements provided by each partner; schedules and event records; individual participant records; planning session records; meeting minutes; agreements with partners; participant tracking records; rosters for events and activities; communications among partners; committee meeting minutes; list of credentials of leaders for activities; and lists of resource persons.

EXAMPLE 9.2   *(Continued)*

Senior Citizen Wellness Center— Documentation Plan, page 2

Goal 4—*Develop and implement single point of entry services for the 1,250 elderly participants by establishing collaborative relationships with service providers so that seniors have one-stop shopping for services and a single personal counselor.*

Our plans for documentation include gathering in the office of the single point of entry coordinator: resource contact persons and profiles of services; Web links to relevant services and information sources; lists of contacts with government agencies; searchable relational database of resources; usage records; lists of commonly asked questions; Web site with key information; agreements and contracts with service providers; planning session records; minutes of meetings; evaluations of services, surveys and questionnaires; participant tracking records; and records of telephone, Internet and personal contacts.

Goal 5—*Monitor, manage, and evaluate project to successfully accomplish all goals and objectives.*

Our plans for documentation include gathering in the office of the project director: meeting minutes; minutes of planning sessions; fiscal reports and audit records; account information; purchasing records; copies of contracts, billing and invoices; evaluation reports; supervisory observations and work sessions; employee records and evaluations; partner agreements and tracking records; procedures and operations manuals; and management by objectives charts and plans.

Example 9.3

Fire and Rescue Project— Documentation Plan

Quad-County Fire and Rescue Association

Goal 1—*Perform project set-up—hire staff, prepare facility and obtain materials—so that the project can effectively serve 1,250 participants.*

Documentation for Goal 1 includes the following records and publications:

- Staff hiring procedures.
- Personnel advertisements.
- Staff qualifications and interviews.
- List of staff hired.
- Set up training facility within the mid-county fire station.
- Set up centralized purchasing office within the Hodges fire station.
- Review and purchase education materials.
- Review and purchase training materials.
- Review and purchase fire prevention campaign materials.
- Review and purchase supplementary materials for junior fire marshal program.

Goal 2—*Increase community outreach through a neighborhood fire prevention program and a junior fire marshal program in schools to reach 47 communities and 22 schools so that fire incidents decrease.*

Documentation for Goal 2 includes the following records and publications:

- Procedures for neighborhood fire prevention program.
- Training plans and documents for neighborhood teams.
- Schedules and assignments for training neighborhood teams.
- Meeting minutes.
- Meeting notices for each community.
- Advertisements and public service notices for each community.
- Flyers concerning neighborhood meetings.

EXAMPLE 9.3   *(Continued)*

Fire and Rescue Project— Documentation Plan, page 2

- Newspaper and media publications and notices.
- Neighborhood fire prevention posters, window placards, and brochures.
- Minutes of neighborhood meetings and rosters.
- Junior fire marshal (JFM) badges, materials, and training materials.
- Procedures for junior fire marshal program.
- Meeting minutes with school officials and rosters.
- Meeting notices for schools, posters and other publicity notices for schools.
- Meeting minutes with students and rosters.
- Training records for students.
- Meeting and presentation records students teaching students.
- Tracking reports of junior fire marshal activities.
- Evaluation reports of neighborhood fire watch and junior fire marshal programs.

Goal 3—*Improve training, recruitment and purchasing by centralizing services for 47 fire and rescue departments so that personnel trained have measurably higher skill, recruitment quotas are met, and costs decrease.*

Documentation for Goal 3 includes the following records and publications:

- Training materials, schedules, and rosters.
- Training evaluations and outcome reports.
- Recruitment planning meeting minutes.
- Recruitment plans and schedules.
- Advertisements and public announcements regarding recruiting.
- Screening procedures for recruits.
- Recruits operations and procedures manuals.
- Lists of recruits, qualifications, and assignments.

(continues)

EXAMPLE 9.3 *(Continued)*

Fire and Rescue Project— Documentation Plan, page 3

- Purchasing manuals with procedures.
- Purchasing agreements and contracts.
- Bid packets.
- Receipts, invoices, bills of lading.
- Order and distribution lists.
- Computer purchasing records.
- Budget reports and cost analyses.
- Audit reports.

Goal 4—Monitor, manage, and evaluate program to successfully accomplish all goals and objectives.

Documentation for Goal 4 includes the following records and publications:

- Supervisory records and reports.
- Minutes and rosters of meetings.
- Management plans and timelines.
- Planning reports.
- Personnel records.
- Evaluation and assessment records.
- Results of surveys, questionnaires, and polls.
- School assessments of junior fire marshal program.
- Incident reports regarding fire safety and rescue.
- Longitudinal studies.
- Fiscal management and audit reports.
- Measurements regarding all goal and objective outcomes.

EXAMPLE 9.4

Alcohol and Drug Abuse Program— Documentation Plan

INNER CITY ALCOHOL AND
DRUG PREVENTION COMMISSION

Goal 1—*Perform project set-up activities—staff hiring, volunteer recruitment, training, obtain materials—to support 1,250 participants.*

All Goal 1 documents will be kept in the office of the project director. The following documents will be available.

- All staff hiring records and personnel manuals.
- Volunteer recruitment records, screening procedures, lists of volunteers.
- Training materials, training contracts, rosters, evaluations, test results.
- Materials review reports, material choices, purchasing records.
- Minutes of planning meetings and rosters.

Goal 2—*Reach 8,000 K–12 young people with anti-substance abuse message with the result that substance abuse decreases.*

All Goal 2 documents will be kept in the office of the outreach director. The following documents will be available.

- Print, advertising, public relations materials.
- Operations and procedures manuals.
- Minutes of meetings with school administrators.
- Minutes of planning sessions.
- Records of education activities and incidents in schools.
- Media reports, public relations messages, and advertisements directed at K–12.
- Records of group meetings and presentations.
- Materials for presentations and classroom sessions.
- Information pieces, flyers, brochures, posters, letters to parents.
- Parent education session records.
- Teacher and administrator education session records.

(continues)

EXAMPLE **9.4**   *(Continued)*

Alcohol and Drug Abuse Program— Documentation Plan, page 2

Goal 3—*Provide comprehensive support and intervention services through a hotline and 24-hour crisis team with the result that drug overdoses decrease and alcohol related crimes decrease.*

All Goal 3 documents will be kept in the office of the outreach director. The following documents will be available.

- Print, advertising, public relations materials.
- Operations and procedures manuals.
- Minutes of meetings with community leaders and neighborhood volunteers.
- Minutes of planning sessions.
- Media reports, public relations messages, and advertisements directed at the community.
- Records of group meetings and presentations.
- Materials for presentations.
- Information pieces, flyers, brochures, posters, letters.
- Records of hotline calls and referrals.
- Records of actions by 24-hour crisis team activities.
- Credentials of hotline managers and crisis team members.
- Incident reports regarding drug overdoses and alcohol-related crimes.
- Longitudinal study reports.
- Patient tracking reports.
- Referral records.
- Patient records.

Goal 4—*Reach community with urgent and impactful anti-substance abuse message so that community knowledge about substance abuse increases, solutions increase, and problems decrease.*

All Goal 4 documents will be kept in the office of the outreach director. The following documents will be available.

- Print, advertising, public relations materials.
- Procedure and operating manuals.
- Minutes of meetings with community leaders and neighborhood volunteers.
- Minutes of planning sessions.

EXAMPLE 9.4 *(Continued)*

Alcohol and Drug Abuse Program—
Documentation Plan, page 3

- Media reports, public relations messages, and advertisements directed at the community.
- Records of group meetings and presentations.
- Materials for presentations.
- Information pieces, flyers, brochures, posters, letters.
- Neighborhood meeting notices and minutes.
- Community records about substance abuse incidents.
- Longitudinal study reports.
- Survey, questionnaire, focus group, and poll reports.

Goal 5—Effectively monitor, manage and evaluate project so that all goals and objectives are successfully accomplished.

All Goal 5 documents will be kept in the office of the project director. The following documents will be available.

- Fiscal reports and audit reports.
- Management plan and monthly reports.
- Evaluation and assessment reports.
- Supervisory records.
- Personnel records.
- Results of all studies.
- Tracking reports of all outcomes for goals and objectives.

Reports available to the public on request

The following publications and documents will be made available to those who want to replicate the project. Fees for copying, packaging and posting are listed beside each publication.

- Publicity materials for K–12 component—$35.
- Procedures and operating records for K–12 component—$75.
- Publicity materials for hotline component—$55.
- Procedures and operating records for hotline component—$65.
- Publicity materials for crisis team component—$35.
- Procedures and operating records for crisis team component—$105.
- Publicity materials for community education component—$85.
- Procedures and operating records for community education component—$55.

Chapter 10

Evaluation Plan

**It is only through evaluation that value
exists: and without evaluation the
nut of existence would be hollow.**

Friedrich Nietzsche[1]

At a Glance

What Else Is It Called?

- Project analysis
- Outcomes
- Project results

When Is It Used?

Always.

Why Is It Used?

Funders want to solve problems. Your connection with the funder is that
you want to solve the same problem. Your solution is a project. Evaluation
is necessary to see if your project was successful. For years, funders have
tried to discover if their investments have been effective. Their efforts have
traditionally been mostly unsuccessful. This has caused funders to actively
seek ways of determining the impact of both their short-term and long-term
investments. Most are gaining sophistication in requiring concrete and
measurable goals with specific outcomes. All are requiring a detailed evaluation plan linked to the goals and objectives of your project. Accountability

---

[1] Friedrich Nietzsche, in *Thus Spoke Zarathustra*, First Part, "On the Thousand and One
Goals" (1883).

is more critical to funding than ever before. This is one of the most important parts of your proposal. Evaluation is proof of success or failure of an activity. Since a grant proposal involves some risk, one learns also from failures.

Key Concepts

- Connect to goals and objectives through outcomes or results of each.
- Measurability is a key.
- Document everything.
- Report progress—include periodic reports in the proposal.
- Have an internal evaluation team even for small projects.
- If the grant involves significant funds, hire an outside evaluation team.

Formatting Issues

Use standard margins, 12-point type and stay within funder's page constraints.

Assistance for Development of an Evaluation Plan

We wrote an entire book about project management and evaluation. It has a disk of guidesheets and templates to use to help you develop evaluation plans. It is *Grant Winner's Toolkit: Project Management and Evaluation* (John Wiley & Sons, 2000).

Connect to Goals and Objectives

Almost all funders will require measurable goals and objectives with clear outcomes or results. Those that don't require measurability yet, will soon. We break goals and objectives into component parts, as we have discussed in the mission, goals, and objectives section in Chapter 6. This insures that we include all of the elements that the funder is interested in and guarantees that we have measurability. We may write the goal or objective in sentence form, or we may include the chart. We suggest you state the goal, at least, and state the outcomes expected from the goal, along with the evidence of evaluation. If you have a curriculum project, the curriculum itself is proof of a goal succeeding. If you have a test tube research project, your findings are proof of a goal completed. If you have a counseling program, records of the people counseled, and the results, are proof of your effectiveness. You do not have to turn every project into a study but you do need to think through what evidence you have that the goal was effectively completed. The following are three examples.

> ***Counseling Research Project Goal Three***—*One thousand senior citizens will have a minimum of 10 counseling sessions with certified psychologists, with 75% reporting better outlook on aging, life, and a more positive outlook.*

> Evaluation Plan for Counseling Research Project Goal Three—*Schedules of counseling sessions will be kept by name of client. Pretests will be given using the standardized tests XYZ Social Contentment Scale and the ABC Life Outlook Exam. After each participant has had five counseling sessions, the tests will be given again. At the end of ten counseling sessions, the tests will be once again administered and a questionnaire will be completed by each participant. The questionnaire appears in Appendix B. Family members will be interviewed six months after counseling and a year after counseling to see if the effects of counseling have lasting impact. All participants will be brought back a year after counseling to retake both tests. Results will be published in a report during project month six, at the end of the ten sessions, and a year after the project has been completed.*

> ***Curriculum Project Goal One***—*A planning session with five area computer aided design (CAD) experts will be led by a planning facilitator to identify the discrete skills and knowledge needed to be a CAD technician in preparation for designing a CAD technician curriculum.*

> Evaluation Plan for Curriculum Project Goal One—*Credentials of each of the five computer aided design (CAD) experts will be available. Each is required to have at least ten years in the field and each will be the supervisor of CAD technicians in his or her respective industry. Our planning facilitation consultant documents the session in detail and completes a comprehensive report of all the skills and knowledge items identified. That report will be sent to the funder of this project.*

> ***Environmental Cleanup Project Goal Three***—*The City Planning Department head along with the local Environmental Protection Agency head, the Sierra Club president, area Forestry Department head, and the head of the State Wildlife Agency will oversee a three month, 300 person volunteer group clean up of the Ripple River within Barnard County.*

> Evaluation Plan for Environmental Cleanup Project Goal Three—*A roster of crew members for 30 teams of ten persons each will be kept along with a schedule for each crew over the three month period of time. Special skills lists indicating the skills of each person in the crew will be kept for each crew. Each crew is assigned specific tasks based on the expertise within that crew. A list of tasks will be kept for each crew. The city planner is responsible for getting a record of progress for every crew chief after each cleanup session. A pictorial record will be kept by each crew chief of progress at each session. These will be combined with inspections by each member of the oversight committee, which will be written into a report.*

About Measurability

Measurability strikes fear in the hearts of potential grantees unless they are involved in research grant projects. We have seen people gasp and practically hyperventilate when faced with having to state measurement and results. This is because of a lack of understanding about grants, and the motivation of funders when they award grants. As we have said several times—the funder is interested in solving a problem. They want to fund well-developed projects they think might provide at least a partial solution to the problem. They know that things might not go exactly as planned.

How many times have you planned a simple meal just to find out that something did not turn out as you expected? A grant project is much more complicated than getting a meal on the table. The funders know that things might not work out exactly as planned. What they want to see is an educated and professional estimate of outcome. If you say 75% of participants will have positive results, and only 60% do, then you have learned something. The funder is not going to make you give back the money. The funder has learned something too—that maybe the project design needs to be revised. This is not a test of results—it is a test of whether you do what you said you would do in your proposal. Do not hesitate to put numbers, percentages, and statistical measurements in your goals and objectives. If you don't, you are not likely to receive funding.

Communication with the Funder

What if you are in the middle of a project, and something you did not anticipate happens? What if you discover something you planned, will just not work? In these cases, and they do happen, decide how to revise your project, write it down along with your rationale for the changes, and contact your funder. Get his or her approval in writing for your changes.

What if you have a budget item that you find out is not the amount you needed, but you can shift funds from another budgeted item? Write down your justification for the change, and contact your funder. Get his or her approval in writing for your budget change.

Funders consider that they are in the project with you. It is their investment, and they will always work with you, if you can justify your changes to them. They do not like to find out later that you spent money on other items than those in your budget, or that you changed the project design without their knowledge. Since the proposal and your award are a legally binding contract, if you make changes without the funders' knowledge, they can require you to pay back the money. Funders would be within their legal rights to do so, and it does happen. Look at funders as friendly partners in the project and treat them as such.

The Role of Documentation

We discuss documentation thoroughly in Chapter 9—the documentation plan, but it deserves another discussion under the evaluation plan. If you document your project, the evaluation is easy. Reports to the funder and others are easy. Documentation is the critical issue in evaluation. What do you document? Document everything that has any bearing on your outcomes. Document everything that shows that you did what you said you would in your proposal.

Internal Evaluation Team

It is a good idea to designate an evaluation person or a team internally to review data and compile evaluation reports. This can be an individual, if the project is a simple one. A team is necessary if the project is complex. This team can be the repository for organizing documents. The individual or the team leader should be the one to address evaluation with the funder. The internal evaluation team, not only provides valuable organizational assistance, but also assures professional communication for evaluation issues.

External Evaluation Team

If the funding is sizeable, most federal funders require an external evaluation team. Find out how much the funder expects to see in the budget for evaluation—the amount can be a sizeable portion of the budget. Find out also the funder's expectations regarding the role played by the external evaluation team so you can write a description into your evaluation plan. Program coordinators for federal funds are good about answering such questions.

Foundations and corporations are just beginning to require external evaluators on projects with sizeable budgets. We expect this trend to continue. Certainly funds are likely to be audited, but beyond that, the more visible funders are beginning to require additional evaluation measures as they strive to get a handle on accountability.

We suggest that you consider getting an external evaluator for any grant of sizeable funds. The external evaluator can act as a partner to keep you from getting into trouble with regard to the evaluation report to the funder.

Checklist—Evaluation Plan[2]

✔ Internal evaluation team?

✔ External evaluator?

---

[2] Remember that a grant maker's directions (instructions/guidelines) take precedence over any and all other considerations. You must absolutely, positively follow the grant maker's directions exactly, precisely, and painstakingly.

✔ What do stakeholders need (want) to know?

✔ What data needs to be collected?

✔ How will the data be collected or gathered?

✔ Do the collection tools exist or need to be developed?

✔ Who will collect the data?

✔ When will the data be collected?

✔ How will the data be analyzed?

✔ Are both formative and summative measures included?

✔ Are both quantitative and qualitative data collected?

✔ Who needs to receive evaluation information?

Last Words

An evaluation plan has two real purposes. One purpose is to determine how effective the project has been, the level, or amount, of success or failure. The second purpose of an evaluation is to provide feedback for course corrections during the operation of the project—to improve the project as it goes along. The measurement of the long-term level of success or failure of project outcomes is called summative. The measurement of project activities during the course of the project is called formative. Most grant makers want to see both formative and summative evaluation measures.

When information is expressed numerically or on a scale, the data is quantitative. Test scores, grades, blood pressure, the number of attendees, and sales figures are all quantitative data. When information is expressed in words as opinions, the data is qualitative. "I am very satisfied" and "this was worthless" are qualitative data. Most grant makers expect to see both quantitative and qualitative data in an evaluation.

Examples of Evaluation Plans for Four Projects

The following four examples (10.1 to 10.4) are examples of evaluation plans for each of the four organizations profiled in this book. The specific elements described within the chapter are reflected in each example.

EXAMPLE 10.1

After School Program—Evaluation Plan

Sunnyvale School District

We will contract with an outside evaluator to provide an objective, unbiased assessment of the results of program activity. In 1997, the district won a technology innovation challenge grant for approximately a million dollars a year for five years. We contracted with an evaluator referred to us by the U.S. Department of Education. Both the department and our district have been pleased with the work of this evaluator. She has proved herself to be thorough and thoughtful, tough but fair, and consistently positive, working to resolve issues in the best interests of both the Department of Education and the district. We contracted with this evaluator for her input during the project development for this proposal.

It will be the responsibility of the evaluator to answer the questions in the numbered list below. The program director will ensure that all program personnel cooperate fully in the collection of evaluation data. The evaluator is responsible for the development of interview guides, questionnaires, data capture sheets, check lists for observations, and other evaluation tools and forms.

1. Determine the effectiveness of the orientation training session
2. Determine the effectiveness of the tutor tutorial
3. Determine the effectiveness of the language arts subject matter mastery test
4. Determine the effectiveness of the mathematics subject matter mastery test
5. Determine the effectiveness of the explanation to school personnel of their responsibilities toward the after school program
6. Determine the effectiveness of the participant recruitment effort
7. Determine the effectiveness of the process for development of the IAP

(continues)

EXAMPLE 10.1 *(Continued)*

After School Program— Evaluation Plan, page 2

8. Determine the effectiveness of the IAP on student achievement

9. Determine the perceptions of staff and participants about the snack

10. Determine the effectiveness of the supervised homework time

11. Determine the effectiveness of the tutoring (one-on-one, two-on-one, and so on)

12. Determine the effectiveness of the language arts supplementary instruction

13. Determine the effectiveness of the mathematics supplementary instruction

14. Determine the effectiveness of the applied learning activities

15. Determine the effectiveness of the effort to expand applied learning activity offerings

16. Determine the attitudes of staff and participants toward recreational activities

17. Determine the effectiveness of the effort to expand recreational activity offerings

18. Determine the attitudes of staff and participants toward social activities

19. Determine the effectiveness of the effort to expand social activity offerings

20. Determine the effectiveness of health services

21. Determine the effectiveness of the effort to expand health service offerings

22. Determine the effectiveness of the parental involvement activities

23. Determine the effectiveness of the program's Web site

24. Determine parent's attitudes toward communications efforts

25. Determine parent's attitudes toward training offerings

26. Determine the change in academic achievement of after school program participants

EXAMPLE **10.1**   *(Continued)*

After School Program—
Evaluation Plan, page 3

27. Determine the change in behavioral problems of after schools program participants

28. Discuss the lessons learned by staff, participants, and parents

The evaluator will deliver an evaluation report to the grant maker and the district as soon as practically possible after the end of each program year.

For internal tracking purposes, each site director will report monthly to the program director the following information:

- Participant recruitment status and numbers
- Staff hiring and retention status and numbers
- Volunteer recruitment status and numbers
- Staff training (types and numbers)
- Student participation numbers for all activities
- Applied learning expansion
- Recreation activity expansion
- Social activity expansion
- Health services expansion
- Numbers of all types of parent contacts
- Numbers of all types of parent visits
- Parent training (types and numbers)

EXAMPLE 10.2

**Senior Citizen Wellness Center—
Evaluation Plan**

The Senior Citizen Wellness Center

For us, evaluation is necessary and valuable because it identifies the project activities that are not producing the expected results, allowing us to make changes and bring the activities back on course. Therefore, we have identified a few key aspects of the project and developed questions. The answers to those questions will guide project improvement and provide a measure of project success. We want to know the answers to the following questions:

1a. How many senior citizens are aware of the health and wellness services?

1b. How many senior citizens know the range of health and wellness services?

1c. How did they learn about the health and wellness services?

1d. How many senior citizens utilize health and wellness services?

1e. What are the judgments of users about the health and wellness services?

2a. How many senior citizens are aware of the social enrichment activities?

2b. How many senior citizens know the range of social enrichment activities?

2c. How did they learn about the social enrichment activities?

2d. How many senior citizens utilize the social enrichment activities?

2e. What are the judgments of users about the social enrichment activities?

3a. How many senior citizens are aware of the single point of entry?

3b. How many senior citizens know what the single point of entry system can do?

3c. How did they learn about the single point of entry?

3d. How many senior citizens utilize the single point of entry?

EXAMPLE 10.2 *(Continued)*

Senior Citizen Wellness Center—
Evaluation Plan, page 2

3e. What are the judgments of users about the single point of entry?

4. What are the partners' perceptions concerning their participation?

5. What are the perceptions of project staff, partner personnel, and volunteers concerning the training they received?

6. What are the perceptions of partners about the value and importance of participating in the project?

7. Has the health of participants in health and wellness services improved?

8. Has the social life of participants in social enrichment activities improved?

9. Has access to services improved for participants in the SPE?

10. What are the "lessons learned" during implementation of the project?

Questionnaires and interview guidelines for the different purposes must be prepared. The questionnaires must be administered (before participation and periodically thereafter), the results tallied and compiled, and the results published in a useable format.

EXAMPLE 10.3

Fire and Rescue Project— Evaluation Plan

Quad-County Fire and Rescue Association

We require an aggressive assessment of the level of accomplishments of this project. Forty-seven community volunteer fire departments have incurred financial obligations based on the belief that the association will improve their community outreach, recruitment, training, and purchasing. We must be able to report to the member departments trustworthy and accurate results of their faith, their commitment, and their monetary contributions.

Our evaluation must tell us the degree of effectiveness of the new community outreach program. Information we need includes the amount of public awareness of fire prevention, the amount of public knowledge about fire prevention, and the rate of reported fires. Over time, we expect the incidence of reported fires to decrease as public awareness and knowledge of fire prevention grows.

For centralized recruiting, success will be that all 47 departments have sufficient manpower to fulfill their responsibilities.

For centralized training, success will be demonstrated by firefighters obtaining the proper certifications while expressing satisfaction that the training is of high quality and relevance.

For centralized purchasing, success will be demonstrated by departments' expending less time and effort while saving money.

With the oversight of an evaluation committee formed from the board of directors (the 47 department chiefs) of the association, the director will be responsible for the performance of the evaluation, using the resources that she and the evaluation committee deem appropriate.

EXAMPLE 10.4

Alcohol and Drug Abuse Program— Evaluation Plan

INNER CITY ALCOHOL AND DRUG PREVENTION COMMISSION

The evaluation will be approached from both the outside and the inside. We have contracted with an outside evaluation team from the mental health department of our state-supported medical university. This team will be tasked with the summative evaluation, including a longitudinal study to measure the ongoing effectiveness of the three main efforts of the project: educational outreach, hotline and crisis teams, and performance art. An internal evaluation team will be tasked with most of the formative evaluation aspects of the project.

A data collection tool will be developed for administration at the beginning of the project and yearly thereafter. At the end of the second school year of the educational outreach effort, we want to see the following outcomes for the approximately 8,000 students in grades K through 12:

- 100% of students are aware of the in-school ATOD prevention program
- 95% of students believe that the ATOD prevention effort is worthwhile
- 95% of students believe that the ATOD prevention effort is relevant
- 95% of students believe ATOD effects are negative
- Student's attitudes toward ATOD trend negative (statistically significant)
- Student's attitudes toward ATOD users trend "negative" (statistically significant)
- Student's use of alcohol, tobacco, and other drugs trends down (statistically significant)

From the formative side, we want to know if sufficient personnel, equipment, materials, and supplies are available to implement the program. We want to know if the volunteer recruitment methodologies are effective and what will make them more

(continues)

EXAMPLE **10.4** *(Continued)*

Alcohol and Drug Abuse Program— Evaluation Plan, page 2

effective. We want to know if the training for volunteers and school staff is perceived to be sufficient, effective, and worthwhile. We want to know if the curricula are effective, worthwhile, and relevant. A data collection tool will be developed for administration at the beginning of the project and yearly thereafter.

Finally, we want to compile the lessons learned by asking volunteers, school staff, and students for their verbal impressions of the program.

It is the responsibility of the project's leadership to take the results of the evaluation, both formative and summative, and to make improving changes in the project.

Chapter 11

Dissemination Plan

**Truth never yet fell dead in the streets;
it has such affinity with the soul of man,
the seed however broadcast will catch
somewhere and produce its hundredfold.**

Theodore Parker[1]

At a Glance

What Else Is It Called?

- Distribution plan
- Publication plan

When Is It Used?

Almost always with federal grants. Requiring a dissemination plan is becoming more prevalent with foundations and corporations as well, though not all require it.

Why Is It Used?

In funding a project, one of the funders' purposes is to plant a seed—to invest funds in a project that has a good chance of solving the problem in which they are interested. Another equally important purpose is to get other organizations to replicate successful projects so the investment is multiplied. However, if no one knows about the project, then it is not likely that anyone will duplicate it. Thus, more and more funders are making it a requirement for the grantee to disseminate information about the project.

---

[1] Theodore Parker, *A Discourse of Matters Pertaining to Religion.*

Key Concepts

- Realistic but comprehensive—don't promise something you are not willing to do or cannot do.
- Plan dissemination locally, statewide, and nationally.
- Plan the types of information you will share.
- Determine what products, if any, will be sold.

Formatting Issues

Use standard margins, 12-point type and stay within funder page limitations.

Local Dissemination

Write a description or make a list of the reasonable things you can do locally to spread the word about your project. The first thing that probably comes to mind is local media—newspaper, radio, and television. Once the award is made, make a personal contact with a specific person in each media market who tends to write or broadcast stories about the topic of your project. In the dissemination plan, state that you will contact each media resource to generate a continuing story about your project. You cannot guarantee that a story will be produced, but you can promise to make the contact.

Another thing you can do locally is to contact local professional journals about writing an article about your project. You can either submit an article yourself or have a staff writer interview you. State in the dissemination plan that you will make contacts with a specific list of local publications.

Presentations can be made at related functions to disseminate information about your project. Make a list of local organizations that you will contact for a presentation about your project.

You can also network with colleagues by discussing your project at professional meetings. In the dissemination plan, discuss the professional groups your staff belongs to, and mention that the project will be discussed within those groups.

State Dissemination

Just as there are media at the local level, there are media outlets at the state level. There are state newspapers and publications—most states have a magazine. There are large television and radio stations that broadcast to a regional audience. All you can do is promise that you will make the contacts to see if a representative will cover your project if it is funded.

At the state level, there might be state clearinghouses that collect information about your project topic. Think about what agency or other organization might be interested in the same topic. Contact the group, and see if they know of a clearinghouse that might be interested in information about your project. A clearinghouse is an entity that collects articles, data, and other information about a particular topic. There are many national clearinghouses, and some states have them as well.

You can contact related professional organizations at the state level to publish information about your project. In the dissemination plan, list organizations that you will contact if the grant is awarded.

If you or your staff holds membership with related professional organizations at the state level, then there are opportunities to spread the word about your project. Staff can make a presentation about your project at a meeting. Gain the commitment of your staff to ask their state organizations about a presentation. For your dissemination plan, make a list of everyone you will contact for presentations if the grant is awarded.

Another way of disseminating information is to hold a seminar about your project, and invite similar organizations who might be interested in replicating your work. This is a more expensive option, and you might want to check with the potential funder to see if they will contribute funds for such an endeavor.

Probably the least expensive way of disseminating information is to establish a Web site and post information about your project. If your organization currently has a Web site, it is a good idea to tell the funder how much traffic the site gets. This will give the funder an idea of how effective your Web site will be in disseminating information about your project.

National Dissemination

You might have a project that will attract major media such as a cable news station or a morning show. If so, make a promise to investigate ways of getting the attention of the key persons who might be interested in profiling your project.

Most people count on national clearinghouses to carry information about their projects. We discussed clearinghouses earlier in this chapter. The following descriptions are from two clearinghouses.

ERIC

ERIC is the Educational Resources Information Center *(ERIC), a federally-funded national information system that provides, through its* 16 subject-specific clearinghouses, associated adjunct clearinghouses, and support components, *a variety of services and products on a broad range of education-related issues.*

ERIC is the world's largest source of education information, with more than 1 million abstracts of documents and journal articles on education research and practice. Our version of the Database, updated monthly with the latest citations available, provides access to ERIC Document citations from 1966 through July 2002 and ERIC Journal citations from 1966 through July 2002.

http://www.askeric.org/

Prevline—Prevention Online—NCADI Services

The world's largest resource for current information and materials concerning alcohol and substance abuse prevention, intervention, and treatment, the National Clearinghouse for Alcohol and Drug Information (NCADI) is a service of the Center for Substance Abuse Prevention, *which is under the* Substance Abuse and Mental Health Services Administration *(SAMHSA).*

http://www.health.org/

National organizations have newsletters. If your organization is a member of a national association or organization, then there is a good likelihood that that organization would welcome an article about your project for its newsletter.

There are nationally distributed magazines that are always searching for good articles. You can do some research to find out a few that might welcome an article. In your dissemination plan, list those publications and state that you will submit an article for publication.

You could consider putting together a national conference or seminar for those that might be interested in replicating your project. Again, this might be something to which the funder might want to contribute. Caution—this is an expensive undertaking. Do not promise this unless your organization is willing to commit to it.

The World Wide Web is another way to publicize your project. Again, it is a good idea to tell the funder what kind of traffic your organization normally has. This will give the funder an idea what kind of response you are likely to get from a Web presence.

Consider Fees

There will be requests for various materials about your project. You need to decide what you will offer and how much it costs to produce them. A Web site with files to download can solve this problem. If you intend to publish information about the project, decide on a fee to cover your costs to produce the information. In the dissemination plan, you should list what documents you are willing to share, and an estimate of the fee you will charge to provide the information. Do not forget about packaging and shipping costs.

Products To Be Sold

Your project may result in products such as a video tape, a computer CD, an audio tape, curriculum materials, an audio CD, and other items. These might generate income to help you continue the project after grant funding runs out. Anticipate these products, estimate a price for each, and include the income in your project design. Discuss these products in the dissemination plan, and list the estimated cost of each product.

Checklist—Dissemination Plan[2]

- ✔ Local presentations at community meetings.
- ✔ State presentations at conferences, conventions, and meetings.
- ✔ National presentations at conferences, conventions, and meetings.
- ✔ Local publishing in newspapers and newsletters (articles and reports).
- ✔ State publishing in state magazines and journals (articles and reports).
- ✔ National publishing in magazines, journals, and clearinghouses (articles and reports).
- ✔ Internet—Web site.
- ✔ Television—local cable access channel.
- ✔ Radio interviews.
- ✔ Video presentation—tape, DVD, or online.
- ✔ Informational pamphlets, leaflets, and brochures.
- ✔ Funds in the budget?

Last Words

Dissemination activities are a key component of the entire grant-making process. One of the main purposes for making grants is to fund model or demonstration projects. It does no good whatsoever to spend money to run model projects if information about the projects does not get out. Dissemination is the process of getting the word out about solutions to problems.

There are three audiences for dissemination—your organization, your community, and your professional peers in the state and nation. Disseminate

[2] Remember that a grant maker's directions (instructions/guidelines) take precedence over any and all other considerations. You must absolutely, positively follow the grant maker's directions exactly, precisely, and painstakingly.

information about the project to the people in your organization so everyone understands what is going on, and to create buy-in among the staff. Disseminate information to the community so people know what your organization is accomplishing, and to sell the community on the idea of supporting the project in the future (continuation). Disseminate to professional peers in the state and nation so other people and organizations working on similar problems will come to know about your solution.

Remember to put funds in the budget to pay for dissemination activities. Money in the budget is a persuasive demonstration that you are serious about performing dissemination activities. Dissemination activities provide a legitimate reason to spend grant funds to get items such as a digital camera, a video recorder, and multimedia software.

Examples of Dissemination Plans for Four Projects

The following four examples (11.1 to 11.4) are examples of dissemination plans for each of the four organizations profiled in this book. The specific elements described in the chapter are illustrated in each example.

EXAMPLE 11.1

After School Program—Dissemination Plan

Sunnyvale School District

The dissemination plan below is divided into three sections. We will first address what we will do locally and then with regard to the state. Finally, we will address what will do to publicize the After School Program (program) nationally.

Local

We have good rapport with the local newspaper. They have written articles about our schools numerous times. There is an education editor that we will contact to do a series of articles about the program as it progresses.

Locally we have a county education foundation that has a newsletter about education issues and happenings in our area. We have contacted them and they would be happy to run a series of articles about our program.

There is no local television station but there is a local radio station that will run public service announcements for us. They will publicize when the program opens and its special events.

Our superintendent is on the board of the local chamber of commerce. He will be able to make a presentation about the program. That will help us get the backing of the business and industry groups and a number of the service providers.

State

All our principals are members of the State Education Association and can make presentations about the program at the state level. In addition, the SEA has a newsletter that will allow us to write articles about the program to be published statewide.

The state magazine occasionally runs articles about education issues. We believe with good photographs and a special project the state magazine might run an article about the program.

There is a key television station, WRAK, that broadcasts regionally. If we have a special project or a kick-off celebration, it is likely

(continues)

EXAMPLE 11.1 *(Continued)*

After School Program— Dissemination Plan, page 2

that the station will cover it. We have had coverage for many of our projects before. We have a friendly relationship with one reporter from that station.

There are several state education foundations and organizations. Each has a newsletter. We are researching a list of contacts to which we can submit articles.

The program will be publicized on our Web site. The State Education Department publicizes our Web site statewide.

National

We will submit articles and information to national clearinghouses such as the Educational Resources Information Center (ERIC) and the Eisenhower National Clearinghouse (ENC).

In conjunction with our partners, we will also hold a seminar at the end of our second year for other schools interested in developing an After School Program. It will be publicized on national education bulletin boards and through Web sites, as well as to those who have contacted us.

EXAMPLE 11.2

Senior Citizen Wellness Center— Dissemination Plan

The Senior Citizen Wellness Center

Locally, our partners are enthusiastic about publicizing the project: first to let senior citizens know of the project and second, to gain support for services. All partners have agreed to publicize the project through their newsletters. But more importantly, they will each make key contacts with newspapers, television stations and with radio hosts. The public affairs officer at the city hospital will coordinate these efforts.

A mailing list of seniors is being compiled from public records and from local agencies. A letter with a brochure will be mailed to each senior. Costs will be covered by a combination of partners through their public relations offices.

State agency counterparts of the partners are keenly interested in this project for replication in other parts of state. The heads of all those agencies have agreed to publicize the project throughout the state. This will be done through newsletters, newspapers, and other media.

In addition, we have a State Clearinghouse on Aging. We will submit articles to the clearinghouse for publication.

Nationally, we will work through the National Association of Counties, the aging clearinghouse. Our county commissioner is active with the association and will help us make the right contacts to get publicity.

We will create a Web site and actively pursue reciprocal links with National information resources for our seniors. We will hire a professional through our partners' public affairs offices to see that we are listed on all relevant search engines.

In addition, we will join all relevant associations nationally and actively pursue publicity for our project. This will be done by submitting articles to newsletters, participating in conferences as speakers and attendees, and seeking reciprocal links to Web sites.

EXAMPLE 11.3

Fire and Rescue Project—Dissemination Plan

Quad-County Fire and Rescue Association

Locally, with 47 Volunteer Fire Departments involved, it will be no problem to get all newspapers to publish articles about our project. There are twelve newspapers in the communities served. Seven are weekly newspapers and will run extensive articles. Three are newspapers with wide distribution. The others are distributed mainly to the communities in which they are published.

There is one regional radio station in our area. That radio station does fundraisers for several volunteer fire departments. Management is very supportive of our efforts. We will be able to get interviews as well as public service announcements.

Each volunteer fire department will distribute flyers in the community about our project.

There are no local television stations. However, there is one regional station in a neighboring county. We believe that with the scope of the project being so broad, we will be able to generate interest in an interview or a special report.

The State Fire Chiefs Association and State Volunteer Fire Department Association are already interested in running articles in their newsletters to inform other departments that might want to replicate our project. In addition, we have been asked to make a presentation at both state conferences.

Regarding the junior fire marshal component, the state newspaper will likely run an article on that program. The state newspaper has been supportive of our other projects.

Through the schools, articles are likely to be run in the state education association newsletter about the junior fire marshal program. Information will be distributed community-wide by school personnel and the students.

Since the combining of efforts of 47 volunteer fire departments is a unique effort, the National Volunteer Fire Department

EXAMPLE 11.3 *(Continued)*

**Fire and Rescue Project—
Dissemination Plan, page 2**

Association will be interested in articles, both on the Web site and in newsletters, as well as a probable presentation at a regional or national convention.

The National Fire Protection Association is already interested in our project because of a contact with the state fire marshal. There is an online newspaper and a hard copy newsletter published by the NFPA.

The regional Fire Chiefs Association is also already interested in our project and if we are funded, they have requested a presentation at the regional conference.

EXAMPLE 11.4

Alcohol and Drug Abuse Program— Dissemination Plan

INNER CITY ALCOHOL AND DRUG PREVENTION COMMISSION

The performance artists component will raise the visibility of the project locally. Presentations will be made at meetings, in schools, and at public gatherings. This component will also gain media attention from the local radio station, the area television station, and the newspaper.

The school district has agreed to send flyers to all the parents and post information on their Web site. In addition, they will attempt to get an article in the State Education Association newsletter.

The hotline and crisis center will be publicized through police, hospitals, clinics, schools, health department, Department of Health and Human Services, all community centers, chamber of commerce, the junior college, all community service clubs such as Kiwanis and Civitan, and through libraries.

The State Substance Abuse Council is already informed of our plans and has agreed to publicize the effort statewide. In addition the Association of Family Counselors and State Association of Psychologists want to study the project for replication in other parts of the state.

The project will have a Web site, and that site will be linked to all relevant Web sites. This will publicize the project locally, statewide, and nationally.

A presentation will be put together, along with a conference display booth for presentations at regional and national conference. The presentation will also be displayed on the project Web site.

Chapter 12

Continuation Plan

**Tradition simply means that we need
to end what began well and
continue what is worth continuing.**

José Bergamin[1]

At a Glance

What Else Is It Called?

- Sustainment
- Institutionalization

When Is It Used?

Always.

Why Is It Used?

Grant makers are interested in good investments. If your solution to the problem in which you are both interested works out well, then both you and the funder want your project to continue. Grant funds do not continue forever. Most are one to five years. There are grant funds that seemingly go on year after year, but they are entitlements like Social Security, Medicare, Title I education funds, food stamps and so forth. And even those can change. But those are not funds you can apply for—they are formula funds. A state entity receives them by formula for the number of people that fit a certain category of need. Funders do not want to make grants to projects that are overnight wonders. They want to invest their money in projects that will continue after their funding has terminated. If you want

---

[1] José Bergamin (1895–1983), Spanish writer. *La Cabeza a Pájaros (Head in the Clouds)*, p. 65 (Madrid: Cruz y Raya, 1934).

to be awarded a grant, it is critical to make a good case for the project to continue after initial grant funding runs out.

Key Concepts

- Buy infrastructure and institutional knowledge with grant funds, not key staff.
- Include letters of support that specifically state how partners will support the project.
- Develop a clear plan to continue the project once funding runs out.
- Do not count on future grant funds to continue the project.

Formatting Issues

Use standard margins and 12-point type.

Why Do Funders Want to Know about Continuation?

Grant funders want to solve problems. Funders want suggestions (in the form of projects), from prospective grant recipients (written in a proposal), from which to choose for an award. Funders want to invest their money as well as possible. In fact, the people responsible for awarding grants would not keep their jobs if they award grants that are bad investments. Grant making is just like any other business. Executives responsible for the funds must perform. Part of performance is to see that good projects that solve problems continue.

Funders aren't in business to give away money over a three-year period for a project, and then have that project disappear. If the project is worth doing, it is worth continuing. The only exception to this rule is a study or a research project with a clear start and end. Otherwise, funders expect that their money will provide the fertile ground for continued success.

With efforts to increase accountability in every area of business, continuation is a hotter topic than it has ever been. Grant makers are becoming wiser when it comes to choosing projects. The guidelines for proposals are stricter than they have ever been. Most funders want to know your investment in the project monetarily, organizationally, and how important the project is to your organization. How important it is to your organization is exhibited by where the project appears in the organizational scheme, and what commitment there is to continue the project once grant funding has terminated.

In summary, grant funders want to make good investments. They do not want to fund a project that runs for a year and then disappears into the sunset. If you were making an investment of your personal funds, you would want to invest in something lasting. Grant funders are no different. They want to be able to point to an ongoing project and proudly state that they helped get it started. Grant makers truly want to solve the problems at the core of their purpose. They are sincere in their focus. Prospective grantees are carefully selected, both because the grant maker believes they have at least a partial solution to the problem in which they are interested, and because the grant maker believes the grantee will make a lasting impact.

What Are the Keys to Continuation?

If you purchase core staff with grant funds, continuation is a tough issue. What do you do when the grant funds run out? How do you continue the project without critical staff members? Under normal circumstances, you cannot continue the project if you purchase key staff with grant funds.

How do you avoid the staff trap? First of all, there are more ways to accomplish a project than throwing people at it. Think in terms of solving the problem without adding staff. What can you buy during the term of the grant (usually from one to five years) that will help you accomplish your project for the long haul? What about purchasing all the necessary equipment and reference materials for your project? What about purchasing consulting services to develop training films and materials for a library of materials to train future staff members? What about hiring a temporary staff member to help you get the project set up, and implemented, and then train your existing staff to take over?

Be creative in thinking about your project—think outside the proverbial box—to find another way to solve your project problems besides adding people. Think about how you can develop institutional knowledge through developing a library of resources, performing training, hiring temporary consulting, adding computers, and performing tasks more efficiently another way.

Think about partners from other organizations that you can join with to get part of the tasks done. Partnerships are required by a lot of funders. Partnerships significantly increase your chances of getting funding because the funder feels that, if there are a number of stakeholders interested in the project, it is more likely to continue. Look to grant funding to support the following:

- Things needed for your infrastructure.
- Funding for studies and planning.
- Training.
- Reference materials.

- Temporary staff to accomplish set-up and initial implementation.
- Consulting.
- Equipment.
- Research.

Do not look to grant funding to:

- Go on forever.
- Support key staff.
- Support ongoing activity.

How Do You Prove You Will Continue a Project?

What do you say to the potential funder to prove your good intentions to continue the project? After all, you cannot tell what is going to happen in three years. In fact, it is hard to predict what will happen one year from now. So how do you convince the funder, if you do not have a disaster, you will continue the project?

First of all, get your managers on board. Management must agree that the project is important for it to be successful. Most projects that don't continue do not have management buy-in. The project should have a prominent place in your organizational structure. It should not be a side issue where management is concerned.

Second, you should develop a plan to continue the project after grant funding runs out—which it inevitably will. Plan to ask for grant funds for things that will help accomplish the goals of the project, but whose costs are onetime expenses. Itemize all the needs for the project. If you have trouble with figuring project costs, our *Grant Seeker's Budget Toolkit* and *Grantseeker's Toolkit*[2] have directions on how to figure out expenses for the project goals and objectives.

Third, your project should be important enough for it to be institutionalized. This means that if your project is successful, it is important enough to your organization to be continued. Institutionalization means the project becomes an integral part of the overall operation of your organization. Grant makers look for signs that the project is important to your mission.

---

[2] Cheryl Carter New and James Aaron Quick, *Grantseeker's Toolkit: A Comprehensive Guide to Finding Funding* and *Grant Seeker's Budget Toolkit*, both published by John Wiley & Sons.

What Is Evidence of Continuation?

Show a clear line of oversight by a top manager. Do not bury your project way down in the hierarchy of your organization. You should state the chain of command showing clearly that it connects to the highest manager possible. If there is room, you can show how the project fits in your organization by using an organization chart.

Have the manager write a letter of support stating how important the project is to the organization. The letter should verify the fact that the manager will be personally supervising the project.

Describe your plan for continuation. Point out that what you are doing with grant funds is buying the set-up (and/or planning) phase and initial implementation. Show how you have not counted on grant funds for continuing activity.

Get any partners to write letters of support specifically stating their investment in the project. Get the partners to state how important the project is to their organization. Letters of support are not just attaboys and attagirls. They should state specific support for the project. Anyone can write "this is a good project and you should give them the money." Those attaboy or attagirl letters are disregarded by the funders.

Show how the project fits with the mission of your organization. Projects that do not clearly mesh with your organization's mission and goals will not have a good chance for funding.

If you have initiated other grant projects, state how you have continued those projects. If you have high-profile related projects that have been successful and have continued over an extended time period, briefly describe your success, even if it was not on a grant. This establishes a track record of responsibility.

Checklist—Continuation Plan[3]

- ✔ Commitments from applicant organization's leadership (board of directors).
- ✔ Commitments from partners.
- ✔ Commitments from community stakeholders.
- ✔ Project structured so continuation cost is low (no grant-paid staff).

---

[3] Remember that a grant maker's directions (instructions/guidelines) take precedence over any and all other considerations. You must absolutely, positively follow the grant maker's directions exactly, precisely, and painstakingly.

✔ Train-the-trainer professional development model (trainers clone themselves).

✔ Increase institutional capacity (does not cost much to continue).

✔ Increase intellectual capital (does not cost much to continue).

✔ No grant-paid worker bees (when the grant stops, the work stops).

✔ Obtain expertise from consultants and contractors, not grant-paid employees.

Last Words

The continuation plan goes to the heart of your sincerity. Grant funded projects are solutions to problems. Ask yourself this question "At the end of the term of the project, will the problem be gone?" Usually, the answer is no. Therefore, when you disregard the continuation plan, you send a message to the grant maker, loud and clear. The message you send is that you are not sincere about solving the problem. What you want is to take the money and run—not a good message. In fact, a message that will prevent you from getting the grant.

At the risk of repetition, if you honestly cannot see any way to continue a project after the grant maker's money runs out, you are not a good candidate for the grant. Grants are not the answer to all funding problems.

The main source of difficulty with continuing a project is the way the project is designed at the start. It is very difficult to convince a grant maker that you can continue a project that is heavily dependent on staff paid with grant funds. Where will the funds come from to pay those salaries? As said before, concentrate on improvements to your organizational capacity and infrastructure. Once in place, these improvements cost very little to continue. Stay away from staff funding and continuation becomes a much easier task.

Examples of Continuation Plans for Four Projects

The following four examples (12.1 to 12.4) are examples of continuation plans for each of the four organizations profiled in this book. The specific elements discussed in this chapter are reflected in each example.

EXAMPLE 12.1

After School Program—Continuation Plan

Sunnyvale School District

The After School Program is a key part of our plans for the future of the Sunnyvale School District. The superintendent is personally supervising the program and the school board is keenly interested.

Our students are mostly from poverty situations where parents have not had good experiences with school and basically are uneducated themselves. Our parents are the working poor. They work in shifts, and most of our children are "latch-key" kids. When the children go home to houses with no adult supervision, they either associate with the older teens or young adults who are out of work and up to no good. Or, they get in trouble themselves because they have nothing productive to do. Homework does not get done. Children do not get fed properly. They do not get in bed until the wee hours of the morning. This does not bode well for success in school. Our district must solve this problem to be able to provide a quality education for our community's children. The school board recognizes the fact. The superintendent recognizes the fact. Both are committed to action to resolve the situation.

Our superintendent and the school board are committed to approaching the city and county councils for funding during the term of the grant. If that does not produce funding, they have agreed to cut administrative staff through attrition to cover the personnel and other costs for the After School Program. Please see letters of support from Dr. Doe, school superintendent, and Dr. Plummer, chairman of the school board, in Appendix A.

EXAMPLE 12.2

Senior Citizen Wellness Center— Continuation Plan

The Senior Citizen Wellness Center

After the grant term is completed, the Senior Citizens Center Project (project) will cover staff salaries through a combination of the following:

- Private insurance payments.
- Medicare and Medicaid payments.
- Sliding fee schedules for those who can pay for services.
- Contributions from the partners.

In addition, support will be provided for equipment and supplies through budgets of the partners and some funding through the city and county councils. Our median age of citizens is over 7 years more than the national average. Thus seniors in our area have significant voting and lobbying power regarding city and county councils—this provides leverage for the project.

The single point of contact component will be continued through our Anytown Foundation, which will initiate a funding campaign from the first month of the project operation. The plan is to establish a trust fund, interest from which will support this component. Supervision will be through the foundation board of directors in conjunction with the project director.

EXAMPLE 12.3

Fire and Rescue Project—Continuation Plan

Quad-County Fire and Rescue Association

The purchasing component, once the equipment and facilities are funded, will operate independently. Our problem with funding this component will be solved by the grant funding.

Recruitment processes and procedures will be tested and revised as a result of grant funding. Grant funding will give us the opportunity to work through the best processes for recruitment, as well as training. Funding training materials could be a problem with such limited operations budgets of our 47 fire departments. We have negotiated an excellent agreement with a local printer to cut costs for manuals and materials. We are considering putting training on a secure Web site. We have a computer security person who is interested in helping us set up the system for free. We will work on options during the term of the grant.

The community outreach program will be no problem except for disposable materials. Again, with limited budgets, the fire departments will only be able to handle a portion of the costs. Our plan is to organize a coalition of small business and large industry managers in our service areas to donate either cash for materials or to actually produce the materials. Several industries have professional printing operations that are fully capable of handling all the materials we need. We feel certain that with a concerted effort, due to the minimal costs to business and industry, we will be able to accomplish continued reproduction of materials.

The junior fire marshal program will be continued by the school districts. There is funding that can be shifted from other line items to continue the program once it has begun. The individual schools will be able to reproduce print material. Once started, the program will be managed at the school level with an advisory board of fire fighters.

For project personnel, each of the 47 fire departments will donate a portion of budget for salaries to cover the costs of a project director and assistant director. Donations will be sought from the community through fundraising efforts to replenish budgets.

EXAMPLE 12.4

Alcohol and Drug Abuse Program— Continuation Plan

INNER CITY ALCOHOL AND DRUG PREVENTION COMMISSION

There are four basic components of the project.

1. Educational outreach to schools.
2. 24-hour hotline.
3. 24-7 crisis team.
4. Performance art to dramatize anti-substance abuse message.

Regarding component one, educational outreach to schools, the ATOD Commission and school district will continue to partner for continuation after the grant funding has terminated. Funding for continuation will come from ATOD Commission outreach budget and from a combination of Title I funding for some materials, from continuation funding through juvenile drug court and through the River City Education Foundation.

The 24-hour hotline will continue by virtue of a coalition of businesses and industries who know the importance of the hotline to both crime prevention and the quality of living of community citizens. Staffing will be handled through an advisory board with ATOD, court, business, and industry representatives.

The 24-7 crisis team is the most expensive of the components. The continuation plan for this component is to fund it with a combination of mental health agency funds, River City Hospital funds, private insurance, medicare, and medicaid. Additionally, the Fraternal Order of Police, Kiwanis, Civitan and the local Shrine Club will hold fundraisers to support the crisis team. It is viewed as a key component for community well-being.

Performance art will charge other counties, schools, and community groups to support its efforts. It will become a regional and statewide touring group after the term of the grant has ended.

Chapter 13

Key Personnel Biographies

Able people can do more.

Chinese Proverb[1]

At a Glance

What Else Are They Called?

- Vitae
- Biographical sketches
- Bios
- Biosketches

When Are They Used?

Almost always.

Why Are They Used?

The funder wants to make sure your key staff members have the right credentials to successfully run the project. You can have the best, most well-planned project and if the staff is not able to handle it, then it will not succeed. Funders know this and read key personnel bios very carefully to see if they believe each person can effectively manage his or her component.

Key Concepts

- One page.
- Only relevant information.
- No job histories.

---

[1] *The Columbia World of Quotations* (New York: Columbia University Press, 1996).

- No resumes unless requested.
- No two inch biographies.
- Be sure to state what position each staff member will hold with regard to the project.

Formatting Issues

Keep it to one page, unless otherwise directed, with standard margins and 12-point type.

Who Are Key Persons?

Key persons are those that oversee important components of your project. The project coordinator or director should be at the top of your list, but others will likely handle other critical functions, and those should be included too. When you are deciding which people are key personnel, you choose people that make a project succeed—without whom the project will fail. If you have broken your project into component parts, key people who head up those components are your key personnel.

Do Not Wait until the Last Minute

Sometimes getting biographical information pertinent to the project is the hardest task you have to perform to get your proposal out the door. For one thing, you are relying on another person. For another, people want to hand you a resume, or worse—they do not have a current one. What you need to know is not typically in a resume. Resumes are job histories—they do not tell the story of skills and knowledge.

Interview

A well-planned interview is the best way to get the pertinent information for a key person's bio sketch. You need to think through the project and develop a guide to questioning the person based on the project. The interview can be done in person or over the telephone, or, if your questionnaire is good enough, it can be done via e-mail.

Name, Rank, and Serial Number

Start your key person's biography with the formal name of the person with any certifications after the name. An example is Elizabeth (not Liz) Carlisle Smith, MSW.

Next, under the name, list the current job title. If the person is not employed by your organization, list the person's current job title and the organization for which the person works.

Third, list the project position for which the person will be hired if the grant is awarded. Be clear—title this section: Proposed Project Position.

Finally, name the project. These bits of information should start your key personnel biography.

Specialties

Describe the special skills of the person as they are relevant to the project. If your project is about firefighting, do not discuss the fact that this person once taught elementary school. That would not be relevant. Think through the position you would hire the person for if you get a grant award. Now, think of the special skills the prospective employee has that would directly affect the job. Describe the skills or knowledge. The following is an example.

Project: Creating a City Park

Mrs. Mullins has a degree in landscape architecture. She specializes in community projects and has been in the business of landscaping for over 15 years. She has won a state park planning award for our community museum park. In addition, she has experience planning a city park for our neighbor city, Wilkesboro. She is a lifelong resident of our community and, as such, knows the community preferences and desires.

Summary

In this section, you provide a summary of the experience the person has that is relevant to the project. Here is where you discuss similar leadership on other projects. This is an expansion of the specialties section of the biography. Using the example of Mrs. Mullins, we might expand her information thus.

In the fifteen year history of her landscape experience, Mrs. Mullins has coordinated planning for twenty similar city parks. Five have won city or state awards. Three have been for communities of the same size and profile as our township. In addition, Mrs. Mullins has experience working with state parks and wildlife agencies. She plans parks that are environmentally sound. This is an important issue in our community because the park will contain a wetland.

Experience

In this section, you list key skills and jobs by name that are relevant to the project. Here is where you might list articles or books written—keep in mind these need to be relevant to the project. Other projects of the same size and scope, along with budgetary responsibility, can be discussed. We will continue with Mrs. Mullins.

Mrs. Mullins created a city park for Jonesboro that had a budget of $350,000 and the project came in under budget and on time. She is highly recommended by the mayor's office of Jonesboro. In the projects she has coordinated for parks the size of ours, budgets have averaged $325,000—our project is estimated at $275,000. She has managed projects of over 300 acres and projects as small as 2 acres. Our project is 50 acres. She is a columnist for Southern Living Magazine *and has written articles such as: "The Perfect City Park," June, 2001 and "Preserving the Environment," January, 2001. Mrs. Mullins is also a contributing editor for* Horticulture Magazine.

Professional Activities

This is where you list relevant association memberships, board memberships and activities that show involvement in areas relating to the project topic. Here are Mrs. Mullins' professional activities.

- *President of Landscape Architect's Association, 1998 and 1999.*
- *Member, State Environmental Action Committee, 1999 to present.*
- *Member, State Parks Planning Board, 2000 to present.*

Education

List relevant degrees and special coursework. Our example continues below.

- *Degree, Landscape Architecture, University of Montana, 1976.*
- *Graduate work in Environmental Issues, California State University, 1984–86.*
- *Graduate of Chamber Leadership Program, 2009.*

Job Description

If you do not have a particular person for a key component, then what do you do? You include a complete job description showing the knowledge and skills needed for the job you want to fill. Inform the funder of the credentials expected, education, and special skills. Normally, this is acceptable if the position is not the project director or coordinator. However, it is a good idea to ask the funder prior to submitting your proposal.

Checklist—Key Personnel Bios[2]

- ✔ One page.
- ✔ Name.
- ✔ Title or position.
- ✔ Education.
- ✔ Experience summary.
- ✔ Accomplishment summary.

Last Words

The task with a key personnel bio sketch is simple—demonstrate that the right person for the job has been chosen. Show that the person selected has the level of education, the background and experience, and the career accomplishments that match the job requirements of the position.

Examples of Key Personnel Bios for Four Projects

The following four examples (13.1 to 13.4) are examples of key personnel bios for each of the four organizations profiled in this book. The specific elements discussed in this chapter are illustrated in each example.

---

[2] Remember that a grant maker's directions (instructions/guidelines) take precedence over any and all other considerations. You must absolutely, positively follow the grant maker's directions exactly, precisely, and painstakingly.

EXAMPLE 13.1

After School Program—
Job Description and Personnel Bios

Sunnyvale School District

Job Description
Site Coordinators—Five
After School Programs

Specialties

All site coordinators must have experience working with parents.
They are also required to be computer literate and capable of
running and troubleshooting computer labs. All five site coordinators
must have supervisory experience. In addition, site coordinators
must have excellent organizational skills.

Experience includes

Site coordinators must have supervisory experience. Each should
have at least 10 years of experience in education. Site coordinators
should have experience leading a team to meet an educational goal.

Professional activities

Site coordinators should be active in the community, because
a part of the success of the After School Program depends on
communication with community resource agencies and
organizations.

Education

Site coordinators must have at least a master's degree in education.
Each must also be a state-certified master teacher.

Christopher Allen, Ph.D.
Current Position—Principal Ripley Middle School
Project Position—Project Director
After School Program

Specialties

Dr. Allen has excellent rapport with both parents and students.
He is a no-nonsense disciplinarian who has respect from staff and
students. He is a mentor trainer with six years of experience in

---

EXAMPLE 13.1   *(Continued)*

After School Program—
Job Description and Personnel Bios, page 2

mentoring. He heads up the technology efforts in his school so will be very valuable in working with computer laboratories. He has superior organizational skills and has headed up major efforts for the school district before. Among these were the institutional reorganization effort, the parent education program, and the development of school district Web sites.

Summary

Dr. Allen has fifteen years of experience as a principal. When he took over the Ripley Middle School, it was a failing school. Last year it won a state award as one of the best middle schools in the state. Student test scores went from way below the state average to among the top performing schools in the state. His institutional reorganization plan was adopted by two other school districts as a model plan. The parent education program has trained over 100 parents a year for three years. All schools now have a Web site and the district has an umbrella site.

Experience includes

Dr. Allen served as an assistant elementary school principal in the Nashville City Schools, Nashville, Tennessee. He was hired as principal of an elementary school for Ripley City Schools in 1989. Seven years ago he took over as principal of Ripley Middle School. He has been the staff representative to the Tennessee Education Association for the past three years.

Professional activities

President of Education Mentors Association, 2001
Ripley district representative for the Tennessee Education
    Association, 2001–2004
Chairman of the Tennessee Teachers for Technology Education, 2000
Board Member, Ripley Library, 1999 to present
Mentor—Big Brothers of Ripley, 1998 to present

Education

Master's in Elementary Education, University of Kansas, 1983
Doctorate in Secondary Education, University of Tennessee, 1989
Postdoctorate work in Public Administration, 2000–01

EXAMPLE 13.2

Senior Citizen Wellness Center— Job Description and Personnel Bios

The Senior Citizen Wellness Center

Aaron Hoyt, Ph.D.
Current Position—YMCA Director
Project Position—Project Director
Senior Citizen Center

Specialties

Dr. Hoyt has 13 years of experience in initiating and leading a major community organization. He has contacts throughout the community with service providers, and is respected as a leader in the service field. Dr. Hoyt literally built the YMCA from the ground up. Our city did not have a YMCA. Dr. Hoyt created it, and grew it, until now it serves over 800 people a week. Dr. Hoyt has experience working with all age groups, including senior citizens.

Summary

The AnyTown city planner recruited Dr. Hoyt to initiate a YMCA for the city. The building was funded by a grant from the Epps Family Trust. Dr. Hoyt met with city council and all the local service resource organizations to develop the programming our communities needed. Now, thirteen years later, he is willing to take on another challenge—the Senior Citizen Center.

Experience includes

Dr. Hoyt acted as town manager of a 20,000 population town, after receiving his doctorate. He spent 5 years of successful management through a 20% growth period for the town. He moved to AnyTown to take over the development of a YMCA to serve the town and surrounding communities with a population of 325,000.

Professional activities

Vice President of State Town Managers' Association, 1987
President of State Town Managers' Association, 1989
Executive Director, AnyTown YMCA, 1991 to present
Board Member, AnyTown College, 1997 to present
Speaker, National YMCA Convention, 1999, 2002
Chairman of the Board, AnyTown Hospital, 2002
Board Member, Chamber of Commerce, 1999 to present

Education

Bachelor of Arts in Education, University of Iowa, 1979
Master's of Public Administration, University of Iowa, 1981

EXAMPLE 13.2   *(Continued)*

Senior Citizen Wellness Center— Job Description and Personnel Bios, page 2

Doctorate in Public Administration, Northwestern University, 1987
Graduate of Chamber of Commerce Leadership Development Program, 1993

April Foote, M.A.
Current Position—Coordinator of Family Services, Department
of Health and Human Services, AnyTown
Project Position—Single Point of Entry Coordinator,
Senior Citizen Center

Specialties

Mrs. Foote has contacts with all the service providers in the area because of her current position. She coordinates a department that serves four communities and over 35,000 cases annually. Her organizational skills are superb. She has completed the DHHS Technical Professional Development program and is adept in working with computers and other related technologies. She has had database development and spreadsheet courses. She also has experience working with advisory boards.

Summary

In her current position, Mrs. Foote works with 18 agencies and service organizations on a contractual arrangement. She works with another dozen agencies when her cases need special services. She has endorsements from the current director of the Department of Health and Human Services (DHHS) and the DHHS board chairman. Her department was recognized for efficiency by the State Department of Health and Human Services.

Experience includes

Mrs. Foote worked eight years as a social worker with DHHS. She was promoted to senior program specialist and finally to coordinator of family services. She has served in her current position for nine years.

Professional activities

Board Member, Girls Club of America, 1995 to present
Advisor to the Community Center Coalition, 1999
President, State Association of Social Workers, 1998

Education

Bachelor of Arts in Psychology, University of Kentucky, 1976
Master's of Social Work, University of North Carolina, 1979
Graduate of Chamber of Commerce Leadership Development Program, 2001

EXAMPLE 13.3

Fire and Rescue Project—
Job Description and Personnel Bios

Quad-County Fire and Rescue Association

Patrick Swift, M.A.

Current Position—Coordinator of Emergency Medical Services
Project Position—Consortium Director
Fire and Rescue Project

Specialties

Mr. Swift has experience in working with police, fire, and emergency medical service organizations. He has the respect of leaders in the community. He is a volunteer fireman in his community and has received training at the state fire fighters school. He was born in our community and has been active in community events for 20 years. He is an active Parent Teacher Association member, is very familiar with the schools, and has worked with the school superintendent and principals. He has successfully led a number of community-wide efforts. Mr. Swift has been trained as a trainer for Emergency Medical Services and has trained trainers for the state agency.

Summary

Mr. Swift has organized community efforts to inform senior citizens about medical hazards. In addition, he led a successful campaign to eliminate fire and medical hazards from our community small businesses. His background in emergency management and firefighting make him strongly suited for the consortium director position. He is also a trained trainer and, as such, can lead the training effort for the staff and community. Mr. Swift has worked with community leaders, and has good rapport with them to gain their cooperation for this fire and rescue project. His experience as coordinator of the Emergency Medical Service exhibits the kind of organization skills needed for the Fire and Rescue Project.

Experience includes

Mr. Swift has five years of experience with the Department of Health, coordinating community education programs. For the past ten years, he has been the coordinator of Emergency Medical Services. He has been a trained volunteer fireman for twelve years.

Professional activities

Board Member, Chamber of Commerce, 2000 to present
Board Member, Central City Hospital, 2002 to present

EXAMPLE 13.3   *(Continued)*

Fire and Rescue Project—
Job Description and Personnel Bios, page 2

Past President, State Emergency Medical Services Association, 2001
Member, State Emergency Medical Services Association, 1994 to present
Member, Central City Shrine Club, 1988

Education

Bachelor of Science Degree in Mathematics, Louisiana State University, 1987
Master's Degree in Public Administration, Auburn University, 1989
Fire Mastery Training, State Fire Training Academy, 1996

James McCarlson
Current Position—Assistant to City Manager
Project Position—Assistant Director
Fire and Rescue Project

Specialties

Mr. McCarlson has skills in documentation and planning. He is also highly
computer literate and has designed programs to capture data for the city. He has
been responsible for communications with community leaders, as assistant to
the city managers. He also has led meetings in the city manager's absence.

Summary

Mr. McCarlson has organizational and technical skills to enhance the Fire and
Rescue Project. There is a lot of documentation and communication involved
in the project. Mr. McCarlson's experience and skills in written and verbal
communications will be invaluable to the director. He is a seasoned coordinator
with eight years of experience assisting in managing city projects.

Experience includes

Computer Technician, Central City Junior College, 1990–1995
Assistant to City Manager, Central City, 1995–2002

Professional activities

Mentor, Junior Achievement, 2000 to present
Secretary, Central City Computing Club, 2001, 2003
Member, Quad-Cities Community Association, 2000–2003
Board Member, ASPCA, 2002

Education

Bachelor of Arts, History, University of Pennsylvania, 1987
Graduate of Bumble Business School Computer User Degree Program, 1990

EXAMPLE 13.4

Alcohol and Drug Abuse Program— Job Description and Personnel Bios

INNER CITY ALCOHOL AND DRUG PREVENTION COMMISSION

Laura Merrell, M.S.W.

Current Position—Coordinator of Outreach, Department
of Health and Human Services
Project Position—Outreach Coordinator
Community ATOD Prevention Project

Specialties

Ms. Merrell has coordinated outreach services in our community
for twelve years. In her capacity with the Department of Health and
Human Services (DHHS), she has developed contacts with leaders in
organizations throughout the county. Her department at DHHS was
in the top 5% of state departments in efficiency and effectiveness,
according to a study last year. The procedures she developed for her
department have been adopted by the state agency.

Summary

Ms. Merrell has the experience with outreach services that the project
needs. She also has established contacts to put the project a step
ahead for implementation. Ms. Merrell has expertise in developing
procedures that work. She has the respect of area service leaders. A large
portion of her work for DHHS has been involved with substance abuse
intervention because of the prevalence of low-income families in our
county. Her work has been exemplary.

Experience includes

Social Worker, River City DHHS, 1984–1988
Coordinator of Outreach, River City DHHS, 1989–present

Professional activities

Advisor, Special Olympics, 1998
Mentor, Girls Club of America, 1995–present
Board Member, County Library Association, 1997–present
Advisor, Association for Disabled Youth, 1994–present

Education

Bachelor of Arts, Sociology, Florida State University, 1982
Master's of Social Work, University of Georgia, 1984

EXAMPLE **13.4** *(Continued)*

Alcohol and Drug Abuse Program— Job Description and Personnel Bios, page 2

Kathryn Brandon, Ph.D.
Current Position—Private Practice Psychologist
Project Position—Director
Community ATOD Prevention Project

Specialties

In Dr. Brandon's private practice, she has specialized in working with alcoholics and drug abusers. She has a vast amount of experience in this community with substance abuse problems. She has worked with the community hospital and other community service organizations to meet her patients' additional needs. She regularly does presentations in the schools on the medical and emotional problems caused by substance abuse. The principals say she is received well, by both teachers and students.

Summary

Dr. Brandon has 15 years of experience working to solve our community's problems of substance abuse. She is a tireless advocate for education as a prevention method. Dr. Brandon initiated a committee of area psychologists, psychiatrists, and physicians to review substance abuse cases and provide expert input on remedies. She has the stature in the community to pull together the various groups the project needs for success.

Experience includes

Internship at Cleveland Clinic, Cleveland, Ohio, 1989
Counselor at Cleveland Mental Health Clinic, Cleveland, Ohio,
    1990–1993
Private Practice in Cleveland, Ohio, 1994–1999
Private Practice in River City, 2000 to present

Professional activities

Advisor, Education Committee, National Association of Psychologists,
    1995–1996
Chairman, Education Committee, National Association of
    Psychologists, 1997
Vice President, State Associations of Psychologists, 2000
President, State Association of Psychologists, 2001
Board Member, River City Hospital, 2002–present

(continues)

EXAMPLE **13.4** *(Continued)*

Alcohol and Drug Abuse Program— Job Description and Personnel Bios, page 3

Visiting Professor, State University, 2000–present
Community Chairperson, Special Olympics, 2002

Education

Bachelor of Arts in Psychology, Ohio State University, 1984
Master's in Psychology, Ohio State University, 1986
Doctorate in Clinical Psychology, Rutgers, 1988
Internship, Cleveland Clinic, 1989

Chapter 14

Timelines

Time goes, you say? Ah, no!
Alas, Time stays, we go.

Henry Austin Dobson[1]

At a Glance

What Else Are They Called?

- Time frames
- Time charts
- Project calendars

When Are They Used?

Almost always with a federal grant maker, but not as often with a foundation or corporation.

Why Are They Used?

Timelines are graphical representations of what will happen when. Timelines are used to inform the funder when benchmarks and major project events are going to happen. Timelines are used to clarify and provide a graphical representation of the project.

Key Concepts

- Uncomplicated.
- Easy to read at a glance.
- Only major events need be noted.

---

[1] Henry Austin Dobson (1840–1921), British poet, author, "The Paradox of Time," st. 1, *Proverbs in Porcelain* (1877).

Formatting Issues

We like to do timelines in terms of project months rather than calendar months. We state what will happen in project month one or project month six. Sometimes a review process is held up. This may cause the reader to question timing, if the project shows a start date before the project will be approved. Listing time frames in terms of project months eliminates that problem. Sometimes it is hard to make a timeline in 12-point type. Always remember the reader—assume that readers do not have 20-20 vision, and make it easy on them to read the chart.

Goals and Major Objectives

On your timeline, you will include your goals and any major objectives that are considered benchmarks. You will only write a few words, or a simple phrase at best, so look at each goal and decide on the focus for your timeline.

Milestones or Special Events

If there are milestones or special events, include them in your timeline. A milestone might be when the first phase of research has been completed, or when a key component of the project has been finished. A special event might be a seminar or an awards ceremony.

Major Reports and Evaluations

It is important to note when reports will be done and which month's analyses will be made. Evaluations are another key item to put in a timeline. Because of the importance of accountability, the funder is keenly interested in these topics.

Important Deadlines

If there is a deadline in your project, it should be noted in the timeline. Deadlines might be for a meeting, a test, or a report to a partner.

Special Requirements of Funder

Any time requirement valued by the funder should appear in the timeline. In fact, you should take every opportunity you can to indicate to the potential funder that you have met all the requirements.

Examples

The following examples show sample formats for timelines.

Project Month	Activity
One	Hire and train staff—set up advisory committee.
Two	Purchase equipment—renovate building.
Three	Enroll students.
Four	Start student classes.
Five	Start parent education classes.

Another example:

Project Month	One	Two	Three	Four	Five
Activity	Assess river damage.	Form work crews.	Work session.	Work session.	Evaluate next steps.

Yet, another example:

Project Month	One	Two	Three	Four	Five	Six	Seven	Eight	Nine	Ten	Eleven	Twelve
Activity												
Planning meeting.	X				X				X			
Set up equipment.	X	X										
Patient intake.		X	X									
Begin therapy.				X								
Patient tracking.				X	X	X	X	X	X	X	X	X
Interim report.												X

Checklist—Timeline[2]

- ✔ Goals.
- ✔ Major objectives.
- ✔ Important milestones.
- ✔ Special events.
- ✔ Major reports.
- ✔ Evaluations.
- ✔ Important deadlines.
- ✔ Any special grant maker requirements.
- ✔ Clean, clear, and uncluttered.
- ✔ Easy to understand.

Last Words

A timeline is a graphical presentation of what and when things happen. This information could be put into a narrative. Why then is a graphical presentation used? The answer is to make the information easier to understand. This simple fact leads into the most important point about a timeline. It must be easy to understand. If it takes careful perusal and several minutes of study to understand a timeline, it has missed the mark. It must be redesigned.

Seek a balance. Show enough detail to draw a complete picture of the project, but not so much detail that the big picture becomes obscured. The forest can disappear behind the trees.

Does it seem as though we keep telling the same story over and over? Perhaps that is because we are doing just that. It goes something like this. The project summary gives a capsule glimpse of the story. The executive summary expands the story to include a few more facts. The problem statement tells the story from the viewpoint of the problems that need solving. Goals and objectives provide the organizational framework, the outline of the story. The project narrative fleshes out the story to its full size. The management plan tells the story from a behind-the-scenes viewpoint. The documentation plan takes the view of saving evidence about the story. The dissemination plan gets the word out about the story. The continuation plan

---

[2] Remember that a grant maker's directions (instructions/guidelines) take precedence over any and all other considerations. You must absolutely, positively follow the grant maker's directions exactly, precisely, and painstakingly.

keeps the story going. The timeline puts the story in perspective chronologically. The budget explains the story from the viewpoint of money. So, do we keep telling the same story over and over? Yes, we do. That is the whole point. The different parts of a proposal, each coming from their own particular direction, come together to tell a complete story, the story of your solution, your project.

Examples of Timelines for Four Projects

The following four examples (14.1 to 14.4) are examples of timelines for each of the four organizations profiled in this book. The elements highlighted in the chapter are illustrated in each example.

EXAMPLE 14.1

After School Program — Timeline

Sunnyvale School District

Goals and Objectives	Project Year One — Project Month											
	1	2	3	4	5	6	7	8	9	10	11	12
Goal 1: Develop Infrastructure	■	■	■									
Obj 1: Hire project director	■											
Obj 2: Hire site directors and snack coordinators	■	■										
Obj 3: Hire teachers		■	■									
Obj 4: Recruit tutors		■	■									
Obj 5: Agreements with contractors		■	■									
Obj 6: Prepare facilities		■	■									
Goal 2: Train Program Personnel												
Obj 1: Staff orientation training			■									
Obj 2: Train tutors			■									
Obj 3: Orient middle school staff			■									
Goal 3: Provide Supplemental Academic Activities												
Obj 1: Recruit participants			■									
Obj 2: Develop academic activity plans			■									
Obj 3: Supervise homework				■	■	■	■	■	■	■	■	■
Obj 4: Tutoring				■	■	■	■	■	■	■	■	■
Obj 5: Language arts supplementation				■	■	■	■	■	■	■	■	■
Obj 6: Mathematics supplementation				■	■	■	■	■	■	■	■	■
Goal 4: Provide Applied Learning Activities												
Obj 1: Schedule applied learning sessions				■								
Obj 2: Hold applied learning sessions				■	■	■	■	■	■	■	■	■
Obj 3: Recruit applied learning providers			■									
Goal 5: Provide Recreational Activities												
Obj 1: Schedule recreational activities				■								
Obj 2: Hold recreational activities				■	■	■	■	■	■	■	■	■
Obj 3: Recruit recreational providers			■									
Goal 6: Provide Social/Health Services Activities												
Obj 1: Schedule social/health activities				■								
Obj 2: Hold social/health activities				■	■	■	■	■	■	■	■	■
Obj 3: Recruit social/health providers			■									
Goal 7: Provide Parental Involvement Activities												
Obj 1: Parent workshops				■								
Obj 2: Open house				■								
Obj 3: Individual parent meetings				■	■	■	■	■	■	■	■	■
Obj 4: After school web page			■	■	■	■	■	■	■	■	■	■
Obj 5: Newsletter				■		■		■		■		■
Obj 6: Solicit parent attendance				■	■	■	■	■	■	■	■	■
Goal 8: Evaluate Program												
Obj 1: Develop evaluation questions		■	■									
Obj 2: Determine needed data		■	■									
Obj 3: Determine measurement methodology		■	■									
Obj 4: Obtain/develop measurement tools			■	■								
Obj 5: Collect data							■	■	■	■	■	■
Obj 6: Analyze data										■	■	■
Obj 7: Publish evaluation results												■
Goal 9: Manage After School Program	■	■	■	■	■	■	■	■	■	■	■	■
Obj 1: Manage project personnel	■	■	■	■	■	■	■	■	■	■	■	■
Obj 2: Manage funds	■	■	■	■	■	■	■	■	■	■	■	■
Obj 3: Make ongoing changes				■	■	■	■	■	■	■	■	■
Obj 4: Disseminate project information	■	■	■	■	■	■	■	■	■	■	■	■
Obj 5: Advisory board		■			■			■			■	
Obj 6: Continue project				■	■	■	■	■	■	■	■	■

EXAMPLE 14.1   *(Continued)*

After School Program—Timeline, page 2

Timeline—After School Program

Goals and Objectives	Project Year One — Project Month											
	1	2	3	4	5	6	7	8	9	10	11	12
Goal 1: Develop Infrastructure	■	■	■									
Obj 1: Hire project director	■											
Obj 2: Hire site directors and snack coordinators		■										
Obj 3: Hire teachers		■										
Obj 4: Recruit tutors		■										
Obj 5: Agreements with contractors		■										
Obj 6: Prepare facilities		■	■									
Goal 2: Train Program Personnel			■	■	■	■	■	■	■	■	■	■
Obj 1: Staff orientation training			■									
Obj 2: Train tutors			■									
Obj 3: Orient middle school staff			■									
Goal 3: Provide Supplemental Academic Activities			■	■	■	■	■	■	■	■	■	■
Obj 1: Recruit participants			■									
Obj 2: Develop academic activity plans			■	■								
Obj 3: Supervise homework				■	■	■	■	■	■	■	■	■
Obj 4: Tutoring				■	■	■	■	■	■	■	■	■
Obj 5: Language arts supplementation				■	■	■	■	■	■	■	■	■
Obj 6: Mathematics supplementation				■	■	■	■	■	■	■	■	■
Goal 4: Provide Applied Learning Activities				■	■	■	■	■	■	■	■	■
Obj 1: Schedule applied learning sessions				■	■	■	■	■	■	■	■	■
Obj 2: Hold applied learning sessions				■	■	■	■	■	■	■	■	■
Obj 3: Recruit applied learning providers				■	■	■	■	■	■	■	■	■
Goal 5: Provide Recreational Activities				■	■	■	■	■	■	■	■	■
Obj 1: Schedule recreational activities				■	■	■	■	■	■	■	■	■
Obj 2: Hold recreational activities				■	■	■	■	■	■	■	■	■
Obj 3: Recruit recreational providers				■	■	■	■	■	■	■	■	■
Goal 6: Provide Social/Health Services Activities				■	■	■	■	■	■	■	■	■
Obj 1: Schedule social/health activities				■	■	■	■	■	■	■	■	■
Obj 2: Hold social/health activities				■	■	■	■	■	■	■	■	■
Obj 3: Recruit social/health providers				■	■	■	■	■	■	■	■	■
Goal 7: Provide Parental Involvement Activities				■	■	■	■	■	■	■	■	■
Obj 1: Parent workshops							■			■		
Obj 2: Open house				■								
Obj 3: Individual parent meetings				■	■	■	■	■	■	■	■	■
Obj 4: After school web page				■	■	■	■	■	■	■	■	■
Obj 5: Newsletter				■		■		■		■		■
Obj 6: Solicit parent attendance				■	■	■	■	■	■	■	■	■
Goal 8: Evaluate Program				■	■	■	■	■	■	■	■	■
Obj 1: Develop evaluation questions				■								
Obj 2: Determine needed data				■								
Obj 3: Determine measurement methodology				■								
Obj 4: Obtain/develop measurement tools				■	■							
Obj 5: Collect data								■				■
Obj 6: Analyze data								■				■
Obj 7: Publish evaluation results												■
Goal 9: Manage After School Program	■	■	■	■	■	■	■	■	■	■	■	■
Obj 1: Manage project personnel	■	■	■	■	■	■	■	■	■	■	■	■
Obj 2: Manage funds	■	■	■	■	■	■	■	■	■	■	■	■
Obj 3: Make ongoing changes						■				■		
Obj 4: Disseminate project information						■				■		
Obj 5: Advisory board		■			■							
Obj 6: Continue project												■

EXAMPLE 14.2

Senior Citizen Wellness Center—Timeline

The Senior Citizen Wellness Center

Goals and Objectives	Project Year 1 — Project Month											
	1	2	3	4	5	6	7	8	9	10	11	12
Goal 1: Preparatory Activities	■	■										
Obj 1: Hire key personnel		■										
Obj 2: Hire project personnel		■										
Obj 3: Recruit volunteers		■										
Obj 4: Train staff and volunteers		■										
Obj 5: Prepare single point of entry facility												
Obj 6: Obtain equipment, materials, and supplies		■										
Goal 2: Health and Wellness Enhancements			■	■								
Obj 1: Health screenings						■	■	■	■	■	■	■
Obj 2: Exercise activities						■	■	■	■	■	■	■
Obj 3: Substance abuse counseling						■	■	■	■	■	■	■
Obj 4: Support groups						■	■	■	■	■	■	■
Obj 5: Food preparation activities						■	■	■	■	■	■	■
Goal 3: Social Enrichment Enhancements			■									
Obj 1: Develop social enrich enhancements			■	■								
Obj 2: Develop foster grandparent program			■	■								
Obj 3: Implement social activities					■	■	■	■	■	■	■	■
Obj 4: Implement foster grandparent						■	■	■	■	■	■	■
Goal 4: Single Point of Entry			■	■								
Obj 1: Complete collaborative agreements			■	■								
Obj 2: Resolve security and privacy issues			■	■	■							
Obj 3: Develop info transfer protocols			■	■	■							
Obj 4: Outreach program			■	■	■	■	■	■	■	■	■	■
Obj 5: Develop operating procedures			■	■	■							
Obj 6: Implement single point of entry					■	■	■	■	■	■	■	■
Goal 5: Monitor and Manage Project	■	■										
Obj 1: Evaluate project	■	■	■	■	■	■	■	■	■	■		■
Obj 2: Manage project personnel	■	■	■	■	■	■	■	■	■	■	■	■
Obj 3: Manage funds	■	■	■	■	■	■	■	■	■	■	■	■
Obj 4: Make ongoing improvements								■	■	■	■	■
Obj 5: Disseminate information											■	■
Obj 6: Seek community involvement							■	■	■	■	■	■
Obj 7: Continue project							■	■	■	■	■	■

EXAMPLE 14.3

Fire and Rescue Project—Timeline

Quad-County Fire and Rescue Association

Goals and Objectives	Project Year One — Project Month											
	1	2	3	4	5	6	7	8	9	10	11	12
Goal 1: Set-up Activities												
Obj 1: Hire consortium director	▓											
Obj 2: Hire consortium staff		▓										
Obj 3: Prepare facility		▓										
Obj 4: Equip consortium		▓										
Goal 2: Increase Community Outreach												
Obj 1: Develop fire prevention program			▓	▓	▓							
Obj 2: Implement fire prevention program						▓	▓	▓	▓	▓	▓	▓
Obj 3: Develop junior fire marshal program			▓	▓	▓							
Obj 4: Implement junior fire marshal program						▓	▓	▓	▓	▓	▓	▓
Goal 3: Improve Training, Recruiting, and Purchase												
Obj 1: Develop centralized training			▓	▓	▓							
Obj 2: Develop centralized recruiting			▓	▓	▓							
Obj 3: Develop centralized purchasing			▓	▓	▓							
Obj 4: Implement centralized training						▓	▓	▓	▓	▓	▓	▓
Obj 5: Implement centralized recruiting						▓	▓	▓	▓	▓	▓	▓
Obj 6: Implement centralized purchasing						▓	▓	▓	▓	▓	▓	▓
Goal 4: Monitor and Manage Project												
Obj 1: Evaluate project	▓					▓						▓
Obj 2: Manage personnel	▓	▓	▓	▓	▓	▓	▓	▓	▓	▓	▓	▓
Obj 3: Manage finances	▓	▓	▓	▓	▓	▓	▓	▓	▓	▓	▓	▓
Obj 4: Ongoing project improvement								▓	▓	▓	▓	▓
Obj 5: Disseminate information												▓
Obj 6: Continue project									▓	▓	▓	▓

EXAMPLE 14.4

Alcohol and Drug Abuse Program—Timeline

INNER CITY ALCOHOL AND DRUG PREVENTION COMMISSION

Project Year One												
Goals and Objectives	**Project Month**											
	1	2	3	4	5	6	7	8	9	10	11	12
Goal 1: Project Set-up Activities	█	█	█	█	█							
Obj 1: Hire project director	█											
Obj 2: Hire project key personnel	█	█										
Obj 3: Hire project personnel		█										
Obj 4: Recruit outreach volunteers			█									
Obj 5: Recruit hotline/crisis team volunteers			█	█								
Obj 6: Recruit performance artists				█								
Obj 7: Orientation training		█			█							
Obj 8: Ready facility	█	█										
Goal 2: Educational Outreach			█	█	█	█	█	█	█	█	█	█
Obj 1: Choose outreach curricula			█									
Obj 2: Train volunteers					█							
Obj 3: Implement outreach in schools							█	█	█	█	█	█
Goal 3: Hotline and 24-hour Crisis Team			█	█	█	█	█	█	█	█	█	█
Obj 1: Develop hotline procedures			█	█								
Obj 2: Train hotline volunteers					█							
Obj 3: Implement hotline						█	█	█	█	█	█	█
Obj 4: Train crisis teams					█							
Obj 5: Implement crisis teams						█	█	█	█	█	█	█
Goal 4: Performance Art					█	█	█	█	█	█	█	█
Obj 1: Develop performances					█	█						
Obj 2: Give performances							█	█	█	█	█	█
Goal 5: Monitor and Manage Project	█	█	█	█	█	█	█	█	█	█	█	█
Obj 1: Evaluate project	█	█	█	█	█	█	█	█		█		█
Obj 2: Manage personnel	█	█	█	█	█	█	█	█	█	█	█	█
Obj 3: Manage finances	█	█	█	█	█	█	█	█	█	█	█	█
Obj 4: Ongoing project improvement							█	█	█	█	█	█
Obj 5: Disseminate information							█			█		
Obj 6: Seek community involvement		█	█	█	█	█	█	█	█	█	█	█
Obj 7: Continue project							█	█	█	█	█	█

Chapter **15**

Budget Summary

A budget takes the fun out of money.

Mason Cooley[1]

At a Glance

What Else Is It Called?

- Budget summary
- Budget request

When Is It Used?

Always.

Why Is It Used?

With the budget, you tell the funder specifically what you are requesting for funding, item by item. A budget is not just a lump sum figure. It is an itemization of how you will spend the funds once you receive the award. All federal funders, and more and more foundation and corporate funders, are requiring first a total project budget, and then, a break out of the request you are making for funding. Funders do not fund the total project budget for any significant project. They want to know that there is enough local investment indicating the project is important to the applicant organization and partners. The funders know if they are the only stakeholders, the project has less chance of success, and little chance of continuation.

Key Concepts

- Be realistic for your project—do not overstate or understate.
- Cost out your project as it is being developed.

---

[1] Mason Cooley (b. 1927), U.S. aphorist. *City Aphorisms* (New York, 1994).

259

- Be thorough—if you forget costs, they will be absorbed by your organization.

- Don't make up figures—get real costs.

- Follow the grant maker's directions—if you have questions, ask.

- Cost out what your organization will spend on the project—both in-kind and cash.

- Cost out what the partners will spend on the project—both in-kind and cash.

Formatting Issues

If the funder provides forms, use them. Use a clear format for the budget that can be read at a glance. Use standard margins and 12-point type.

Budget Assistance

We have written an entire book on budgets. It is the *Grant Seeker's Budget Toolkit.*[2] The book describes how to cost out a project step-by-step. There is a detailed analysis of every part of a budget with examples. In addition, there is a CD included with spreadsheets to use for every part of the budget process, and worksheets for project budget development. This book cannot go into detailed specifics of the budget, as the *Budget Toolkit* does. If you still have questions, we suggest that you either purchase a *Grant Seeker's Budget Toolkit* or find one at your local library.

Introduction

Goals are steps to accomplish your mission. Objectives are steps to accomplish your goals. Goals and objectives are detailed and measurable, as we have discussed. Each indicates actions to accomplish your project mission. Where there is activity, there are costs. As you develop your project goals and objectives, cost out exactly how much funding it takes to accomplish them. It is important to your project, but also important to funder research, to do this. One does not go to a $25,000 funder for $100,000, and one does not go to a $300,000 funder for $500. You need to match your project budget to the funder as well as to the problem it intends to solve. The

---

[2] Cheryl Carter New and James Aaron Quick, *Grant Seeker's Budget Toolkit* (Hoboken, NJ: John Wiley & Sons, 2001).

following are some examples to show how to cost out project goals and objectives.

Goal 3

What?	What approach?	When?	How many or how much?	Result/outcome
Enroll patients in cancer study.	Notify doctors, hospitals, and clinics in a 100-mile radius and supply with packets of information.	Project month two.	To enroll 260 patients.	Sufficient patients fitting profile are enrolled for double-blind research.

Costs associated with this goal include the following.

- Development of packets—in-house, 80 hours @ $20 an hour = $1,600 in-kind.
- Printing of 2000 packets at $5 each = $10,000.
- Envelopes for packets = $200.
- Stamps for mailing at $1.25 per packet = $2,500.
- Development of mailing labels—in-house, 30 hours @ $20 an hour = $600 in-kind.
- Packaging, stuffing and application of labels and stamps—in-house, 10 hours at 4 people @ $20 an hour = $800 paid temp service.

The following is a second example.

Goal 2

What?	What approach?	When?	How many or how much?	Result/outcome
Hire mentor coordinators and train staff.	State personnel guidelines and five-day course.	Project month three.	Hire 2 staff and train 22.	Two mentor coordinators hired and staff is trained on mentoring techniques.

Costs associated with this goal include the following.

- Place ads in are newspapers—$325.
- Advertise on Web site—no cost.
- Place ads in state newsletters—$250.

- *Post ad on state personnel Web site—no cost.*
- *Interview potential mentors—12 hours @ $32 an hour = $384 in-kind.*
- *Hire two mentors—$43,000 each and 17% fringe benefit each = $100,620.*
- *Consultant training for staff—$2,000 a day for five days = $10,000.*
- *Materials for 22 staff @ $50 each = $1,100.*
- *Conference room for a week @ $100 a day = $500 in-kind.*
- *Catering for 25 @ $20 a day for five days = $2,500.*
- *Pens and legal pads for 22 = $44.*

In-Kind

In-kind items are the contributions your organization can make to the project without going outside to hire the services or purchase the goods. For example, almost every project will require tasks by your support staff. Estimate the hours your staff will have to work on the project times their hourly rate to get your in-kind contribution. If someone in your organization will supervise the project as a part of an existing job, then estimate the percentage of time it will take to provide supervision and multiply by salary and fringe benefits. Most people forget things like copying on in-house copy machines. You can charge the going rate per page for use of your internal copy machines as in-kind. If your project uses phone lines, a percentage of your system costs can be allocated as in-kind contributions.

In-kind is not "funny money." In-kind contributions are real costs that your organization incurs as a result of running the project. Grant makers recognize in-kind as part of the contribution you and your partners make to the overall project budget.

There will be other things you will actually purchase for the project. Those should be separated from in-kind contributions. You will show actual cash expenditures for the project, and then a separate item for in-kind contributions.

The following are some items that can be included as in-kind.

- Employee time and fringe (percentage or hourly).
- Use of equipment at the going rate.
- Use of materials, including software licenses and books.
- Supplies.
- Volunteer time at fair market value of donated time.
- Facilities.

• Access to special support services such as technical consulting.

The value of in-kind contributions is defined as the fair market value of contributed personnel, facilities, equipment, services, materials, and supplies.

Direct Costs

Direct costs are costs that can be assigned to a specific cost center. In our case, the cost center is the grant project. For example, if a staff member will spend half-time working on your grant project, half of that person's wages (plus fringe) is a cost directly attributable to the total cost of the project. If the person is paid from your organization's normal funds (not from the grant), half the person's wages (plus fringe) is an in-kind contribution from your organization to the direct costs of the budget of the project.

Indirect Costs

Indirect costs are costs that are difficult, or impossible, to assign to a specific cost center. Let's say, for example, that you will use grant funds to hire a project director. The project director's wages and fringe are a direct cost, because you know exactly the "cost center" to which the expense should be assigned—in this case, your grant project.

When the project director reports for work, your organization will provide a desk, a chair, lighting, a trash can, a toilet that flushes, pens, pencils, and such. How much does all this cost? It's difficult or impossible to say. These are indirect costs.

Accountants use a formula to arrive at a general indirect cost rate, a percentage. For grant proposal budget purposes, obtain your organization's indirect cost rate from the people who handle the finances.

To determine indirect costs, simply multiple total direct costs times the indirect cost rate. It is worth noting that some grant makers do not allow indirect costs on equipment costs. For those grant makers, the equipment costs must be subtracted from the total direct costs before computing indirect costs.

Overhead

An accountant may disagree, but for all practical purposes, overhead is the same thing as indirect costs. Business and industry tend to speak in terms of overhead. Government and nonprofit organizations tend to use the term indirect costs. They are referring to the same thing (I feel accountants cringing everywhere)—those costs for which it is difficult or impossible to assign to a specific cost center.

Items Included in Budgets

- Personnel—wages for project personnel at their annual salary times their percentage involvement in the project, or at their hourly rate times the number of hours dedicated to the project.
- Fringe—includes FICA, SUTA, FUTA, worker's compensation insurance, health insurance, retirement benefits, and any other cash costs incurred by an employer because of a person's employment—usually expressed as a percentage of wages.
- Travel—lodging, mileage, airline tickets, meals, taxi, shuttle, and lease cars.
- Contractual—Any contract services such as leases, rents, consulting costs, contractors, software licenses, and training.
- Construction or renovation—actual material costs for the construction or renovation—architectural or contractor costs will normally appear under the contractual line item.
- Materials—reference materials, training materials, software, and books.
- Supplies—postage, copy paper, pens, CDs, pencils, and paper clips.
- Equipment—items with a longer life span than materials and supplies, usually three years minimum, such as furniture, computers, copy machines, fax machines, laboratory equipment, and telephone systems.
- Indirect costs—the expense for items such as heat, lights, space, air conditioning, and so on, items for which it is difficult or impossible to ascertain exactly how much is expended for a particular activity or project.

Formatting the Budget

Generally, grant makers provide applicants with a budget form. All that is necessary is to fill in the blanks. Over the years, we have worked with hundreds of budget forms. At first glance, it can seem as though there is a tremendous variety, but looking with care will show that layout and formatting aside, there simply cannot be that much difference among budget forms. There are only so many ways to categorize the expenses of a project. But, however one decides to group the expenses, the categories become line items, and the sum of all the direct cost line items always becomes the total direct costs. Adding the indirect costs to the direct costs always yields the total costs.

EXHIBIT 15.1

Generic Budget Form

	Line Item Description	Grant Request	Matching Funds		Match Totals	Project Totals
			Applicant	Partners		
1	Personnel					
2	Fringe					
3	Travel					
4	Equipment					
5	Materials and Supplies					
6	Contractual					
7	Capital Expense					
8	Other					
9	Total Direct Costs					
10	Indirect Costs					
11	Total Costs					

Some grant makers, usually foundations, have applicants use their own budget format. For those occasions, we have included an example of a generic budget form in Exhibit 15.1. Note that you may not need all the columns we have included. It will depend on what information the grant maker requires.

A. Line Item Description Column:

Line Items 1 through 8 are direct costs. Line items come in two types: expense categories and functional. Functional line items describe a specific type of expense, such as travel, printing, or the project director. Expense categories are general groupings of items without any specific identification. Most grant makers use both types on their budget forms, with travel being the most often used functional line item.

1. Personnel—Wages—salary and/or hourly.

2. Fringe—Cash cost incurred by employer over and above employee wages.

Fringe = personnel cost × fringe rate.

Obtain fringe rate from payroll personnel.

3. Travel—A functional line item with the function being, obviously, travel and all its associated expenses such as parking, tolls, tips, and meals. Another functional line item sometimes used is printing, though both travel and printing are contractual services.

4. Equipment—Items with a useful life span of several years (usually at least three but sometimes more) that also cost over a set amount (a common minimum is $500 but it's often more). The life span and cost are dependent on an organization's accounting procedures. Both criteria must be met. For example, a small audio cassette player may have a useful life span of five or more years, but it costs only $30, so it is not considered to be equipment.

5. Materials and Supplies—Items that do not meet the criteria to be equipment.

6. Contractual—Generally, the cost of services performed by individuals, organizations, or companies, though the expense could be for an intangible such as a royalty. The fundamental difference between contractual services and personnel costs is that payroll taxes are not withheld from the amount paid to contractors.

7. Capital Expense—Land, buildings, improvements, fixtures, and so forth. Equipment is a specific type of capital expense.

8. Other—At times labeled miscellaneous. This line item should always be zero. There are no expenses—absolutely none—that will not fit into one of these categories: personnel, fringe, equipment, material/supplies, contractual, and capital expenses.

9. Total Direct Costs—The sum of all direct costs. In our example, this is the sum of line items 1 through 8.

10. Indirect Costs—Indirect costs = total direct costs × indirect cost rate.

    Some grant makers require that equipment and capital expenses be subtracted from total direct costs before computing indirect costs.

11. Total Costs—The sum of total direct costs and indirect costs, Lines 9 and 10.

B. Grant Request Column

This column contains the amounts being requested from the grant maker. Often, these are the only figures required by a grant maker, though it is well to keep in mind that there are always expenses incurred by an organization implementing a grant project.

C. Applicant Matching Funds Column

Matching funds can always be in-kind contributions unless the grant maker uses the precise phrase "cash match." Matching funds denotes in-kind contributions. Only the phrase "cash match" requires the expenditure of cash.

D. Partners Matching Funds Column

When an applicant is required to produce a specific match, for example one-to-one, the project partners can be a source of matching funds (in-kind contributions). If an organization is truly a partner, they are doing something on behalf of the project. That "something" has a value. That value is an in-kind contribution to the budget of the project. Keep in mind that a person or organization that gets paid is *not* a partner. A person who gets paid would be an employee or a contractor, but not a partner. An organization that gets paid would be a contractor or a vendor, but not a partner. Discounts do not a partner make. In this case, a word—partner—means one thing in business and quite another thing in grant seeking. Don't confuse the two.

E. Match Totals Column

At times, a grant maker will ask to see the total of matching funds (in-kind contributions) from all sources. A column such as this one might be used when a grant maker requires a specific percentage match. This column enables a quick and easy check of the matching funds against the project total.

F. Project Totals Column

The total cost of running a project is *always,* without exception, more than the grant request. A grant maker may not require an applicant to compute those costs, but they still exist. These costs are so real, in fact, that grant makers do not make large grants to small organizations. Small organizations do not have the resources (personnel or funds) to effectively spend large amounts of money. This truth goes down hard with almost everyone who serves in small nonprofits. The off-the-cuff response is: "Of course I can spend millions of dollars. Just give it to me and watch." However, the fact is that spending large amounts of money is very expensive. For example, your organization gets a million dollars to spend on equipment. What is the first thing that must happen? Decisions must be made about exactly how to spend the funds. Who makes these decisions? How much time will it take? What happens to the other work the person was performing before the new task appeared? Once decisions are made, orders must be placed. How much time will it take to complete the paperwork to order a million dollars worth of equipment? Finally, the stuff begins to show up. Who gets all the stuff out of the boxes? Who cleans up the mess? Who keeps up with the paperwork and the warranty information? Who installs all the equipment? Well, you get the idea. And, this is just the tip of the iceberg. The usual response to this discussion is that the grant funds can be spent to hire all that work done. OK, fine, hire people. Who manages the people you hire to ensure that the work gets done properly? Who maintains quality control, security, and financial responsibility? And if it is you, who is doing the job you did before? Just keep in mind that the total cost of a project is always greater than the grant request. The amount might not be much, and it might be very manageable, but the cost always exists.

Checklist—Budget Summary[3]

- ✔ Spreadsheet the budget form.
- ✔ Create computer version of budget form.
- ✔ Complete the budget justification (narrative) section first.
- ✔ The phrase "matching funds" means in-kind contributions.
- ✔ The phrase "cash match" means money in the bank.
- ✔ Personnel costs—Allowed? Restrictions?
- ✔ Fringe rate—within allowable range?
- ✔ Fringe = personnel cost × fringe rate.
- ✔ Equipment—Allowed? Restrictions?
- ✔ Materials and supplies—Allowed? Restrictions?
- ✔ Contractual services—Allowed? Restrictions?
- ✔ Capital expenses—Allowed? Restrictions?
- ✔ Other—zero ($0.00).
- ✔ Total direct cost = Sum of all direct cost line items, both categorical and functional.
- ✔ Indirect cost rate—Within allowable range?
- ✔ Indirect cost—Allowed? Restrictions?
- ✔ Indirect cost = Total direct costs × indirect cost rate.
- ✔ Total costs—Within allowable range?

---

[3] Remember that a grant maker's directions (instructions/guidelines) take precedence over any and all other considerations. You must absolutely, positively follow the grant maker's directions exactly, precisely, and painstakingly.

Last Words

First and foremost, the figures on the budget form are not the budget. They are a summary of the budget. This proposal section is always placed in front of the budget justification or narrative, giving the impression that it is created first, which it is not. The figures for this section are compiled from the budget justification or narrative. Much of the difficulty grant seekers experience during development of a project budget comes from attempting to create a summary before the itemization. The itemization comes first, then the summary. Use the budget form to structure the budget justification or narrative. Except for doing that, forget the budget form until the real budget has been completed.

It is easily worth the investment of time to use a computer to recreate the budget form with spreadsheet software. Set up the spreadsheet to perform all the calculations automatically. This way, when changes must be made in budget amounts—and changes will most certainly occur—fringe costs, indirect costs, and all the various totals will recalculate automatically as the new amounts are entered.

The amount entered into the "Other or Miscellaneous" line item should always be zero. First, every expense known to human kind fits nicely into a budget category without using "Other." All expenses fall neatly into three types: (1) purchase of tangible items, such as books, computers, buildings, and hot dogs, (2) payment of employee wages, and (3) purchase of intangibles, such as the knowledge and skill of a contractor, or a service such as the telephone. Type one expenses fall into equipment, materials, supplies, or capital expenses. Type two expenses fall into personnel. Type three expenses fall into contractual services. It does not matter that tangible results often follow the purchase of an intangible. A consultant generates a report, a tangible, but the consultant is not being paid for the physical fact of the report. The consultant is being paid for the knowledge, skills, and experience used to create the report.

In reality, the "Other" expense category is used as a hedge against mistakes in other parts of the budget. We all fear that we have forgotten some little something in the budget that will rise up to bite us six months into the project. We allocate a few thousand dollars to "Other" just in case. It's the slush fund. It's the cushion, the insurance against that rainy day when the budget comes unraveled. You know it. We know it. Grant makers know it.

So, what message do you send to the grant maker by requesting funds as "Other?" The message is one of uncertainty and trepidation. Instead, go boldly and assuredly to the grant maker with an "Other" expense of zero. Go with confidence that the budget figures will stand the test of time.

Send the message that even if the budget figures are not exactly correct, the problem will be easily handled when the time comes.

As often as not, grant makers place restrictions on spending, usually one or both of two types. The first type of restriction simply forbids expenditures for specific items. One grant maker will not pay for travel. Another will not allow equipment purchases. Another forbids stipends to project participants.

The second type of restriction limits the amount of the grant that can be spent on an expense. A typical example is a limitation on the amount that can be spent on equipment. The limit is often expressed as a percentage of the total grant request. For example, a grant maker may limit equipment purchases to no more than 15% of the grant.

Another expenditure of time that can pay dividends is to recreate the budget form as a computer document. It may take a little time, but once the budget form is exactly duplicated as a word processor or spreadsheet file, the budget figures can be entered directly into the cells neatly and cleanly. Clean original copies can be printed as needed directly from the software. Applicants are often relegated to using a typewriter to complete budget forms. The results are often less than professional. Taking the time to create a computer-generated version of the budget form, takes one more step on the path of presenting your application in the best possible light.

Examples of Budgets for Four Projects

The following four examples (15.1 to 15.4) are examples of budgets for each of the four diverse organizations described in this book. The elements discussed within this chapter are implemented in each example.

EXAMPLE 15.1

After School Program—Budget Summary

Sunnyvale School District

Project Year 1

	Line Item Description	Grant Request	Matching Funds Applicant	Matching Funds Partners	Match Total	Project Total
1	Personnel	$ 620,250	$ 94,600	$109,500	$ 204,100	$ 824,350
2	Fringe	186,075	28,380	32,850	61,230	247,305
3	Travel	22,000				22,000
4	Equipment		375,000		375,000	375,000
5	Supplies		103,200		103,200	103,200
6	Contractual	68,800		107,500	107,500	176,300
7	Construction					
8	Other			16,000	16,000	16,000
9	Total direct costs	897,125	601,180	265,850	867,030	1,764,155
10	Indirect costs	125,598	84,165	37,219	121,384	246,982
11	Training stipends		58,000		58,000	58,000
12	Total costs	$1,022,723	$743,345	$303,069	$1,046,414	$2,069,137

Project Year 2

	Line Item Description	Grant Request	Matching Funds Applicant	Matching Funds Partners	Match Total	Project Total
1	Personnel	$496,200	$218,650	$109,500	$ 328,150	$ 824,350
2	Fringe	148,860	65,595	32,850	98,445	247,305
3	Travel	22,000				22,000
4	Equipment		125,000		125,000	125,000
5	Supplies		103,200		103,200	103,200
6	Contractual	55,040	13,760	107,500	121,260	176,300
7	Construction					
8	Other			16,000	16,000	16,000
9	Total direct costs	722,100	526,205	265,850	792,055	1,514,155
10	Indirect costs	101,094	73,669	37,219	110,888	211,982
11	Training stipends		58,000		58,000	58,000
12	Total costs	$823,194	$657,874	$303,069	$ 960,943	$1,784,137

(continues)

EXAMPLE 15.1   *(Continued)*

After School Program—Budget Summary, page 2

Project Year 3

	Line Item Description	Grant Request	Matching Funds		Match Total	Project Total
			Applicant	Partners		
1	Personnel	$372,150	$342,700	$109,500	$ 452,200	$ 824,350
2	Fringe	111,645	102,810	32,850	135,660	247,305
3	Travel	22,000				22,000
4	Equipment					
5	Supplies		$103,200		103,200	103,200
6	Contractual	41,280	27,520	107,500	135,020	176,300
7	Construction					
8	Other			16,000	16,000	16,000
9	Total direct costs	547,075	576,230	265,850	842,080	1,389,155
10	Indirect costs	76,591	80,672	37,219	117,891	194,482
11	Training stipends		58,000		58,000	58,000
12	Total costs	$623,666	$714,902	$303,069	$1,017,971	$1,641,637

Project Year 4

	Line Item Description	Grant Request	Matching Funds		Match Total	Project Total
			Applicant	Partners		
1	Personnel	$248,100	$466,750	$109,500	$ 576,250	$ 824,350
2	Fringe	74,430	140,025	32,850	172,875	247,305
3	Travel	22,000				22,000
4	Equipment					
5	Supplies		103,200		103,200	103,200
6	Contractual	27,520	41,280	107,500	148,780	176,300
7	Construction					
8	Other			16,000	16,000	16,000
9	Total Direct Costs	372,050	751,255	265,850	1,017,105	1,389,155
10	Indirect Costs	52,087	105,176	37,219	142,395	194,482
11	Training Stipends		58,000		58,000	58,000
12	Total Costs	$424,137	$914,431	$303,069	$1,217,500	$1,641,637

EXAMPLE 15.1   *(Continued)*

After School Program—Budget Summary, page 3

Project Year 5

	Line Item Description	Grant Request	Matching Funds		Match Total	Project Total
			Applicant	Partners		
1	Personnel	$124,050	$ 590,800	$109,500	$ 700,300	$ 824,350
2	Fringe	37,215	177,240	32,850	210,090	247,305
3	Travel	22,000				22,000
4	Equipment					
5	Supplies		103,200		103,200	103,200
6	Contractual	13,760	55,040	107,500	162,540	176,300
7	Construction					
8	Other			16,000	16,000	16,000
9	Total direct costs	197,025	926,280	265,850	1,192,130	1,389,155
10	Indirect costs	27,584	129,679	37,219	166,898	194,482
11	Training stipends		58,000		58,000	58,000
12	Total costs	$224,609	$1,113,959	$303,069	$1,417,028	$1,641,637

Personnel Budget—Project Year 1

Indirect rate 14.00%

Position	Quantity	Salary	Total
Project director	1	$45,000	$ 45,000
Assistant project director	1	32,000	32,000
Administrative assistant	1	24,000	24,000
Site director	5	35,000	175,000
Assistant site director	5	28,000	140,000
Snack director	5	6,450	32,250
Teachers	25	6,880	172,000
		Total	$620,250

Fringe rate 30.00%

Position	Quantity	Salary	Total	Weeks	Hrs	Rate
Bus Driver	5	$5,160	$25,800	43	10	$12
Security	5	9,460	47,300	43	20	$11
Maintenance	5	4,300	21,500	43	10	$10
		Total	$94,600			
Contractors	20	3,440	68,800	43	4	$20

(continues)

EXAMPLE 15.1   *(Continued)*

After School Program — Budget Summary, page 4

Other

Student	Number	Average Amount	Total
Mini-grants	400	$40	$16,000

	Number	Per Amount	Total
Supplies	1,200	$86.00	$103,200

	Number		Total	Weeks	Hrs	Rate
Partner—contractual	20	$5,375	$107,500	43	5	$25

	Number	Sessions	Amount	Total
Training stipends	58	10	$100	$58,000

Partner Personnel	Percent Involvement	Salary	Total
1	50%	$60,000	$ 30,000
2	50%	$55,000	$ 27,500
3	50%	$48,000	$ 24,000
4	50%	$56,000	$ 28,000
			$109,500

EXAMPLE 15.2

Senior Citizen Wellness Center— Budget Summary

The Senior Citizen Wellness Center

	Line Item	Project Year			Project Total
		One	**Two**	**Three**	
1	Personnel	$210,000	$220,500	$231,525	$ 662,025
2	Fringe	77,385	81,254	85,317	243,956
3	Travel				
4	Equipment	26,000			26,000
5	Supplies				
6	Contractual	25,000	15,000	5,000	45,000
7	Other				
8	Total direct costs	338,385	316,754	321,842	976,981
9	Indirect costs	62,601	58,600	59,541	180,742
10	Total costs	$400,986	$375,354	$381,383	$1,157,723

Personnel Budget—Project Year 1

Personnel	Salary	Quantity	Total
Project director	$65,000	1	$ 65,000
Single-point-of-entry director	55,000	1	55,000
Administrative assistant	26,000	1	26,000
Social worker	32,000	2	64,000
Total			$210,000

Fringe rate	36.85%
Indirect rate	18.50%

EXAMPLE 15.3

Fire and Rescue Project—Budget Summary

Quad-County Fire and Rescue Association

Personnel	$ 0
Fringe	0
Equipment	65,000
Materials and supplies	22,000
Contractual	130,000
Other	0
Total costs	$217,000

EXAMPLE 15.4

Alcohol and Drug Abuse Project— Budget Summary

INNER CITY ALCOHOL AND DRUG PREVENTION COMMISSION

	Line Item Description	Grant Request	Matching Funds	Project Total
1	Personnel	$ 86,000	$116,000	$202,000
2	Fringe	16,125	21,750	37,875
3	Travel			
4	Equipment	30,000		30,000
5	Materials and supplies	15,000		15,000
6	Contractual	40,000		40,000
7	Other			
8	Total direct costs	187,125	137,750	324,875
9	Indirect costs	17,777	13,086	30,863
10	Total costs	$204,902	$150,836	$355,738

Fringe rate   18.75%
Indirect cost rate   9.50%

Grant Request Positions	Salary
Outreach coordinator	$32,000
Director of performing arts	32,000
Administrative assistant	22,000
Total	$86,000

Match Positions	Salary
Project director	$ 48,000
Hotline manager	32,000
Assistant director	36,000
Total	$116,000

Chapter 16

Budget Justification

The man of science has learned to believe
in justification, not by faith, but by verification.

Thomas Henry Huxley[1]

At a Glance

What Else Is It Called?

• Budget narrative

When Is It Used?

Always.

Why Is It Used?

Your budget is a summary. It does not show where you got your figures—
just the final numbers. The funder wants to see how you came up with
your budget figures and thus the budget justification. The budget justification explains the budget. Most grant writers do the budget justification
first and then do the budget. If you are applying for a three-year project,
you will show three years of budgets. Normally, grant funds will be less
the second and third years of a project.

Key Concepts

• Write the budget justification in the same order as the line items.
• Put the budget justification in the order the funder lists line items.
• Explain fully where you got the figures for the budget summary.

---

[1] Thomas Henry Huxley (1825–1895), British biologist and educator. *Reflection #4, Aphorisms
and Reflections,* selected by Henrietta A. Huxley (London: Macmillan, 1907).

- Do not include actual bids from vendors unless the funder requests them, and then put them in the appendix.

Formatting Issues

Clear and concise are watchwords for the budget justification. Just show where you got your figures. Write in 12-point type and normal margins.

Personnel

Personnel can either be figured by the hour or at a percentage of an annual salary. If figuring by the hour, you show how many hours should be expended times the hourly rate. If figuring based on a percentage, you decide what percentage of time will be devoted to the task, state the annual wage, and take that percentage of it. If a staff member will be totally devoted to the project, then you show the salary. Figure these costs without fringe benefits; there is a separate category for fringe benefits. See the following examples below.

- *The executive director will supervise the project at 10% of his time. His annual wage is $102,500. At ten percent, the project will be charged with $10,250 for his time.*
- *A project coordinator will be hired with project funds at $57,000 annually.*
- *Two support staff will spend 40 hours each on the project. Their hourly wage is $21.25. The total for these two staff members is $1,700.*
- *Two teachers will spend 20% of their time with the project. Their annual salary is $43,560. The total for their time is $17,424.*

Fringe Benefits

Fringe benefits include: FICA, SUTA, FUTA, worker's compensation insurance, health insurance, and retirement benefits. Fringe benefits are usually expressed as a percentage of salary. If you do not know what the fringe benefits for your staff are, the person who processes payroll does. The following are several examples.

- *A project coordinator will be hired at the rate of $57,000 annually. Our fringe benefits are 19.23% of salary. The total fringe benefit for this position is $10,961.10.*
- *Two counselors will be hired for the project at a salary of $47,500 annually. Our fringe benefits are 17.22% of salary. The total fringe benefit for these two positions is $16,359.*
- *Two support staff will spend 40 hours each for a total salary of $1,700. Our fringe benefits are 20.15%, so the fringe benefits are $342.55.*

- *The executive director will spend 10% of his time supervising the project for a wage total of $10,250. Our fringe benefits are figured at 25.25%, so his fringe benefit is $2,588.13.*

Travel

Travel includes: lodging, mileage, airline tickets, meals, taxi, shuttle, lease cars, parking and tips. With the Internet, it should not be a problem to research any costs necessary for travel purposes. The funder knows that airline tickets could change prices, so if you have to shift funds to cover an increased cost, the funder will understand. However, do not figure such things as airline tickets at the cheapest rate when you are not assured you will qualify. Figure at full price. The following are examples.

Lodging

- *Two people will spend four days training in Baltimore at a nightly rate of $105.45 including tax and fees. The trip involves five nights each. The total is $1,054.50.*
- *Four people spend two nights for a meeting in Washington, D.C. The nightly rate is $125.76 including tax and fees. The total is $1,006.08.*

Mileage

Most organizations have a mileage rate they normally pay. It is expressed as a certain figure per mile.

- *Staff will spend a total of 300 miles a month traveling among clinics. Our mileage rate per mile is $0.40. Staff will travel among clinics for 12 months. The total for mileage is $1,440.00.*
- *Staff will take two trips to the state capitol for meetings at a round trip distance of 145 miles per trip. Our mileage rate is $0.38 per mile. The total mileage for this activity is $110.20.*

Airline Tickets

- *Two staff members will travel to Houston, Texas, for the state counseling convention. Airline tickets, coach fare, are $527.50 each. The total for this activity is $1,055.*
- *The project coordinator will travel to Washington, D.C., for a mandatory meeting. The airline ticket, coach fare, is $1,250.89.*

Meals

Meals can be expressed at a per diem amount that the traveler will be allowed for meals. Or, there can be a set amount per meal. The following are examples.

- *Two staff will travel to training in Atlanta, Georgia. They will be eating three meals a day for three days. Our organization allows $55 a day per person for a major city. The meal allowance will be a total of $330.*

- *The project coordinator will travel to Hobson, South Carolina, for two state meetings. Our organization allows $35 a day per person for a minor city. The meal allowance will be a total of $70.*

- *Four staff will attend a lunch meeting in Willard, New Hampshire. Our organization's allowance for a lunch meal is $12 per person. Meals will cost $48.*

- *Three staff will be traveling to Lexington, Kentucky, overnight for a training session. They will eat an evening meal; lunch is included in registration fees. Our organization's allowance for evening meals is $20 and for breakfast is $10. The total for this activity is $90.*

Taxi

Most hotels can tell you how much a taxi costs to major locations in cities. Taxi services can also be reached on the Internet or by telephone, if you need estimates. Chambers of commerce or tourist bureaus have numbers for taxi services. The following are examples.

- *Two staff will travel between the hotel and the agency offices for four meetings. Taxi service, one way, costs $10 including tip. The total will be $80.*

- *The project coordinator will take a taxi to and from the airport to the hotel for the state meeting (a shuttle is not available). Taxi fare is $23 including tip, one way. The total is $46.*

Shuttle

Some shuttles are free but it is usual to tip the driver. Some shuttles are for hire as are taxis. One can find out if shuttles are available through the hotel, chamber of commerce or the tourist bureau. The following are examples.

- *There is a free shuttle to and from the airport from the hotel. However, it is customary to tip the driver. There will be a total of four trips for two staff. An allowance of $12 has been allowed for tips.*

- *During the conference there is a shuttle service to the coliseum. Four staff will be going to the conference for a week each. A week pass on the shuttle costs $25 per person. The total fee is $100.*

Lease Cars

The Internet is invaluable for figuring lease car costs. The following are examples.

- *The project coordinator must travel to Harrisburg, Pennsylvania, for two mandatory state meetings. A car will be leased for these trips with unlimited mileage. Each trip will be two days in length. Car lease is $54.76 per day for the four days for a total of $219.04.*

- *Six staff will travel to the state conference for nurses. The conference is a week-long conference. A van will be leased for the trip at a discount rate for the week of $425.*

Parking

Hotels usually have a fee for parking. Convention centers frequently have fees for parking as well. It is best to learn these costs ahead of time so they can be figured into the budget. The following are examples.

- *The hotel where the ABC Training is held has a $5 a day charge for parking. The staff will be at the hotel for four days. The total for parking is $20.*
- *The convention center charges $10 a day for parking. Six staff members will be in two cars for the convention. They will be at the convention for three days. The total parking fee is $60.*

Tips

It is best to include tips with the various fees for meals, taxi or shuttle. However, there is still the sometimes sizeable amount for tips at hotels. It is best to determine an allowance for tips.

Contractual Services

Any contracted services such as leases, rents, consulting costs, contractors, software licenses, and training constitute contractual services. If you have a contract for the service, it goes under this line item. The following are examples.

- *For the week long training session, we are leasing a conference room from the Marriott Hotel for $150 per day. The total contract is for $750.*
- *The clinic will pay a monthly facilities rent of $1,200. For the grant year, the total will be $14,400.* ＋ 2300 per month for 54ft ＝
- *Blueprints for the building renovation will be supplied by the architect for a fee of $10,500.*
- *Technical support will be provided for installation of the computer systems for $50 per work station for 25 work stations for a total of $1,250.*
- *Landscaping will be provided by Atkins Nursery for $5,670.*
- *The leased telephone system costs $325 per month. One year costs $3,900.*
- *Software license for the patient tracking system costs $1,000 per workstation. There are five workstations. The total is $5,000 per year.*

Construction or Renovation

You would put the actual costs for materials used in construction or renovation and architectural or contractor costs under the contractual services line item. Examples follow.

- *Concrete for the basketball courts is figured at 300 yards at $20 per yard for a total of $600.*
- *Total cost of wood for the playground equipment will be $550.*

- *Showers will be installed for the women's swim team dressing room. There are five showers at a cost of $350 each for a total of $1,750.*

Materials

The materials line item includes reference materials, training materials, software, and books. Examples follow.

- *Workbooks for 30 people for mentoring training cost $40 each. The total is $120.*
- *National Geographic Maps software cost $596 each. We are equipping each of 15 libraries with the maps. The total is $8,940.*
- *We are purchasing a set of Golden World books for every classroom at a discount of $120 a set. There are 20 classrooms. The total is $2,400.*

Supplies

Supplies include such things as postage, copy paper, pens, CDs, pencils, and paper clips. Examples follow.

- *We will mail a notice to all patients listing support groups and meeting dates every month. There are 1,000 patients and 8 months of mailings during the first year. Cards cost $0.55 each to mail. The total is $4,400.*
- *We estimate that a ream of copy paper will be needed for the parent activity workroom each month. A ream costs $38. For 12 months the total is $456.*
- *Students will burn 20 CDs per month, for 12 months, to store project data. A case of 120 costs $140. We need two cases for the year for a total of $280.*

Equipment

Equipment is not expendable, and it includes such items such as computers, copy machines, fax machines, research laboratory equipment, and telephone systems. Examples follow.

- *We are equipping two computer labs with a desktop computer and printer. There will be 25 workstations in each lab. At our discount rate, the cost will be $2,050 per workstation. The total is $102,500.*
- *Each laboratory has to have a fax machine for communicating with the pharmacy and hospital. There are three labs. Each high-speed fax costs $200. The total is $600.*

Indirect Costs

Indirect costs include factors for heat, lights, space, and air conditioning—basically, the building costs where projects are housed. These can be figured exactly or can be based on a percentage. Your financial officer will know the percentage to apply. Examples follow.

- *We will devote two classrooms to the project. Our monthly electrical bill for the building of 20 classrooms averages $2,050. Factoring for the two rooms of electricity comes to $205 per month. For a 12-month period, the indirect cost for the two rooms is $2,460.*
- *Our indirect cost is 11% of the budget. The budget is $100,000. Our indirect cost is $11,000.*

Checklist—Budget Justification[2]

✔ Budget summary line item totals.

✔ Major components of each line item total.

✔ Building blocks of each major component.

✔ Are salaries in line with local wage scales?

✔ Show multiple factors (# sessions × # people × material cost = total material cost).

✔ Show as much detail as possible.

✔ Show which goals and objectives depend on major cost items.

✔ Any "out of line" amounts explained fully.

✔ No padding.

✔ Real amounts, no rounding to thousands.

Last Words

This is another of those straightforward sections that, in some ways, is more difficult to explain than to create. The whole idea is to explain the source of the numbers. Follow these four steps.

1. Start with a line item total from the budget summary form.
2. Break the total into its components. For example, the personnel total may be comprised of the salaries of two positions. Show the amounts

---

[2] Remember that a grant maker's directions (instructions/guidelines) take precedence over any and all other considerations. You must absolutely, positively follow the grant maker's directions exactly, precisely, and painstakingly.

for the two positions. The fact that the two amounts total to the line item amount shows how that figure was totalled.

3. Take each component figure from step 2 and either explain it, or break it down, into smaller components. In the example, take each salary figure and explain why such a wage is justified.

4. Keep breaking figures down until the basic figures that were used to compile the budget are reached. Explain the origin of the numbers. For example, buried in the materials and supplies line item total of $25,000 is an amount of $3,000 for workshop materials. The final explanation is that there will be 30 workshops with ten participants, each of whom will receive a $10 packet of materials. Thus, 30 workshops × 10 participants/workshop × $10 materials/participant = $3,000 materials.

So, keep it simple. Begin with a budget summary line item total. Break it into its components. Explain each component. If possible, break the component into smaller blocks. Explain each smaller block. Keep going as far as necessary, though two steps are usually all that are needed.

Keep it short. Long explanations are not necessary. Say what needs to be said, but don't rattle on and on. If the grant maker asks what time it is, do not explain how to build a clock. It is your responsibility, however, to explain completely any anomalies in the budget.

A workshop participant complained to us that her proposal was rejected because the amount for travel was deemed excessive. It turns out her service area was on both sides of the Grand Canyon. To get from one side to the other, about four miles as the crow flies, took a hundred mile drive—fifty miles up to the first crossing and fifty miles back to the other side. The fault, however, was with the applicant, not the reviewer. It is up to the applicant to realize when a budget figure needs explaining. Grant makers have heard it all. You will not surprise them with your circumstance, but you cannot expect them to approve odd budget figures without explanation. It's called budget justification for a reason.

A little tip to keep in the back of the mind is that, while the project narrative probably has a tight page limit, budget narratives almost never have a size limitation. Here is the place for a lot of explaining that can not be squeezed in anywhere else. This also means you should not waste space in the project narrative explaining anything that can reasonably go in the budget narrative. Here, you have all the space you choose to use.

The more detail the better. A detailed budget justification demonstrates a thorough and careful approach to the project. It shows competence and confidence, traits important to convey to the grant maker.

One last thing—use real figures. Look at these two line item totals.

Materials and Supplies $10,000

or

Materials and Supplies $9,876

Which amount looks like it was plucked straight out of thin air? Which amount looks like it may have been the result of adding together a list of actual costs? Reality, or at least verisimilitude, should be worth $124. Enough said.

Examples of Budget Justification for Four Projects

The following four examples (16.1 to 16.4) are examples of budget justification for each of the four organizations profiled in this book. The elements discussed within this chapter are highlighted in each example.

EXAMPLE 16.1

After School Program—Budget Justification

Sunnyvale School District

1. Personnel (grant request) **$620,250**

Project director $45,000

    Salary range in our location for a person with the required
    education and experience is $42,000 to $52,000

Assistant project director $32,000

    Salary range in our location for a person with the required
    education and experience is $30,000 to $38,000

Administrative assistant $24,000

    Salary range in our location for a person with the required
    education and experience is $22,000 to $28,000

Site directors—5 @ $35,000 $175,000
(one for each school site)

    Salary range in our location for a person with the required
    education and experience is $33,000 to $39,000

Assistant site directors—5 @ $28,000 $140,000
(one for each school site)

    Salary range in our location for a person with the required
    education and experience is $26,000 to $36,000

Snack coordinators—5 @ $6,450 each $32,250
(one for each school site)

    These are part-time positions

    Salary range in our location for a person with the required
    education and experience is $6,000 to $8,000 for the
    time required

Teachers—25 @ $6,880 each (five for each school site) $172,000

    These are part-time positions

    Salary range in our location for teachers with the required
    certification and experience is $6,000 to $10,000 for the
    time required

Personnel total (grant request)   **$620,250**

EXAMPLE 16.1   *(Continued)*

After School Program—Budget Justification, page 2

1. **Applicant matching funds** **$94,600**

   Bus drivers—5 @ $5,160   25,800
   (one for each school site @ established district rate)

   Security—5 @ $9,460   47,300
   (one for each school site @ established district rate)

   Maintenance—5 @ $4,300   21,500
   (one for each school site @ established district rate)

   Personnel total (applicant matching funds)   **$94,600**

1. **Partner matching funds** **$109,500**

   Partner 1—one person @ 50% involvement with $60,000 salary = $30,000
   Partner 2—one person @ 50% involvement with $55,000 salary = $27,500
   Partner 3—one person @ 50% involvement with $48,000 salary = $24,000
   Partner 4—one person @ 50% involvement with $56,000 salary = $28,000

   Personnel total (partner matching funds)   **$109,500**

   Personnel total matching funds   **$204,100**

2. **Fringe (grant request)** **$186,075**

   Fringe rate = 30%
   Fringe = 30% of $620,250 (grant request personnel total)

3. **Travel** **$22,000**

   This amount is for the travel, lodging, and meals required
   for grantor-required meetings

4. **Equipment** **$0**

   No grant funds are being requested for purchase of equipment

5. **Materials and supplies** **$0**

   No grant funds are being requested for purchase of materials and supplies

6. **Contractual services** **$68,800**

   20 contractors at an average of $3,440 each
   The evaluator will be paid with district funds   *(continues)*

EXAMPLE 16.1   *(Continued)*

After School Program—Budget Justification, page 3

7. **Construction** **$0**

   No grant funds are being requested for construction

8. **Other** **$0**

   No grant funds are being requested for other costs

9. **Total direct costs** **$897,125**

   Total direct cost is the sum of line items 1 through 8

10. **Indirect costs.** **$125,598**

    Indirect rate = 14%
    Indirect costs = 14% of $897,125 (total direct costs)

11. **Training stipend costs** **$0**

    No grant funds are being requested for training stipend costs

12. **Total grant request** **$1,022,723**

    Total grant request is the sum of line items 9 through 11

EXAMPLE **16.2**

Senior Citizen Wellness Center—Budget Justification

The Senior Citizen Wellness Center

1. **Line item 1—Personnel** **$210,000**

   The total for this line item consists of the salaries of four positions.

Project director	$65,000
SPE director	$55,000
Administrative assistant	$26,000
Social workers (2 @ $32K)	$64,000

2. **Fringe** **$77,385**

   The fringe rate is 36.85%.
   Total fringe is 36.85% of $210,000

3. **Travel** **$0**

   The applicant will cover any costs of travel incurred during the project.

4. **Equipment** **$26,000**

   These funds will be used to equip the single point-of-entry system.

   Center-based SPE

Desktop computers	$7,000
Peripherals	$1,500
Communications and database software	$2,000

   Home visit SPE

Laptop computers	$9,000
Peripherals	$1,500
Satellite communications hardware and software	$5,000

5. **Supplies** **$0**

   All costs of supplies will be borne by the applicant and project partners.

(continues)

EXAMPLE **16.2**   *(Continued)*

Senior Citizen Wellness Center— Budget Justification, page 2

6. **Contractual** **$25,000**

These funds will be used to purchase the services of various companies, organizations, and individuals—services that we cannot obtain without charge from a partner. The areas in which services will be purchased include nursing, medical laboratory analysis, mental health, exercise, weight training, dance, swimming, cooking and nutrition, and various miscellaneous skills such as instruction in arts and crafts.

7. **Other** **$0**

Any incidental or unforeseen project costs will be borne by the applicant or the project partners.

8. **Total direct costs** **$338,385**

Total direct cost is the sum of line items 1 through 7

9. **Indirect costs** **$62,601**

Indirect cost rate is 18.5%.

Indirect cost is 18.5% of $338,385 (total direct costs)

10. **Total costs** **$400,986**

Total cost (total grant request) is the sum of line items 8 and 9.

EXAMPLE 16.3

Fire and Rescue Project—Budget Justification

Quad-County Fire and Rescue Association

Total grant request is $217,000.

No grant funds are being requested for personnel and fringe costs. The applicant consortium is covering the salary and fringe costs of project personnel.

$65,000 is being requested for the purchase of *Equipment*.

This amount will be used to purchase the hardware and software to establish a computer network among the 47 member departments for the purpose of information flow for community outreach, recruitment, training, and purchasing.

$22,000 is being requested for *Materials and Supplies*.

This amount will be used to purchase the start-up materials for the community outreach program including the junior fire marshal program in the schools. No grant funds will be used to purchase office supplies for normal functioning of the association. This expense is covered through departmental allocations.

$130,000 is being requested for *Contractual* services.

These funds are for renovation of a building that has been donated to the association. Once renovated, the facility will house office space for the centralized purchasing, including a shipping and receiving area. Space for centralized training will also be prepared.

No grant funds are being requested for the *Other* budget category.

EXAMPLE 16.4

Alcohol and Drug Abuse Program—
Budget Justification

INNER CITY ALCOHOL AND
DRUG PREVENTION COMMISSION

1. Personnel (grant request) **$86,000**

Outreach coordinator	$32,000
Director of performance art	$32,000
Administrative assistant	$22,000

1. Personnel (matching funds) **$116,000**

Project director	$48,000
Hotline manager	$32,000
Assistant project director	$36,000

2. Fringe (grant request) **$16,125**

Fringe rate is 18.75%

Fringe is 18.75% of grant request personnel costs ($86,000)

2. Fringe (matching funds) **$21,750**

Fringe rate is 18.75%

Fringe is 18.75% of matching funds personnel
   costs ($116,000)

3. Travel **$0**

4. Equipment **$30,000**

Multiline telephone system for hotline	$12,000
Cell phones/radios/pagers for crisis teams	$4,000
Two computers with peripherals for hotline and crisis teams	$5,000
Database and communications software	$2,000
Staging equipment for performance art	$7,000

5. Materials and supplies **$15,000**

Curriculum material for educational outreach	$9,000
Performance props and supplies	$2,400
Miscellaneous office supplies	$3,600

EXAMPLE 16.4   *(Continued)*

Alcohol and Drug Abuse Program—
Budget Justification, page 2

6. **Contractual** **$40,000**

    Consultants for educational outreach training $6,000

    Consultants for hotline and crisis team training $10,000

    Outside evaluation team $15,000

    Telephone, wireless, and pager service $9,000

7. **Other** **$0**

8. **Total direct costs (grant request)** **$187,125**

    Total direct cost is the sum of grant request line items 1 through 7.

8. **Total direct costs (matching funds)** **137,750**

    Total direct cost is the sum of matching funds line items 1 through 7.

9. **Indirect costs (grant request)** **$17,777**

    The indirect cost rate is 9.5%.

    Indirect cost is the indirect cost rate times the total
       direct costs ($187,125).

9. **Indirect costs (matching funds)** **$21,750**

    The indirect cost rate is 9.5%.

    Indirect cost is the indirect cost rate times the total
       direct costs ($137,750).

10. **Total costs (grant request)** **$204,902**

    Total cost is the sum of line items 9 and 10

10. **Total costs (matching funds)** **$150,836**

    Total cost is the sum of line items 9 and 10.

Chapter 17

Appendix

Funders no longer award grants based on poundage of proposals.

Cheryl Carter New

At a Glance

What Else Is It Called?

- Supplementary material

When Is It Used?

Often, especially with federal grant proposals. Almost always, with complex projects and larger funding requests.

Why Is It Used?

The appendix exists so there is no confusion between the body of the proposal, and material that can be presented at the end of the document. The appendix is the right place for letters of support and key personnel biographies, as well as other materials that provide further illustration of important parts of the proposal. If a funder specifies what is to be in the appendix, do not add information they do not request. Keep appendix materials to a minimum. Include only information that is critical to the understanding of the proposal. Always refer to the appendix section in the body of your proposal. Don't assume that the reader will read the appendix sections.

Key Concepts

- When in doubt, leave it out.
- Include information the funder requests.
- Include only essential material.

Formatting Issues

Use standard margins and 12-point type, with clearly labeled sections. Place a clearly labeled cover page before each appendix section. Normally appendices are labeled Appendix A: Key Personnel Biographies, Appendix B: Letters of Support, and so forth.

Items to Include

The appendix is one of the most misused sections of a proposal. Proposal writers seem to think that the thicker the proposal the better, when the opposite is true. The name of the game is to be concise and clear. In fact, readers have very little time with each proposal, and you risk irritating them with extraneous and superfluous material. It is important to think and rethink your inclusions in the appendix. As we said, when in doubt—leave it out.

Some items that belong in an appendix are as follows.

Biographical Sketches of Key Personnel

Unless the funder tells you to put biographical sketches in the body of the proposal, put them in the appendix. Clearly label a cover page for the biographical sketches and refer to the section in the body of the document several times, so the reader does not think you have not included the information.

Organization Chart

If there is not room in the body of the proposal to put your project organization chart, then you can put it in the appendix. Again, refer to it in the body of the proposal. Clearly label a cover page for the organization chart. Examples can be found in Exhibits 17.1, 17.2, and 17.3.

EXHIBIT 17.1

Sample Organization Chart

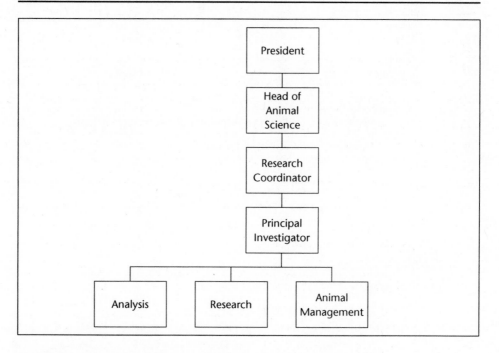

EXHIBIT 17.2

Another Organization Chart

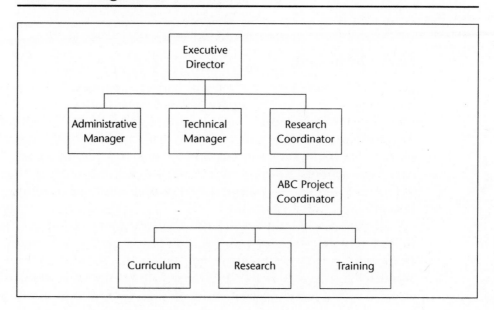

Timeline

If there is not room in the body of the proposal to put your timeline, then it can go in the appendix. Refer to it in the body of the proposal and clearly label a cover page for the timeline. Examples follow.

Project Month	Activity
One	Hire and train staff—set up advisory committee.
Two	Purchase equipment—renovate building.
Three	Enroll students.
Four	Start student classes.
Five	Start parent education classes.

Another example:

Project Month	One	Two	Three	Four	Five
Activity	Assess river damage.	Form work crews.	Work session.	Work session.	Evaluate next steps.

Yet another example is shown in Exhibit 17.3.

Letters of Support

Letters of support should always go in the appendix. But, what are letters of support? Letters of support should come from partners and organizations who are contributing something concrete to the project itself. Anyone can get people to write, "These are good people, give them the money" letters. We call those letters attaboy and attagirl letters. The funders pay no attention to those letters. However, they do pay attention to letters that indicate real support, either monetarily or in-kind contributions.

All partners should specify the things they are contributing to the project activities. If there is an organization or person contributing something, but they are not a partner, get a letter of support from them as well. You will likely have to write the letters of support, or at least provide guidance, so do not leave this task until last. Letters of support should be typed

EXHIBIT 17.3

Sample Timeline

Project Month	One	Two	Three	Four	Five	Six	Seven	Eight	Nine	Ten	Eleven	Twelve
Activity												
Planning meeting.	X				X				X			
Set up equipment.	X	X										
Patient intake.		X	X									
Begin therapy.				X								
Patient tracking.				X	X	X	X	X	X	X	X	X
Interim report.												X

on the organization's letterhead. Paragraphs from good letters of support follow.

- *The XYZ Organization will provide recruitment and oversight of volunteers for the project. In addition, we will keep timesheets on all volunteer activity.*

- *As executive director for the ABC Agency, I have committed our organization to provide counseling services to parents of the children who are brought before the juvenile court for criminal activity. This service will be done through our community outreach program. Support groups will be organized for parents who wish to participate.*

- *The DEF Foundation will contribute $2,000 toward development of educational programming for public television on the topic of consequences of drug abuse.*

- *Design Graphics will donate expertise to develop graphics for brochures for parent education classes. Our staff will provide camera ready art for additional flyers for the project, as well.*

- *The Small Business Association of Everett County will collect outdated computers to be refurbished by students. These computers will be donated to low-income families.*

- *Volunteers from local churches will cook and serve meals to the homeless. First Baptist will coordinate volunteers and develop menus for the meals.*

- *Noon meals will be prepared and served daily to the homeless in our Central City Recreation Center. Our center can seat 150 persons.*

- *The local physicians exchange will provide free screenings for senior citizens for skin cancers. This will be done on the first and third Mondays of each month at local clinics.*

Survey, Test, and Questionnaire Results

If there is a survey, test, or questionnaire that is key to your problem statement, then include a summary of the results in the appendix. Also include a sample survey, test, or questionnaire. Do not include all the surveys completed—only a summary of results. An example follows.

State Achievement Test Results about the Plan to Evaluate State Test Results

The plan for evaluating state test results calls for comparing results for students as they move from one grade to the next. This longitudinal analysis compares grade-level results from one year to the next. This is cohort analysis.

In the case of both longitudinal analysis and cohort analysis, the desired outcome is that students would move from the lower categories (below basic and basic) to the high categories (proficient and advanced). A negative value in the difference column for the first two categories and a positive value for the higher categories show that the desired outcome has occurred.

Summary of Results

For the longitudinal analysis, which tracks the same students from one grade to the next, the English/Language Arts results show a reduced number of students in the below basic category for all grades except the 2000 6th grade.

The Mathematics results show a reduced number in the below basic group in all grades except the 2000 7th grade.

The cohort analysis, which looks at grade level results for different student groups, shows movement from the below basic category for all grade levels in Mathematics.

The English/Language Arts results shows movement from the below basic category for all grade levels except Grade 8 (see Exhibit 17.4).

Equipment Descriptions

If there is an unusual piece of equipment in your budget, you might want to include a description and picture of it in the appendix. If you are purchasing a well-known piece of equipment such as a computer, there is no

Exhibit 17.4

State Test Results—Longitudinal Analysis

Percent	Below Basic	Basic	Proficient	Advanced
99 3rd Grade	41	39	19	0
00 4th Grade	24.4	42.3	30.4	2.9
Difference	−16.6	+3.3	+11.4	+2.9
99 4th Grade	37	39	23	1.0
00 5th Grade	24	53	22.3	0.7
Difference	−13	+27	−0.7	−0.3
99 5th Grade	35	45	18	1.0
00 6th Grade	38.5	38.7	19.7	3.1
Difference	+3.5	−6.3	+1.7	+2.1
99 6th Grade	42	47	11.0	0.0
00 7th Grade	37.3	44.7	17.3	0.6
Difference	−4.7	−2.3	+6.3	+0.6
99 7th Grade	48	41	11	1.0
00 8th Grade	44.1	41.6	13.5	0.7
Difference	−3.9	+.6	+2.5	−0.3

need to include equipment descriptions in the appendix—in fact, you should not include them. The following is an example.

Macroscopic Chemical Imaging Systems— for Large or Irregular Samples

The CONDOR family of macroscopic chemical imaging systems brings visible and NIR spectroscopy coupled with the power of widefield chemical imaging to the analysis of large or irregular samples. They are non-invasive and non-destructive platforms that can reveal and characterize original sample structure. Widefield chemical imaging is combined with digital imaging techniques to provide molecular images that reveal material morphology, composition, structure and concentration. Three members make up the family of systems. The VIS model is used for measurements in the 400 to 700 nm range. The NIR-sw model covers the 700 to 1100 nm range of wavelengths. The NIR-mw allows measurements from 1000 to 1700 nm. All three can be configured for transmission or reflectance measurements.

(ChemIcon Inc., 7301 Penn Avenue, Pittsburgh, PA 15208.)

Lists of Advisors and Board Members

If your advisors or board members will impress the funder, then you might want to include a list in the appendix. By impress the funder, we mean that the board members are either easily recognized, or have impressive credentials, in the project field. Some funders request this information and expect it in the body of the proposal.

Checklist—Appendix[1]

✔ Grant maker's requirements.

✔ Observe page limit.

✔ Number all appendix pages consecutively.

✔ Key personnel bio sketches.

✔ Organization charts.

✔ Flow charts.

✔ Timeline.

✔ Letters of support (commitment).

✔ Consultant and service contracts.

✔ Partner collaborative agreements.

✔ Survey instruments and compiled results.

✔ Focus group guidelines and compilation of results.

✔ Equipment technical specification sheets.

✔ Project advisory board member list.

✔ Tax-exempt letter.

✔ Organization's audited budget.

✔ Organization's board of directors.

---

[1] Remember that a grant maker's directions (instructions/guidelines) take precedence over any and all other considerations. You must absolutely, positively follow the grant maker's directions exactly, precisely, and painstakingly.

17

Last Words

If an item is not referenced directly in the body of the proposal, what is it doing in the appendix? Honestly now, do reviewers peruse the appendix in search of really cool stuff? The simple rule is that anything in an appendix must be there in response to a direct reference in the narrative. The exception is, as always, if the grant maker directs that specific items be included in the appendix.

Examples of Appendices for Four Projects

The following four examples (17.1 to 17.4) are examples of appendices for each of the organizations profiled in this book. The elements described within this chapter are depicted in each example.

EXAMPLE 17.1

After School Program—Appendix

Sunnyvale School District
One Academy Lane • Sunnyvale, Mississippi 39200

August 31, 2004

Sarah Smith, Ph.D., Director
After School Grant Program
Office of Elementary and Secondary Education
U.S. Department of Education
Washington, D.C. 20500

REF: September 1, 2004—After School
      Grant Program Competition

Dear Dr. Smith:

It is with enthusiasm that I commit to the After School Program for Sunnyvale School District. We need this program in order to be able to provide a chance for our children. Otherwise, our children will return to the cycle of poverty and lack of productivity they were born to.

I have personally committed that while the grant program is in process I will make numerous presentations to City and County Councils for supplementary funding for the key positions of Project Coordinator and Site Coordinators. If they will not fund the positions, with the aid of the School Board, I will cut enough administrative positions to cover the personnel costs for the After School Program. This will not be difficult due to normal District attrition.

The entire District and community are committed to the After School Program.

Sincerely,

John J. Doe, Ph.D.
Superintendent

JJD/kbf

EXAMPLE 17.1   *(Continued)*

After School Program—Appendix, page 2

Sunnyvale School District

One Academy Lane • Sunnyvale, Mississippi 39200

August 31, 2004

Sarah Smith, Ph.D., Director
After School Grant Program
Office of Elementary and Secondary Education
U.S. Department of Education
Washington, D.C. 20500

REF: September 1, 2004—After School
      Grant Program Competition

Dear Dr. Smith:

The Sunnyvale District School Board is committed to the
After School Program. In fact, it will solve a problem we have
recognized for years. Our children go home mostly to empty
houses—they get in trouble. Our crime rates and substance
abuse rates are high.

We have agreed with Dr. Doe, the Superintendent, that we will
lobby City and County Council for funding during the entire
time the grant is operating. If all else fails we will cut
administrative staff to cover the key positions of Project
Coordinator and Site Coordinators.

We thank you for the opportunity to apply.

                                        Sincerely,

                                        Allyson A. Plummer, PhD
                                        Chairman, Sunnyvale
                                        School Board

AAP/dap

EXAMPLE 17.2

Senior Citizen Wellness Center—Appendix

City Hospital
111 A Street
P.O. Box 2002
AnyTown, AnyState 10022
857-245-9871

Sally Stevens
Project Director
ABC Foundation
St. Paul, Minnesota 34567
Re: Support for the Senior Center Project

Dear Ms. Stevens:

City Hospital administration enthusiastically supports the Senior Center Project. Our contribution to the project is as follows:

- Space for therapy and for other activities
- Expert staff to pre-screen participants
- Expert staff to provide oversight for activities
- Physicians and nurse practitioners to monitor health of participants and to recommend therapy
- Funds for supplies and testing kits

The Senior Center is a tremendous need in our community because we are a retirement center and as such we have a population dominated by senior citizens.

Thank you for the opportunity to submit the grant proposal.

Regards,

Dr. Samuel Stevens
Hospital Administrator

EXAMPLE 17.2   *(Continued)*

Senior Citizen Wellness Center—
Appendix, page 2

AnyTown Public Health Department
211 Main Street
AnyTown, AnyState 99884
987-432-6789

Sally Stevens
Project Director
ABC Foundation
St. Paul, Minnesota 34567
Re: Support for the Senior Center Project

Dear Ms. Stevens:

The Senior Center Project is a critical need for this community. Our citizenry is largely elderly. We see serious conditions that could have been prevented with earlier intervention. We also have a large number of indigent citizens who need to be informed of precautions to take so they do not wind up in our hospital emergency room or our Exigent Center.

We will contribute a conference room for classes. We also will teach some of these classes as the need arises. In addition, we will provide flu and pneumonia shots at no charge. We can do this because of a grant from a local foundation.

Our nurses will provide on site blood pressure checks, weight measurement and other similar tests as identified.

Our nutritionist will provide cooking classes at the YMCA and will provide transportation for participants.

Thank you for the potential funding of our project

Sincerely,

Rachel Greene, RN
Special Projects Director

EXAMPLE 17.2 *(Continued)*

Senior Citizen Wellness Center— Appendix, page 3

Harmony School of Dance

14 SOUTH MAIN STREET • ANYTOWN, ANYSTATE 32456
867-233-5454 • FAX 867-233-4567

Sally Stevens
Project Director
ABC Foundation
St. Paul, Minnesota 34567

Re: Support for the Senior Center Project

Dear Ms. Stevens:

Our studio will provide free dance lessons once a week for senior citizens at our studio. Once every two months we will sponsor a dinner dance for participants of the Senior Center.

Our space and instructors are donated.

Sincerely,

Susan Gardener
Owner

EXAMPLE 17.3

Fire and Rescue Project—Appendix

Center City Public Schools
10 Hawthorne Street
Center City, AnyState 23456
867-654-8761

Dr. Joseph Moses
Executive Director
XYZ Foundation
Portland, Oregon 98745
Re: Quad City Fire Marshal Program

Dear Dr. Moses:

We enthusiastically support the Fire Marshal portion of the Quad City Fire Prevention Project. We have a large number of low income families in our service area. Most have substandard heating units such as rusty kerosene heaters, fireplaces, wood stoves and oil stoves. During the past winter we had three families whose houses burned to the ground due to the use of dangerous heating devices.

In addition, our community has numerous sub-standard houses with poor wiring. This is another fire hazard.

We will provide materials for training and the publicity campaign. We will provide space and a forum for presentations to our student bodies. After the term of the grant is over we will fund the program ourselves.

We appreciate the opportunity to submit our proposal.

Regards,

Dr. John Jones
Superintendent

EXAMPLE 17.3 *(Continued)*

Fire and Rescue Project—Appendix, page 2

Quad-County Fire and Rescue Association
123 Middle Junction Road
Central City, AnyState 12345

Project Board of Advisors

James Blake, AnyState Fire Chief
56 E Street
State Capitol, AnyState 23456
234-765-4567

Dr. John Jones, Superintendent
Center City Public Schools
10 Hawthorne Street
Center City, AnyState 23456
867-654-8761

Nathan Yerty, President
AnyState Purchasing Managers Association
123 Oak Drive
Jonesville, AnyState 67458
345-765-8793

Matthew Cox, Area Fire Marshal
567 Lakeview Drive
Morristown, AnyState 45678
456-567-3456

Mark Restin, Public Relations Specialist
78 West Main Street
Fletcher, AnyState 23456
987-652-3432

EXAMPLE 17.4

Alcohol and Drug Abuse Project—Appendix

Lake County Consolidated Schools
P.O. BOX 1234, RIVER CITY, ANYSTATE 12345, 234-956-2456

Melissa Martin
Program Director
Department of Health and Human Services
234 State Street—Suite 567
Washington, D.C. 20202

Re: Support for the Drug Prevention Project

Dear Mrs. Martin:

Our schools are facing a serious problem with substance abuse. We have some children who have experimented with drugs at the age of eight. In an anonymous survey of students, over 40% of our high school students have at least tried some drug. Last year 25 students were arrested for drug possession with intent to distribute.

We enthusiastically welcome the grant project as a way of community agencies working together to stop substance abuse in its tracks. We welcome the assistance.

We will provide space for meetings. Also, we will sponsor presentations in each school.

We have a sizeable printing operation and will print materials, posters, training materials and brochures for the project gratis.

We will also sponsor early morning and evening awareness sessions for family members of our students. We will attempt to offer sessions to meet all schedules.

In addition we will educate all teachers and administrators to look for signs of drug abuse and will set up an intervention policy.

We believe we can create a model project to be publicized to other districts across the country through our Web site.

Thank you for your kindness in answering our questions.

Sincerely,

Quinton Cole, EdD
Superintendent

EXAMPLE 17.4 *(Continued)*

Alcohol and Drug Abuse Project— Appendix, page 2

Lake County Consolidated Schools
P.O. BOX 1234, RIVER CITY, ANYSTATE 12345, 234-956-2456

Substance Abuse Survey Results

School	Question	Total Students	Students Answering Yes
Bowen Senior High School	Have you ever had a drink of beer, liquor, or wine?	1345	867
	Have you ever smoked pot?	1345	467
	Have you ever used Ecstasy?	1345	87
	Have you ever used any other type of illegal drug?	1345	124
Stevenson Senior High School	Have you ever had a drink of beer, liquor, or wine?	1657	989
	Have you ever smoked pot?	1657	503
	Have you ever used Ecstasy?	1657	45
	Have you ever used any other type of illegal drug?	1657	245
Martin Middle School	Have you ever had a drink of beer, liquor, or wine?	678	234
	Have you ever smoked pot?	678	67
	Have you ever used Ecstasy?	678	4
	Have you ever used any other type of illegal drug?	678	46
Sanders Middle School	Have you ever had a drink of beer, liquor, or wine?	987	345
	Have you ever smoked pot?	987	198
	Have you ever used Ecstasy?	987	24
	Have you ever used any other type of illegal drug?	987	125

EXAMPLE 17.4 *(Continued)*

Alcohol and Drug Abuse Project— Appendix, page 3

Lake County Consolidated Schools
P.O. BOX 1234, RIVER CITY, ANYSTATE 12345, 234-956-2456

School	Question	Total Students	Students Answering Yes
Merrell Middle School	Have you ever had a drink of beer, liquor, or wine?	904	278
	Have you ever smoked pot?	904	89
	Have you ever used Ecstasy?	904	12
	Have you ever used any other type of illegal drug?	904	95
Jefferson Middle School	Have you ever had a drink of beer, liquor, or wine?	1013	378
	Have you ever smoked pot?	1013	245
	Have you ever used Ecstasy?	1013	46
	Have you ever used any other type of illegal drug?	1013	432
All Primary Schools	Have you ever had a drink of beer, liquor, or wine?	4056	1023
	Have you ever smoked pot?	4056	567
	Have you ever used Ecstasy?	4056	23
	Have you ever used any other type of illegal drug?	4056	312

Chapter 18

Bibliography

Personally I think we're over-specialized. Why it's getting so we have experts who concentrate only on the lower section of a specimen's left ear.

Martin Berkeley and Jack Arnold[1]

At a Glance

What Else Is It Called?

- References

When Is It Used?

Whenever you quote studies, books, magazines, interviewed persons, television, radio or movies, you must include a bibliography. You might include footnotes throughout your document. If you wish, you might also include a bibliography.

Why Is It Used?

A bibliography shows the importance and current state of your research. It is also a protection against plagiarism.

Key Concepts

- Include only recent or landmark references.
- Do not include references you have not used in your proposal.
- If the potential funder has a study out, it is a good idea to quote it.

---

[1] Martin Berkeley and Jack Arnold. Prof. Clete Ferguson (John Agar) in *Revenge of the Creature*, talking to Helen Dobson as she studies the creature (1955). Story by William Alland.

Formatting Issues

There are many ways to do a bibliography. Some examples are shown in this chapter. Choose one way and be consistent in the use of it. Format in standard margins and 12-point type.

Include Only Recent or Landmark References

Funders will look at your references to determine the depth of your research. They will look for current references. If there is a landmark, but old, study or reference—note that it is a landmark reference. If all your research is outdated, what does it say about the basis for your project? It indicates that your project is not on a firm foundation. Funders like to fund well-developed and solidly founded projects—remember they are making an investment.

Do Not Include References Not Used in Your Proposal

We have heard of people getting a printout from the library on the project topic and including it as a bibliography. That will not fool the funder. It only shows laziness. You do not want the funder to think you are lazy. If so, what kind of a job will you do on the project itself? Only include references you have actually made in your proposal.

Include a Bibliography, Even if You Have Footnotes

Always make it easy on the reader. The reader appreciates a page where the reference information is all together. If your references are to have impact, they are easier to read, all on a page or two.

Quote Studies from the Potential Funder

Remember, the funder is interested in solving the same problem as you are. It is likely, then, that the funder may have published a study or article on the problem. You should thoroughly research the funder to see if you have a match for funding. Ask for any documents the funder has published. Or, if they are posted documents on a Web site, be sure to read them. It is a good idea to quote the funder's own studies in your proposal. The funder will not argue with your research.

Examples of Bibliographical Formats

- Andre, Elizabeth. *Earth Science,* Volume III. Bradham Publishers, 2002.
- Carter, Aaron. Passages from *Serendipity,* pages 123–126. Patrick and Sons, 2000.
- Merrill, B.M. *The Dynamics of Learning.* University Press, March 2002.
- New, L. "The Importance of Pantothenic Acid," *Pharmaceutical Digest,* April 2001.
- Tildon, John. "The Problem with Children," *Parents Digest,* June 2001.

Checklist—Bibliography[2]

- ✔ Recent only.
- ✔ Keep it short.
- ✔ Tell the truth; include a reference only if used.
- ✔ No URLs.
- ✔ Do not reference Internet sites—use title of work, author, and organization name.

Last Words

Make citations in the body of the narrative. A grant proposal is not an academic paper. It is a sales pitch.

Examples of Bibliographies for Four Projects

The following four examples (18.1 to 18.4) are examples of bibliographies for each of the organizations profiled in this book. The elements highlighted within this chapter are illustrated in each example.

---

[2] Remember that a grant maker's directions (instructions/guidelines) take precedence over any and all other considerations. You must absolutely, positively follow the grant maker's directions exactly, precisely, and painstakingly.

EXAMPLE 18.1

After School Program—Bibliography

Sunnyvale School District

Brown, Jennifer. *No Supervision*. John Wiley & Sons, March 2001.

Cox, Michael. "Criminalization of Our Children." *Parents Digest,* November 2000.

Martin, Wallace. *The Danger for Our Children*. Brookings Institute Study, December 2000.

Selby, Margaret, ed. *County Statistics*. Research Group, State Development Board, June 2000.

Tilly, Susan, and Albert Williams. *Latch Key Kids*. National Education Association, May 2001.

EXAMPLE 18.2

Senior Citizen Wellness Center—Bibliography

The Senior Citizen Wellness Center

Bartholmew, Matthew. *Preventive Medicine for Geriatric Patients.* National Institutes of Health Study, March 2000.

Haloran, James. *Why Our Elders Are Dying.* John Wiley & Sons, December 2000.

James, Lauren, ed. *Heart Smart for Seniors.* National Heart Association, February 2000.

Macon, Margarie. *Physical Therapy for Geriatric Patients.* National Physical Therapy Association, January 2001.

Sanger, Anne Bates, ed. *Briley County Statistics.* County Health Department, June 2000.

Stewart, Linda. *Therapy for Senior Citizens.* John Wiley & Sons, November 2000.

EXAMPLE 18.3

Fire and Rescue Project—Bibliography

Quad-County Fire and Rescue Association

Glick, Captain Howard. *Fighting Fire With Education.* National Fireman's Association, June 1999.

Howard, Mark. *A Guide to Rural Fire Fighting.* National Fireman's Association, March 2001.

Johnson, Thomas, ed. *County Fire Statistics.* State Development Board, February 2002.

Norris, Melissa. *Guide to Household Fire Hazards.* John Wiley & Sons, January 2000.

EXAMPLE 18.4

Alcohol and Drug Abuse Program— Bibliography

INNER CITY ALCOHOL AND DRUG PREVENTION COMMISSION

Marino, Anthony. *Substance Abuse Intervention Techniques.* National Institutes of Health, July 2001.

Robertson, John. *Setting Up a Substance Abuse Program.* John Wiley & Sons, January 2001.

Stevenson, Michael, ed. *The Substance Abuse Problem Our Nation Faces.* National Health Organization, March 1998.

Stuart, Aileen. *Educating the Population About Substance Abuse.* National Committee on Substance Abuse, November 1999.

Walters, Robert, ed. *County Statistics.* State Development Board, January 2002.

Chapter 19

Introduction and Forms

A good preface must be the root and the
square of the book at the same time.

Friedrich Von Schlegel[1]

When at last we are sure / You've been properly pilled, /
Then a few paper forms / Must be properly filled /
So that you and your heirs / May be properly billed.

Theodore Geisel (Dr. Seuss)[2]

At a Glance—Introduction

What Else Is It Called?

- Foreword

When Is It Used?

You write an introduction when the funder requires it. There are several introductions within the body of the average proposal. One is written in the problem statement and again in the project description. However, sometimes a funder will require an introduction. If the funder does not tell you what to put in this introduction, describe your organization and give a brief summary of the problem.

Why Is It Used?

When the funder requires it.

---

[1] Friedrich Von Schlegel (1772–1829), German philosopher. "Aphorism 8" in *Selected Aphorisms from the Lyceum (1797),* translated by Ernst Behler and Roman Struc, *Dialogue on Poetry and Literary Aphorisms,* Pennsylvania University Press, (1968).

[2] Theodore Geisel (Dr. Seuss), *You're Only Old Once!* Random House, 1986.

Key Concepts

- Brief and concise.
- Follow the funder's directions for content.
- Describe your organization.
- Provide a brief summary of the problem you are addressing.

Formatting Issues

Stay within page limitations. Format with normal margins and 12-point type.

Follow the Funder's Directions for Content

If the funder tells you what to put in the introduction, follow directions explicitly. Write what the funder tells you to, in the order in which the items are mentioned.

Describe Your Organization

Describe your organization as it relates to the project. Talk about the following topics.

- Location (urban, rural, suburban, state, type of environment).
- Mission of your organization.
- Size and reach.
- Experience with project leadership.
- Reason for the decision to attack the problem.

Provide a Brief Summary of the Problem You Are Addressing

Look at your problem statement. Choose the key points and write a paragraph from those points. Key in on the issues that caused you to feel that your project was a match for this funder.

At a Glance—Forms

What Else Are They Called?

Templates

When Are They Used?

Always, for federal programs. There will commonly be budget forms for foundations and corporations. Occasionally, the whole proposal will be submitted to a foundation or corporation on a series of forms.

Why Are They Used?

Federal forms are used to make certain portions of the proposal uniform. This is most common with a cover form and the budget. But, there are other forms the federal government requires such as a lobbying form. The lobbying form provides assurance to the government department that your organization has not lobbied for grant funds. There are numerous forms for research projects involving issues such as use of human subjects, and for procedural matters relating to legal issues. Every department of the federal government has its own procedural forms.

Most foundations and corporations will have only a budget form. Some will have a cover form. A few will have a questionnaire to fill out as a preliminary application, to see if there is a match for funding.

Key Concepts

- If forms are required, complete each and every one.
- Fill out each form completely.
- If you do not understand, then ask the contact person.
- Use the forms you are given.
- Put forms in the proposal in exactly the order in which you are directed.
- Complete each form, even if it is to state that it is not applicable.
- Complete each form neatly and legibly (you may need to use a typewriter).
- Save the originals for signatures.

Formatting Issues

Follow directions.

If Forms Are Required, Complete Each and Every One

Do not leave a form out. There is likely to be a check box for indicating the form does not apply to your project. If one is not applicable, then write *"Not Applicable"* on the form and include it in the appropriate place in the proposal. If you do not understand an item on the form, call the contact person and ask. The contact person may refer you to a book of rules or procedures, but you will get direction.

Use the Forms You Are Given

In an age of technology, this can be really irritating. Even the Federal government does not have forms formatted to use on the computer. If you can access them on the computer, you generally cannot fill them out on the computer. This is gradually changing, but it cannot come fast enough for those of us who have forgotten how to space things on a typewriter. It is likely you will have to use old technology in filling out forms. People, especially bureaucrats, are enamored of their forms. So, grit your teeth and fill out the forms you are given.

Put Forms in the Proposal in Exactly the Order in Which You Are Directed

It is important that you follow directions, and place the forms in exactly the right place in a proposal. If the initial reviewer does not find the form in the right place, your proposal (and all your hard work) may be thrown out. Number the forms exactly as directed. Save out the originals for signatures.

Complete Each Form Neatly and Legibly (You May Need to Use a Typewriter)

Be sure that anyone can read the form, once you complete it. Messy or illegible forms do not indicate that you will be more careful with the project.

Checklist—Introduction and Forms[3]

- ✔ Project title—clever but not cute.
- ✔ Project title—three to five words.
- ✔ Project title—check acronym, it may spell something unfortunate.

---

[3] Remember that a grant maker's directions (instructions/guidelines) take precedence over any and all other considerations. You must absolutely, positively follow the grant maker's directions exactly, precisely, and painstakingly.

✔ Return all forms.

✔ Complete all forms.

✔ Page number forms.

✔ Separate entry in table of contents for each form.

✔ Signatures in blue ink (identifies the original).

Last Words

Never fail to return a form, and never return a blank form. If a form has no relevance to your organization, your application, or your project, then scrawl on it a big "Not Applicable" in broad bold marker strokes, but do not return that form blank. A typewriter sits forlorn in a back room in our office for the single purpose of completing forms. First choice is to produce the form on a computer. The only other choice is to use a typewriter.

The forms and the project summary are the two proposal parts that get left to last—big mistake. Forms always take much longer to complete than expected. The nightmare scenario is that the person who must sign a form just went on vacation to Antarctica.

Index

CPSIA information can be obtained at www.ICGtesting.com
Printed in the USA
BVOW02n1134091014

370054BV00010B/14/P